# BANDITS AND POL... LANDLORD AND PEASANT VIOLENCE IN HUALGAYOC 1900–30

## LEWIS TAYLOR

*Lecturer in Latin American Politics*
*University of York*

CENTRE OF LATIN AMERICAN STUDIES
UNIVERSITY OF CAMBRIDGE

Other publications of the Centre of Latin American Studies include: *Land, People and Planning in Contemporary Amazonia* (ed. Francoise Barbira-Scazzocchio).

Copyright © Centre of Latin American Studies
History Faculty Building, West Road,
Cambridge, U.K.

ISBN 0-904927-29-6
ISSN 0266-7541

Typeset by University Printing Services, Cambridge.
Printed in Great Britain at the University Press, Cambridge.

*FOR JANINE*

'Competition of Riches, Honour, Command,
or other power, enclineth to Contention,
Enmity, and War: Because the way of one
Competitor, to the attaining of his desire,
is to kill, subdue, supplant, or repell
the other'.

Thomas Hobbes

£5-95

# Contents

# Preface

To date the study of agrarian structures and peasant movements has dominated scholarly research on Andean society in Peru. Although peasant communities and kinship patterns have also been analysed in some depth, few detailed investigations into local level political behaviour and power structures have yet been published. This is especially true with respect to the period 1890 and 1930. In addition, the department of Cajamarca remains one of the least researched regions of highland Peru. Hopefully this book will make a contribution to filling some of these gaps and encourage others to undertake research into the area.

Any study of brigandage and factional politics faces the problem of sources. Few bandits leave detailed accounts of their motives and exploits. Factional leaders tend to operate through word of mouth and not put their instructions on paper. What documentation exists consequently tends to be of an *oficialista* kind and presents a one-sided picture. This difficulty has partly been overcome in the present work because faction leaders and some bandits did write to the authorities giving their opinions about particular incidents. These papers can mostly be found in the sub-series *Particulares* in the prefectural collection of the Archivo Departamental de Cajamarca. Criminal cases being tried before the court in Cajamarca also contain many affidavits from non-official sources. Wherever possible conversations were held with people from Hualgayoc to verify certain events. Despite such precautions no doubt unfortunate instances exist where I have unwittingly fallen into error and accepted as fact incidents that may have been only partially true. In a study of this nature such difficulties are perhaps inevitable, but after thoroughly checking all the available sources, I am convinced that the story presented here is as reliable as is possible in the circumstances.

I am grateful to Evelio Gaitán, Flaminio Alvarez, Cecilia Barrantes and Rossina Urteaga, archivists in the Archivo Departamental de Cajamarca. Without their co-operation and friendship this book could not have been written. Support for field research was forthcoming from the British Academy. David Brading suggested that I write the book, gave me encouragement during its preparation, and passed useful comments on the text. I also owe much to Rory Miller who read the manuscript and offered worthy advice. The usual disclaimers apply. Thanks are due to Alison Roberts, who typed part of the text and initiated me into the computer age. David Lewis sketched the cover design. Finally, I owe a deep debt to Janine, who was burdened with additional domestic responsibilities while this book was being written and gave me invaluable support.

# CHAPTER 1

# Introduction

In the early part of this century the provinces of Hualgayoc, Chota and Cutervo in northern Peru were the scene of internecine strife. Brigandage, commonly related to clan conflict, also attained endemic proportions. The outcome was a wave of violence unmatched in the Peruvian Andes between 1900 and 1980. The most important leader within this violence in the northern region of Cajamarca, one of the largest and most populous departments in Peru, was Eleodoro Benel. Born in 1873, by 1910 Benel had established himself as one of the largest entrepreneurs in northern Cajamarca. Apart from engaging in a wide range of economic activities, Benel became a prominent local caudillo deeply embroiled in factional strife. His political involvements eventually led Benel into open confrontation with the government of Augusto Leguía in 1924. After a guerrilla struggle lasting nearly three years, Benel was assassinated in 1927.

Surprisingly, these events have been largely neglected as a theme for detailed investigation. Although a few interesting studies have appeared, the field is still dominated by local balladeers and novelists of dubious merit. Into this latter category falls the work by Salomón Vílchez entitled *Fusiles y machetes*.[1] Set in Cutervo province, the story centres on a conflict between peasant *guerrilleros* and the state. It seeks to retell in literary form the battles waged by Eleodoro Benel and Avelino Vásquez against the regime of Augusto Leguía. Although the plot is thin, the characters stereotyped and the style poor, the novel contains snippets of useful information, since Vílchez was an adolescent living in Cutervo when these disputes arose. In similar vein, but offering much more detail, is Carlos Vigil's *La rebelión del caudillo Andino*.[2] For Vigil's father was a foreman in the employ of Eleodoro Benel and the author maintained close *compadrazgo* ties with the Benel family, a link which provides a key to understanding the strengths and weaknesses of the work. On the one hand, the role of Benel and his *guapos*, or pistoleers, was grossly idealised. The author regarded Benel as 'Cajamarca's Pancho Villa', and his followers as 'revolutionaries' who were together seeking the overthrow of an oppressive dictatorial regime.[3] No responsibility for the murder, rape and pillage committed by his *clientela* was laid at Benel's doorstep. Vigil also chose to ignore Benel's role as a supporter of the social status quo in Hualgayoc and his activities on behalf of the most conservative tendency within the Partido Civil. On the other hand, Vigil's close connections with the Benel family enabled the author to assemble much useful background information on the personalities and alignments of many individuals caught up in factional imbroglios.[4]

Various other authors have also commented on politics and banditry in northern Cajamarca during the period under review. Unfortunately, their analyses suffer from a lack of detailed archival research into the causes and nature of these phenomena. This leads them to make statements that are unsupported by documentary evidence, an approach that allows for any number of divergent opinions. Wilfredo Kapsoli, for example, imbues Benel with some of the qualities of a 'social bandit'.[5] In contrast, Manuel Burga and Alberto Flores Galindo see the caudillo as an archetypal traditional landlord bent on 'violently resisting the expansion of the state'.[6] Perhaps Eric Hobsbawm comes closest to grasping the real character of these developments. He lays stress on the relationship between 'the virtual breakdown of government authority, in a combination of political and personal rivalries, vengeance, political and economic ambitions, and social rebellion'.[7] Confusion about the real form of the violence that characterised this zone prior to and during the Leguía period is heightened by the definition of Cajamarca as a feudal society.[8] The logical outcome of this well-entrenched perspective is the claim that 'In 1940 there were even feudal wars in the highlands of La Libertad and Cajamarca', a highly debatable statement, even if we ignore the fact that the author fixes on the wrong decade.[9]

The study of banditry is also in its infancy with respect to other regions of Peru, with many authors tending to fall into the trap of viewing their subjects as romantic highwaymen in the Robin Hood mould.[10] The title by López Albújar is the most perceptive. He observed that banditry thrived in localities with a history of village feuds. Robbers also tended to congregate around key trade routes, especially at points where secure mountain retreats were near at hand. The incidence of brigandage rose in districts where land was unequally distributed, with traditional haciendas proving a breeding ground for bandits, a development encouraged by ineffective state control. On the other hand, in zones where agrarian capitalism was more advanced, rural entrepreneurs moved to control brigandage, enlisting effective state support to accomplish this task. Landlord oppression, the monopolisation of water supplies, the abuse of tenants by over-zealous foremen, as well as trickery practised against the peasantry by unscrupulous labour contractors, or *enganchadores*, – all acted to heighten discontent and promote peasant involvement in criminal activity. Finally, López Albújar suggested that where such features were absent, as in the southern departments of Moquegua and Tacna, no brigandage arose.[11] Our study of politics and banditry in Hualgayoc confirms most of López Albújar's observations. Nevertheless, it should be noted that prior to 1930 all districts in Cajamarca department were plagued by outlaws, irrespective of their level of commercial agriculture. Cajamarca province, the most developed and the area where the presence of the state was felt most strongly, also spawned significant levels of bandit activity. Robbers were attracted to the zone by the greater intensity of commerce and by the most important trade route leading from the department of Cajamarca to the coast. The most powerful landowning family in Peru, the Gildemeisters, proved unable to combat rustling on their highland properties before 1930, even though they hired private law enforcers.

Detailed investigations into local political bossism, known as *gamonalismo*, in Peru are surprisingly scarce.[12] Víctor Andrés Belaúnde, in his numerous writings on Peruvian society and politics during the 1910s never advances his discussion of this topic beyond the level of generalities.[13] A similar criticism can be levelled at the essays of José Carlos Mariátegui, who saw the *gamonales* as abusive feudal lords standing at the centre of an intricate web of dependents. They were consequently able to dominate politics and the local state, and acted as a brake on the socio-economic development of highland Peru.[14] The claim that these individuals were feudal landlords needs questioning. Our study shows that local power brokers in Hualgayoc also engaged in a wide range of economic activities and were primarily concerned with capital accumulation, not seigneurial prestige. Neither did all *gamonales* own large estates. Several were medium-scale farmer-merchants, others, like Tiburcio Barrantes in San Miguel, were *tinterillos*, or quack-lawyers. The only detailed study of *gamonal* activity at the regional level has been written by José Tamayo, who shows that in the department of Puno local bosses came from a variety of backgrounds and occupations. They also maintained close ties with brigands.[15]

Fortunately, the literature on *caciquismo* and brigandage elsewhere in Latin America is richer, much of it stimulated by the pioneering work of Hobsbawm and the debate his ideas provoked.[16] Brazil is the most studied country, and in English the work of Billy Jaynes Chandler and Linda Lewin merits special mention. In her study of Paraíba during the Old Republic (1889–1930), Lewin highlights the central role of extended family networks (*parentelas*) in political organisation and conflict.[17] Northeastern society is shown to be vertically divided along factional lines, with each clan engaging in a violent struggle for local domination. At the grass roots level these vendetta wars were fought in the *municípios*, an administrative unit roughly comparable to the district in Peru. To further their ambitions, powerful élite families hired gangs of armed retainers, many of whom were brigands. Conversely, in order to survive, bandits sought integration into local patronage structures.[18] Outlaw guns were consequently used to sustain a system of political bossism (*coronelismo*), which lived on electoral chicanery, the use of the local state for partisan ends, and the harassment of political enemies.[19] The present study shows that all the essential features of factional politics in northeastern Brazil were also to be found in Hualgayoc over the same decades. In Paraíba a cotton boom at the turn of the century engendered more intense clan warfare to control land and commerce.[20] Likewise, in Hualgayoc increased trade after 1890 brought heightened strife to the province. Other striking similarities between the northeast of Brazil and Hualgayoc are the weakness of the state, its lack of a monopoly over the use of violence, and the ability of bandit gangs to outgun the police prior to the 1920s. In Paraíba and northern Cajamarca, endemic banditry was linked to vertical power structures controlled by local magnates, and created important obstacles to the development of class based peasant movements. The

3

prevailing climate of insecurity and violence encouraged the rural poor to enter into protective alliances with their social superiors.[21]

Many of these social traits can also be gleaned from the work of Chandler. His excellent book on the notorious Lampião provides additional points of comparison between banditry in Brazil and Hualgayoc. In both cases state governments attempted to compensate for a weak coercive capability by hiring bandits to eradicate political opponents intent on their overthrow.[22] Vengeance killings did not only claim the lives of male heads of households; women and children often figured among the victims; the displaying of corpses as trophies was practised in both countries. Efficient intelligence networks, safe retreats and bandit-police collusion helped Lampião's career span more than two decades. These have also been found to be factors influencing the longevity of brigands in Hualgayoc. Finally, betrayal decided the fate of bandit chiefs in both localities.

Colombia is another country justifiably renowned for its bandits. The bloody years of 'la Violencia', that commenced in the 1940s, dragged on to the mid-1960s, and is still in evidence in the shape of guerrilla warfare, has earned Colombia a reputation as a nation saturated with rural violence.[23] Here again a number of similarities with the events described in this book can be discerned. An agrarian structure analogous to that found in Hualgayoc developed in parts of the Colombian Andes. This provided an economic framework for the establishment of clientage relations. Organised into rival factions, landlords and merchants strove to win local power by terrorising their opponents. To this end they formed armed bands of gunmen, known as pájaros, to intimidate and eliminate enemies. These were frequently recruited from the rural dispossessed and individuals already engaged in banditry. The struggle for local domination intensified traditional animosities and spawned new feuds, initiating a wave of killing that spun out of control. A weak state was unable to impose its authority or act as a mediator between competing clans. Political clashes unfolding at the national level served to exacerbate local conflicts. Vengeance assassinations elicited both feelings of admiration and fear among the populace. The rural poor were forced to establish ties with one of the rival factions for reasons of security. Simultaneously, a sense that the outlaws were acting in a manly fashion and somehow enjoyed greater control over their own destiny, led many country people to envy them. Such sentiments permitted the emergence of folk-hero mythologies. In the popular consciousness bandits became a symbol of rebellion against an unjust and seemingly unalterable social order.[24] The Colombian experience again illustrates the lesson that once brigands found themselves deprived of the protective cover offered by local power structures, their vulnerability increased and their eradication became more probable.[25] Like their counterparts in Hualgayoc, many Colombian bandits who began their careers as common highwaymen or pistoleers in the pay of a rural racketeer, ended up fighting a primitive guerrilla war for or against the national government.[26] Part-time brigandage appears to have been practised in Colombia, with combatants working as labourers during the coffee harvest.[27] A similar pattern arose in Hualgayoc, where pistoleers alternated thievery and political violence in the highlands with seasonal work on the coastal sugar plantations.

More has been written on Mexican history than any other Latin American country. Studies on banditry, however, remain scarce. In English the only publication of note is Paul Vanderwood's *Disorder and progress*.[28] Important points of convergence between Vanderwood's findings and the situation in Hualgayoc include the dislocative impact of capitalist development in the countryside, weak central authority and the blurred distinction that existed between outlaws and the police (*rurales*). Brigands frequently donned official uniforms and attained the status of law enforcement officers. Many *rurales* moved in the opposite direction, engaging in a wide range of criminal activities. Drunkeness and corruption were rife, just as in Hualgayoc. If detailed works on Mexican banditry are relatively rare, the literature on *caciquismo*, or political bossism, is far richer, a result of the all-important role of local caudillos and their bands of armed followers during the Revolution.[29] Like many of their *cajamarquino* counterparts, caudillos in Mexico were primarily concerned with local matters. Nevertheless, they invariably became embroiled in national conflicts. Less astute at operating outside the realm of provincial politics, involvement in these wider imbroglios brought greater risks and eventually led several to destruction.[30] After making alliances on the basis of a mistaken estimation of the balance of political forces, several caudillos in Mexico rebelled and fell victim to the development of the state. Similar errors of judgement resulted in the demise of Eleodoro Benel, a principal figure in the events described in this book.

Clan politics clearly played a key role in Latin American society during the first decades of this century. With regard to its organisation and operation close resemblances are to be found with southern Europe. The three-tier structure existing in Hualgayoc mirrors that found in Andalucía.[31] The class and occupational background of individuals occupying positions at different levels in a faction's hierarchy is also largely comparable, despite the important socio-economic distinctions that existed between the two regions. Electoral malpractice appears to be another common phenomenon.[32] Both southern Spain and northern Peru boasted a long tradition of bandit activity, although it is difficult to argue that outlaws in Hualgayoc assumed the qualities of 'social bandits', as some of their brothers in Andalucía are reputed to have done.[33]

In Italy also, managed elections fought on no well-defined issues of principle were the norm in the late nineteenth century. Central government control was ineffectual over large areas of the country, especially in the south. Consequently, power and authority were exercised informally at an individual level, rather than through formal or procedural structures. Rural entrepreneurs employed private violence to attain economic and socio-political goals. Crimes of honour frequently occurred, remained unpunished by a corrupt judicial system, and sparked off new vendetta feuds or intensified

5

existing hatreds.[34] Mass political parties intent on acquiring a popular base by mobilising around a common ideological programme were still in their infancy. Local rather than national issues dominated political competition, reflecting a poorly developed national consciousness. Another important similarity between southern Italy and northern Cajamarca is the central role of clientage relations in social and political life. These were rooted in the landlord control of resources and an increasingly precarious peasant economy. Demographic growth, land fragmentation, accelerating market contact and peasant proletarianisation, encouraged the establishment of patron-client ties in southern Italy, just as they did in Hualgayoc.[35] Politics thus revolved around the affairs of local clan networks. The *mafiosi*, in their struggle to control additional resources in a capital scarce society, utilised bands of armed retainers to cow and eliminate opponents. Poor communications, the absence of a strong state and a widespread distrust of government also created conditions in which banditry could flourish. To survive and prosper, outlaws needed to align themselves with a *mafia* network. Like their counterparts in Brazil, Colombia and Peru, successful Italian brigands of necessity became 'political'. Once they moved outside the protective cover provided by a *cosca*, or clique of local political power brokers, life became far more hazardous.[36] Finally, involvement in quixotic political causes of a populist inclination led at least one infamous Sicilian bandit to a fate similar to that which befell Hualgayoc's Eleodoro Benel as described in this book.[37]

Like the present volume, several of these studies have been influenced by the seminal writing of Eric Hobsbawm on the phenomena of pre-modern social movements and banditry. Many of the arguments advanced by Hobsbawm as to the origins and nature of brigandage are supported in this case study on Hualgayoc. Hobsbawm notes that the dislocative impact of agrarian capitalist development contributed to the spread of banditry.[38] In Hualgayoc growing proletarianisation and market contact stimulated many rural inhabitants to engage in non-legal activities. So too did the socio-economic impact of war and breakdown in the political system.[39] The present study stresses the role of Chilean invasion and civil war in encouraging an upsurge in factional strife and criminality. Outlaw inability to evolve even a minimal programme of social reform and produce 'ideas other than those of the peasantry', is a further point of convergence.[40] Hobsbawm notes that on occasions normal bandit activity may degenerate into 'epidemics of cruelty and massacre', a development fomented by uncontrolled blood-feuding and the outlaws' need to instil fear in the local populace.[41] Terror and vengeance assassination form recurrent themes in the story told in this volume. Finally, evidence from Hualgayoc confirms Hobsbawm's contention that 'noble robbers' are not a common breed, and backs his claim that anti-social bandits form the typical representatives of their profession.[42]

In other respects brigandage in Hualgayoc departs from the characteristics mentioned by Hobsbawm. Hobsbawm suggests that banditry 'is rural, not urban'.[43] Several important outlaw chiefs in Hualgayoc alternated their residence between town and country. Many townspeople worked smallholdings. The small highland settlements were focal points of commercial life in the province. Robbers thus looted in both sectors. Given that all bandit gangs eventually became linked to one of the rival factions, and that political competition centred on the district capitals, outlaws were of necessity drawn into urban-based squabbles. For a number of economic and political reasons, therefore, the distinction between rural and urban life remained blurred. Rural banditry was also urban. A second difference between the general characteristics outlined by Hobsbawm and the situation in Hualgayoc concerns the social composition of robber bands. Based on evidence from the Mediterranean world, Hobsbawm concluded that brigands tended to be drawn from the rural unemployed and under-employed, escaped serfs, those fleeing conscription, deserters and men discharged from the army who experienced difficulty reintegrating themselves into peasant society. Shepherds were another occupational group exhibiting a propensity towards banditry, along with individuals who 'are unwilling to accept the meek and passive social role of the subject peasant'.[44] According to Hobsbawm, bandits were normally drawn from the ranks of the 'young and single or unattached'.[45] A dependent family and a tied holding, made it difficult for 'an adult peasant to turn bandit'.[46] While many robbers in northern Cajamarca possessed backgrounds similar to those pinpointed by Hobsbawm – for example, Avelino Vásquez became an outlaw after resisting conscription – some important differences merit attention. Smallholding peasants with dependants, either residing inside estate boundaries or on their own land, formed the hard core of Hualgayoc's bandit gangs. Fugitives from the law frequently sought protection by offering their services to prominent landowners. If acceptable, these would normally be allocated a plot of land and so settle down. The logistics of peasant farming meant that they needed to form a relationship with a local woman and establish a family. Given the pervasiveness of patron-client relations and factional divisions at all social levels, numerous adult peasants invariably became involved in clan imbroglios. On most occasions, no clear dividing line could be drawn between politically motivated conduct and acts of brigandage. Part-time robbery was consequently customary among many male heads of household. Rather than being a hindrance, adult males with dependents possessed certain advantages that permitted the pursuance of a successful outlaw career. Demographic patterns are important here. Families tended to be large, and it is perhaps no coincidence that the most successful bands were based on fathers, sons, brothers and cousins. The kernel of the Ramos, Vargas, Díaz, Vásquez and Avellaneda bands was made up of close relatives. They owned holdings and had families. Ties of blood were usually more trustworthy than loot and provided greater internal cohesion.

Neither were peasants in Hualgayoc 'meek and passive'; bellicosity and bloodshed proved commonplace. Often indistinguishable, a complexity of personal and factional feuds coalesced to produce an extremely violent

7

environment. Just one story will serve as a starting point for what follows. In March 1892 José Encarnación Reaño paid a social call on fellow peasant Manuel Cubas. Cubas then insisted that his guest drink several glasses of sugar cane alcohol (*aguardiente*). While drinking together Cubas started to address his neighbour:

> 'I have seen five doctors and they can't find anything wrong. They say I suffer from idleness. I have visited a wizard (*brujo*), who tells me that you have put a spell on me in order to ruin my health and farm'.[47]

Reaño replied that these accusations were false and there was no proof that a spell had been cast, whereupon Cubas flew into an uncontrollable rage, grabbed his rifle and shouted 'This is the proof!' as he shot Reaño through the heart.[48] Hopefully this book will throw some light on the causes of such behaviour.

# Chapter 2

# Politics and society in late nineteenth century Hualgayoc

## I

The province of Hualgayoc was founded in August 1870, when the province of Chota was divided in two. This newly formed administrative unit was carved out of the southern half of Chota and comprised the seven districts of Bambamarca, Hualgayoc, Llapa, Niepos, San Gregorio, San Miguel and Santa Cruz (see Map 1). Human activity in the province's central area was restricted by the presence of a high *meseta*, which ran from north to south at altitudes of between 3,200 and 3,800 metres. Covering most of the district of Hualgayoc and parts of Bambamarca, Llapa, San Miguel and Santa Cruz, these bleak *jalcas* (moorlands) sustained grasses that were able to survive in the thin acidic soils and withstand the cold nights. Here livestock rearing was the most important human occupation: sheep and cattle roamed freely, grazing the poor quality pastures under the shadow of craggy peaks that in places topped 4,600 metres. Little husbandry was undertaken. Below 4,000 metres some potatoes and other varieties of Andean tubers were sown in sheltered spots, as was *quinua* (quinoa). Demographic density in this ecological zone was low. Isolated homesteads battered by icy winds clung onto the desolate landscape. The only urban settlement was the provincial capital, Hualgayoc, a squalid mining town 3,508 metres above sea level.

A succession of narrow mountain valleys cut by fast flowing rivers broke up the monotonous *jalca*. Sited at altitudes of 2,000 to 2,800 metres, these held relatively fertile soils and provided a hospitable climate for human habitation. The largest valley surrounds the town of Bambamarca, covering an area nearly 15 kilometres wide and 20 kilometres long. Most other valleys have a much smaller extension, such as that adjacent to Llapa, which has a width of 7 kilometres and a similar length. A majority of Hualgayoc's rural population was settled in this ecological zone (around 70 per cent in 1876), living in adobe and wood constructed dwellings topped by red tiled roofs. These homesteads were dotted all over the countryside surrounded by small fields sown with temperate grains (mainly maize and barley), pulses, tubers and vegetables. Livestock rearing was widely practised, animal growth and reproduction being facilitated by the more clement environment. As well as housing the bulk of the rural population, the greater part of Hualgayoc's urban dwellers were settled in the small valley towns of Bambamarca, Llapa, Niepos, San Gregorio, San Miguel and Santa Cruz (see Map 2).

On Hualgayoc's western flank, the central *meseta* rapidly meets the coastal desert in the districts of Niepos, San Gregorio and Santa Cruz. Narrow low-lying valleys gouged by Pacific bound rivers sustain a hot sub-tropical

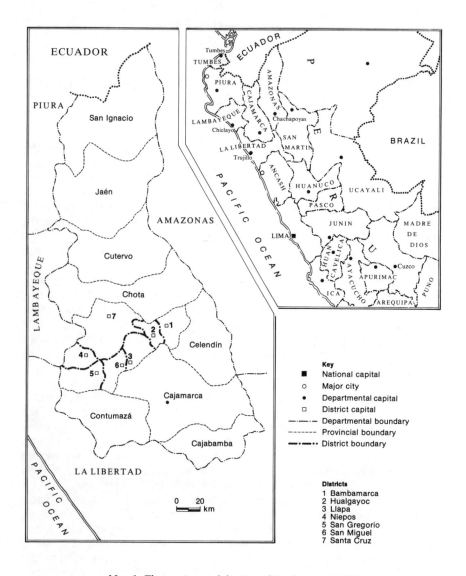

Map 1: *The province and districts of Hualgayoc, c. 1900*

Key
- ■ National capital
- ○ Major city
- ● Departmental capital
- □ District capital
- —·—·— Departmental boundary
- — — — Provincial boundary
- ■—··—··■ District boundary

Districts
1 Bambamarca
2 Hualgayoc
3 Llapa
4 Niepos
5 San Gregorio
6 San Miguel
7 Santa Cruz

10

climate that permitted the cultivation of rice, cassava, sugar cane, avocado, mangos and citrus fruits. Due to a combination of tropical diseases and a limited area of cultivable land, in 1876 these tapering valleys supported only 10 per cent of the province's population.

By the late nineteenth century at least 80 per cent of Hualgayoc's inhabitants obtained a major portion of their living directly from some form of agricultural work. Within the rural economy land was unevenly distributed, large estates covering several thousand hectares claiming ownership of 60 to 70 per cent of the province's surface area.[1] If on these haciendas agricultural innovation was slow and production techniques generally backward, nevertheless estates continuously engaged in commodity exchange. Livestock and foodstuffs were retailed both in coastal markets and in highland towns. The mining industry, centred on Hualgayoc district, also provided an outlet for food products, timber, charcoal and beasts of burden. Most estates were organised along *gutherrschaft* lines, whereby one section of the property was directly under landlord control, with other areas divided up amongst quit-rent tenants (*arrendatarios*), labour-service tenants (*colonos*) or sharecroppers. Competition in the highland labour market, emanating from the mines and coastal agricultural enterprises, meant that cash payments to hacienda employees were more prevalent than has hitherto been assumed.[2]

A majority of landowners resided in their estates for most of the year, enabling them to sustain regular contact with the foremen, tenants and wage labourers in their employ. This face-to-face nature of rural life, coupled with grossly skewed resource allocation, created an environment conducive to the establishment of patron-client relations. Paternalism in the form of calculated gift-giving, when allied to a relatively lax work regime, enabled strong bonds to be formed between the landowning élite and their social inferiors. Such ties were not restricted to the rural world. Several wealthier landlords owned shares in mines and most engaged in mercantile activities. Consequently, their influence extended to Hualgayoc's small urban settlements, which were populated by merchants, artisans, casual labourers, petty traders and a few professionals.[3] This combination of landownership with commerce also supported a numerically small, but socially and politically influential class of small to medium farmer-merchants.

Although large estates monopolised the soil, peasant freeholders comprised at least 70 per cent of Hualgayoc's rural population.[4] A majority of smallholders participated in on-farm and off-farm pursuits because of land fragmentation and an inability to meet subsistence needs. Semi-proletarianised peasants sought seasonal employment in the mines and coastal agriculture.[5] They traded food and artisan products in highland and coastal towns. Muleteering, animal dealing and cattle droving to the coast were other well-subscribed activities.[6] Local taxation also forced peasant households to participate in product and labour markets.

Thus, in the decades leading up to 1900, extra-estate peasant households in Hualgayoc were by no means isolated from the national economy. On the

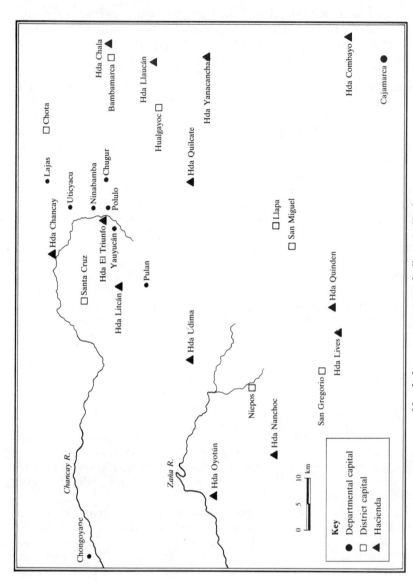

*Map 2: Important estates and villages in Hualgayoc*

contrary, a majority were already caught up in a process of proletarianisation, regularly migrating to the coast in search of work or for trading purposes, and freely engaged in commodity exchange. Participation in these pursuits created a highly mobile peasantry with an intimate knowledge of terrain, — advisable prerequisites for successful brigandry or guerrilla warfare.

## II

Throughout the latter half of the nineteenth century, Hualgayoc was prone to personalist, as opposed to ideological, socio-political conflict. Although divisions along class lines did occur, the population most commonly decided its political allegiances on the basis of personal acquaintance or social expendiency.[7] Indeed, given the face-to-face nature of rustic life, the low incidence of urbanisation, and the total absence of well-organised political parties capable of rallying mass support around a common ideological programme, it was only natural that political competition revolved around men instead of ideas.[8] Rural society was, therefore, vertically segmented on 'political' issues, so that at any given moment every small town, village or rural parish tended to be divided into two or even three rival bands, with each political group a poly-class amalgam in which landlords, merchants, smallholding peasants, quasi-urban artisans and rural labourers participated. At the departmental and provincial level, factional leaders were normally the most important landowners or wealthier mineowners and merchants, with leadership in the districts usually assumed by medium-scale farmer-merchants or the occasional quack lawyer. The third tier in a faction's informally organised hierarchical structure was most commonly composed of *coqs de village*, richer peasants or the more prosperous artisan-farmers, who nurtured their own and their superiors' political and economic ambitions at hamlet level.

Clientage bonds within a political faction were not forged and sustained around a collection of commonly held political ideas, but through the more practical medium of economic advancement. If, for example, a member of one faction managed to attain appointment as provincial subprefect, he generally strove to have his followers named as governors of the various districts, as lieutenant governors in each parish housing over three hundred inhabitants, and as mayors presiding over a supportive majority on the town councils. Since the governors and lieutenant governors were charged with supervising the collection of head taxes (the *contribución personal*), land taxes, duties on livestock being marketed outside the province, duties on sugar cane alcohol production and sale, as well as other retail taxes, opportunities for financial gain were abundant. These officials were also charged with the marshalling of collective labour on public works, such as highway construction and repair, maintaining public buildings or the local water supply. Furthermore, it was the same men acting in co-ordination with the subprefect, who organised the selection of conscripts for the army, and decided the composition of the local militias, who were subject to their command. Control over the collection of head and land taxes was important not only due to the fact that it presented opportunities for graft, or that the collector was allowed to retain a percentage of the proceeds as a commission. Arbitrary tax collections could be (and were) imposed, using the slightest pretext.[9] Tax collection also provided the means through which supporters of one's own faction might be rewarded by exempting them from payment or alternatively lowering the amount paid. New loyalties could thus be fashioned and existing ties strengthened. At the same time, members of the opposing camp could be harassed into prompt payment and made to pay sums in access of the legally stipulated figure. Similarly, a blind eye could be turned to one of the governing partys' business of driving cattle to the coast or conducting a brisk trade in liquor, while an opponent performing the same commercial activities would be closely watched and taxed accordingly. Apart from being victim to this kind of discriminative behaviour, rivals of the local governor tended to find that their sons were being shanghaied into the army, or only released by the recruiting squad after the payment of a hefty bribe, while the governor's supporters remained unmolested by military conscription. Control over the local militia had obvious ramifications, insofar as it was invariably composed of members belonging to the governor's faction and acted according to his whims, with little effort being made to disguise arbitrary actions behind a veneer of official impartiality.

Given this situation, it can be appreciated that the outcome of inter-factional competition had important implications for all aspects of rural life, ranging from everyday economic well-being, to family stability, and ultimately, to physical survival. This meant that the struggle for local domination was fiercely fought and frequently terminated in violent confrontation.

By the 1850s the personalist mode of political competition between rival factions was already well established. Throughout Peru in 1854 a civil war raged between supporters of Ramón Castilla and those of president Echenique. Castilla's victory led to the establishment of a 'liberal' government (1854–56) which abolished slavery and Indian tribute as part of a political manoeuvre to gain support at Echenique's expense. These policies provoked a backlash in the shape of general Vivanco, who rose against Castilla in late 1856, so initiating a period of factional dispute (1856–58) that eventually resulted in the 'conservative' semi-restoration of 1860.[10] Events such as these, fought out on a national plane, had important repercussions in the Cajamarca region. Indeed, the department itself was founded as a consequence of the liberal 'revolution' that occurred on 3 January 1854. This liberal victory, however, was not peacefully accepted by the pro-Echenique/Vivanco faction in Cajamarca, with the result that violent confrontations took place in 1855 and following years. On 19 January 1855 Hualgayoc town was attacked by an armed band led by Juan Montoya, the right-hand man of José Manuel

14

Osores, a prosperous merchant whose commercial affairs were centred on the town of Chota. Osores had been subprefect of the province during the toppled Echenique regime, and was faction leader for that group in the zone. A majority of the populace of Hualgayoc had opted for the rival cause, and in his eagerness to wreak revenge on the townspeople, Osores managed to effect several deaths through gun-shot wounds. In the words of the then subprefect:

> 'These innocent liberal citizens were sacrificed by the rabid supporters of Echenique. They were unmercifully gunned down at close range by the *nacionales* from Chota, who were led by ex-subprefect Don José Manuel Osores under the command of Don Juan Montoya, to stifle the wishes of the people'.[11]

Similar incidents were to take place throughout 1855 and 1856. For example, in December 1856 Montoya was once again on the attack, on this occasion entering Bambamarca, where he raised a band of twelve well-armed men from the ranks of his faction's allies among the townsfolk. Responding to events occurring at the national level, Montoya 'proclaimed general Vivanco as the Regenerator of Peru' and announced that he was the new subprefect.[12] The existing governor rallied his supporters, a gun-fight developed, and Montoya was chased out of town.

### III

Events such as these were not uncommon in the 1860s and 1870s, especially when elections were taking place or at moments when national political conflicts became particularly intense. But although acts of violence occurred, politically motivated assassination and despoilation was far from endemic. By the 1880s this situation had radically altered. Playing a crucial role in this new development was the impact of war on the rural populace, and the period of civil war that swept through highland Cajamarca over the years 1882–85. The events taking place in Cajamarca during the War of the Pacific were of an extremely complex nature, and due to considerations of space cannot be fully detailed here.[13] Some comment, nevertheless, needs to be made on a few essential points.

Upon declaring war on Peru in April 1879 the Chileans marched northwards, quickly registering military victories in the southern departments of Peru. Thereafter, Peru's military position degenerated, the decisive battles of the war being fought on the outskirts of Lima in January 1881, when the Chileans routed the badly organised, poorly trained and ill-equiped defending forces. The Chilean army also launched an expedition to conquer and plunder northern Peru, entering this region in September 1880. Notwithstanding the fact that Peru was engaged in a war, had suffered humiliating defeats and that a Chilean invasion of Cajamarca appeared imminent, the

15

political factions in Hualgayoc province found it impossible to establish a united opposition to the enemy and to pool their human and material resources in an attempt to repel the invaders. Instead, long established animosities continued to dominate. Thus, in Bambamarca a plan to defend the town by constructing a network of trenches and stockades could not be implemented due to:

> 'a political plot that has caused a shameful division among the people and led to the deplorable situation of spilling human blood. While this is a worthwhile sacrifice in the defence of our sacred and wounded Nation, certain evil intentioned individuals value this less than the furtherance of their own personal interests...Don Luis García, in whose house flutters the national flag, and where cries of support for Peru and general Montero can be heard, has placed at my disposal the arms that he possesses to defend his home'.[14]

García's house was besieged and the roof set ablaze by the rival *iglesista* faction. 'On the other hand', continued the subprefect:

> 'the lieutenant governor supports the opposing band, which publically utters cries of 'Death to general Montero' and 'Long live the Iglesias and Santolallas'. The mayor and lieutenant governor show open rebellion and insolence. It is urgent that twenty-five soldiers be sent to restore public order, as well as collect arms which are being used in the useless spilling of blood, and are undermining public morale and social stability. The townsfolk should be trying to defend Peru and not fighting factional conflicts'.[15]

Others used the war as a pretext for personal economic advancement and criminal behaviour against the civilian population, as is illustrated by the following letter from the governor of San Miguel to the prefect:

> 'Don Simón Soberón and the group of individuals that he commands left this town on the road to Santa Cruz, without committing additional crimes from those that I have already informed you about. But one league outside the town, this band began to fire rifle shots as if they were in combat...no doubt with the intention of terrorising people living in the hamlets they passed through, and to rob them at gun-point of whatever took their fancy. This happened to citizen Don Domingo Chuquilín, a resident of Rodeopampa in this district. He was hung by his testicles and tortured, after which Soberón's men looted his house, robbing S/.1,800 in franked silver, gold and silver jewels, clothing and horses. They have not even left him with a bed to sleep in. Moreover, Soberón has been threatening that on his return next February, people will feel the severity of his character, and it is very likely that the outrageous crimes that he has been committing since receiving his commission from His Excellency the President of the Republic will be repeated'.[16]

16

The governor proceeded to note that San Miguel had contributed its share to the war effort and should not be:

'the victim of abuses of authority by arrogant officers who come here pretending to be defenders of the Nation, demanding that their slightest whims be immediately satisfied. They have kept the horses that were lent to them, and it appears that they want to fleece the population. With *guerrilleros* such as these life has no guarantee . . . under the pretext of *guerrilleros* they are destroying the places they visit, worsening the disastrous situation that has befallen us due to the savage War'.[17]

In part this situation is indicative of the debility of the Peruvian state at this juncture, as well as the predominance of a localised outlook and a poorly-developed national consciousness among the local population. This is understandable insofar as war against Chile was but a passing event brought about by non-local issues, whereas the inter-factional struggle was an indigenous phenomenon that grew out of the pores of Hualgayoc society, and one that would continue long after the Chileans had departed.

Personal and factional, as opposed to national, sentiments dominated to such an extent that they prevented the formation of a unified army. Local caudillos and factional leaders invested themselves with military titles, formed armed columns of their own supporters and set off to do combat. Miguel Iglesias (1830-1909) was departmental chief of the *pierolista* faction and occupied the post of Minister of War in Piérola's government. Iglesias was one of Hualgayoc's most important landlords, owning the 50,000 hectare hacienda Udima in San Miguel. In 1879 he formed an armed column of upwards of five hundred men, many of whom were drawn from tenants housed on his estate. Heading the rival faction was José Mercedes Puga (1836-85), who in the late 1870s emerged as a leading *civilista* caudillo. Puga was landlord of La Pauca and Huagal estates. These contiguous properties in the district of San Marcos covered a little under 50,000 hectares, and supported a population of 898 at the time of the 1876 census. As in the case of Iglesias, their inhabitants formed the core of Puga's force of between four to five hundred irregulars.[18] Although neither man had any formal military training or experience when war broke out, Iglesias proclaimed himself a 'general' and Puga more modestly adopted the rank of 'colonel'.

Representatives of a national military hierarchy in name only (the Peruvian state rapidly disintegrated after the fall of Lima and responsibility for conducting the war rested on the shoulders of regional caudillos), Iglesias and Puga pursued separate campaigns and found it impossible to co-operate. Indeed, the harassment of factional opponents was more often than not conducted with greater gusto than attacks against the Chileans. Within the Iglesias camp, such attitudes prevailed to an extent that a Chilean victory was regarded as a lesser evil than the military success of the Cáceres-Puga faction. Favourable progress by Cáceres and Puga on the battlefield, it was argued, would enhance their rivals' political prestige, combat capacity and undermine efforts being made by Iglesias to terminate the war. For example, at the time of the battle of Huamachuco (10 July 1883), Iglesias was actively co-operating with the Chilean forces, so condemning the troops led by general Cáceres to defeat. His faction in Cajamarca celebrated the Chilean victory as their own, going so far as to congratulate the Chilean commander Gorostiaga on his success.[19]

Already in 1882, and more markedly by 1883, the nodal point of factional conflict turned on the question of whether or not to continue the war. Eager to end hostilities and prevent further economic destruction through waging what he considered to be a futile war against a stronger enemy, in October 1883 Miguel Iglesias signed the Treaty of Ancón and was declared president of Peru with Chilean backing. Cáceres and Puga, on the other hand, despised this collaborationist behaviour and determined to continue the struggle employing guerrilla tactics. Thus, the scene was set for the bitter civil war which raged between 1883 and 1885. More than any other single issue, the question of continuing or terminating the war was to raise political passions and determine factional loyalties in Cajamarca for two generations.

Under guidance from local caudillos, each town and hamlet divided on this contentious topic. Puga's armed column of *montoneros*, or rebels, swept through Hualgayoc and Chota, occupying Chiclayo in August 1884. By mid-1884 Puga's supporters dominated large areas of highland Cajamarca. They then proceeded to launch a series of campaigns against *iglesistas* in Trujillo, Huaraz and Huamachuco. Amid growing chaos gun rule was the order of the day, as rival bands committed murder to even up past scores, or engaged in acts of common criminality. Thus, in May 1884 the governor in Niepos informed the subprefect that:

> 'ex-governor don Antonio Pérez, Agustín Vásquez and his broth-ers, Francisco Torres and other criminals continue their armed attacks on this town, as they have been since Wednesday of last week. On 29 April they robbed and burnt down my farm Céquez, causing more than S/.8,000 in damage. They also robbed me of a good mule. From this valley they have stolen more than twenty-five cattle. The animals have been sold on the coast in order to attain cash with which to buy men, arms and ammunition. The outlaws are breaking into houses in the countryside and robbing whatever they find. These vandals have pickets of armed men watching the roads'.[20]

Over the following three years politically motivated bloodletting and economic pillage was so prevalent in Niepos that many families abandoned the district and sought refuge on the coast.

Similar conflicts were taking place in Bambamarca, where in April 1884 the governor was a member of the Cáceres-Puga alliance. The subprefect, an *iglesista*, wanted him removed and replaced by a member of the ruling faction. He alleged that the governor and his backers were smuggling arms into the town from Chota as well as maintaining a clandestine correspondence with José Mercedes Puga. According to a confidential letter that had been intercepted by the subprefect's spies, even the priests in Bambamarca were plotting with the Puga faction.[21] On 7 October 1885 Puga's *montoneros* led by 'colonel' Tomás Romero launched a major offensive, attacking the departmental capital. The prefect reported to Lima that the rebel forces numbered 1,843 'well-armed and supplied' men.[22] Several hours of fierce street combat took place. It was claimed that 109 of Puga's men were killed and a further 151 taken prisoner before the attempt to capture Cajamarca town was abandoned. Following this defeat the most intensive phase of the civil war came to an end, but animosities continued to simmer long after the assassination of José Mercedes Puga in Huamachuco.[23]

On 3 June 1886 general Cáceres was installed as president, a political development that motivated a further bout of bloodshed in Hualgayoc. Puga's supporters sought revenge for the persecutions they had suffered at the hands of the *iglesista* faction, who in turn strove to oust Cacerist officials by fair means or foul. In June 1887 a group of armed 'bandits' led by the Díaz brothers entered Bambamarca and began to fire their rifles in the streets. When the Cacerist governor attempted to restore order, he was gunned down. The assassins, reported the subprefect, 'obey a political plan . . . encouraged by the support they receive from many *azules* (blues) in this province'.[24] The subprefect pleaded for troops to be sent on the grounds that 'all the caudillos of Iglesias are to be found in this province, as well as many of those from Chota. I cannot sustain my position without a permanent force, if need be consisting of citizens from here, choosing the most dependable'.[25] Factional schism of this genre was to continue in all districts up to the end of the century and beyond.[26]

A second sequel to the war and the civil war that succeeded it was a marked upsurge in lawlessness, most commonly in the form of banditry. During the hostilities rival armies travelled throughout the countryside, leaving behind the customary trail of economic disruption. Crops and livestock were requisitioned, special taxes to finance the war exacted, while the Chilean forces placed *cupos*, or ransoms, on the inhabitants of every locality they visited. Consequently, the septennium 1879–85 brought a rapid decline in an already precarious peasant economy.[27] Many labourers, peasants and artisans turned to banditry as a solution to their economic difficulties. In this they were aided by a collapse of the state as a source of law enforcement and coercion. Furthermore, large numbers of peasants armed themselves during the period 1879–85, becoming acquainted with handling firearms.[28]

Groups of bandits were thus operating in all of Hualgayoc's districts by the late 1880s, making the highways unsafe for travellers. In Niepos and San Gregorio a group of sixty-four bandits was engaged in robbing cattle and making exactions from merchants, artisans and peasants alike. The leaders of this band were the brothers Agustín, Edilberto and Rosendo Vásquez. Agustín Vásquez was governor of Niepos at this time, using his official position as a tool for personal enrichment and a cover for illegal activities.[29] Matters became so bad that during 1887 the subprefect mounted two expeditions to crush the Vásquez gang. Both failed miserably, due to the criminal's preparedness and good equipment: according to the subprefect 'they are well armed with weapons belonging to the state'.[30] As a result, this bandit group was able to continue unhindered its main line of 'business', that of rustling cattle in the highlands, driving them down to the coast and selling them to landlords in the Zaña valley. Those landowners who benefited from this trade protected the brigands 'under the pretext of employing them as tenants and labourers'.[31]

Armed bands also stalked the moors around Bambamarca and Hualgayoc, stealing from neighbouring haciendas as well as peasant freeholders. From time to time they invaded local towns to perpetrate acts of pillage and violence against personal enemies or innocent bystanders.[32] Other bandit groups operated along coast-bound trade routes in San Miguel and Santa Cruz. Although periodic attempts were undertaken to quell banditry in the zone, state officials lacked coercive capacity, tact or zest, so their efforts proved largely futile. Moves to control brigandage were especially hampered because each armed group developed ties with one or other of the political factions competing for dominance in Hualgayoc, and received protection from them. The career of Daniel Díaz is indicative in this respect. It was Daniel Díaz who shot the Cacerist governor of Bambamarca in June 1887. Díaz enjoyed the protection of *iglesista* supporters in the province, notably that of Leopoldo Santolalla, a prominent member of Hualgayoc's mining élite. With *iglesista* assistance he managed to elude the posse sent to apprehend him after the governor's assassination. He was finally captured in Hualgayoc town on 15 March 1888, while enjoying a drinking session with political associate and lawyer Eloy Carranza. Both were 'completely drunk and shouting against the authorities . . . and even against His Excellency General Cáceres, saying he was a crook and a wretch unfit for office'.[33] Boasting that he had more than forty rifles at his command, Díaz was thrown into jail, but escaped thanks to outside *iglesista* assistance on 29 April 1888, fleeing to the hacienda Yanacancha, whose owner was a prominent sympathizer of the *iglesista* faction.[34] Captured again in early 1890, Díaz was bailed out of prison by Leopoldo Santolalla, and fled the night before he was due to be sentenced. On this occasion he sought refuge in the hacienda Combayo, owned by the Santolalla family, and once more formed his armed band under *iglesista* patronage. Resuming his bandit activities, Díaz remained a wanted man until 1895, when the *iglesista* faction in Hualgayoc regained control over the bureaucracy upon Piérola's accession to the presidency. This event transformed Díaz's status overnight: from common outlaw he became a custodian of law and order in the province. Receiving arms and ammunition from the subprefect, he was instructed to hunt down the Tello gang, which had more than forty members, and was the largest outlaw group in the Hualgayoc-Bambamarca area not in the pay of the *iglesistas*.[35]

20

This tendency to use control of official positions in order to arm supporters of the dominant band, confiscate weapons possessed by the opposing faction and harass them to the utmost in all walks of life, meant that there could be no pretence that the representatives of the state were neutral. Impartiality gave way to active intervention in partisan politics, thus further debilitating an already weak state at the local level by depriving it of any semblence of moral authority and legitimacy.[36] Rather than being a prerogative of the state, authority was mostly exercised by individuals through control of a well-armed bandit group, and was on a personal basis. Legitimacy was also vested in individuals rather than in the state. This was attained either through ownership of wealth and the concomitant ability to establish patron-client relations, or via the charismatic qualities of a particular individual, as was the case with many bandit chiefs of peasant origin.

## IV

The institutionalised disorder that characterised local politics from the 1880s through to the early decades of this century was also mirrored at the national level. Formally, Peruvian politics was dominated by competition between parties, but these were divided more by personal jealousies and ambitions than by principle. Like their local counterparts, parties in Lima were unstable coalitions headed by caudillos, a situation noted by Víctor Andrés Belaúnde, who emphasised the high level of infighting both within and between the various groupings in Congress. Personalised conflict, he argued, was especially prevalent inside the ruling party, where rivalry for the spoils of office was intense, resulting in low internal cohesion and 'anarchy'.[37] Political schism was exacerbated by the lack of adherence to a common ideology that could discipline and bind parliamentary groups, a situation which induced Belaúnde to comment that:

'One commits a grave error if the study of Peruvian politics is conducted according to the following formula: conservatives and liberals, consolidators and reformers, elitist or democratic tendencies, individualist or socialist currents. All this vocabulary has no meaning in Peru. The first thing an impartial and intelligent observer of the political scene has to do is to ignore all this cheap terminology. Neither should the political parties be taken seriously into account; even less as to what is attributed to them by way of programme or characteristics. Our parties are imaginary entities, abstract nouns, inconsistent and ephemeral personal groupings...Everyone who has studied Peruvian politics and history agrees that we are not a democracy, and not even an oligarchy. In varying degree the Peruvian system is personalist'.[38]

Thus, in the 1870s Peruvian politics was dominated at the national level by the conflict between the Partido Civil, formed by Manuel Pardo, president

21

between 1872 and 1876, and the followers of Nicolás de Piérola, the Minister of Finance under president Balta, who, in 1869, had deprived the Peruvian élite of the lucrative business of exporting guano in return for loans to the government. Piérola, a demagogic but fundamentally conservative figure, became *de facto* president of Peru after the flight of the *civilista*-backed head of state Mariano Ignacio Prado in 1879. In 1884 Piérola founded the Democrat Party as a vehicle through which he could further his political ambitions. At the same time military caudillo Andrés Cáceres used the Constitutional Party as a tool to contest political office with the *civilistas* and Piérola's Democrats. Cáceres and his followers, supported in the late 1880s by sectors of a deeply split Partido Civil, formed administrations from 1885 until 1895, when they were ousted by a *montonera* uprising backed by Democrats and *civilistas*. Although Piérola assumed the presidency, it was the Partido Civil, a coalition of landowners, businessmen and representatives of the Lima middle class, who increasingly dominated national politics. In 1897 the political scene was further complicated when Augusto Durand and his circle of associates in parliament broke with Piérola and the Democrats, eventually founding the Liberal Party in 1901.[39] Consequently, three of Peru's four parties were dominated by caudillos, while the fourth, the *civilistas*, suffered from deep internal divisions caused by personal and familial rivalries. These problems within the Partido Civil deepened after 1909, during Leguía's first administration, and the splits were never healed. The result was a decade of political instability which included the two-year presidency of Guillermo Billinghurst, who had a strong popular appeal and who was removed from office by a coup d'etat early in 1914 led by military officers and members of all the major parties. This did not resolve the crisis and after the four-year adminstration of José Pardo, which began in 1915, Leguía seized the presidency, occupying the post until 1930. His eleven-year dictatorship brought an end to the *república aristocrática* and to outright oligarchic rule in Peru.

In Congress representatives of regional élites and their lawyer assistants gathered around national caudillos like Piérola, Cáceres and Durand, as well as leading politicians in the Partido Civil. These *caciques parlamentarios* provided a vital link between the national leaders and their circles of associates in the provinces.[40] If the dominance of Lima, the effective residence of much of the coastal oligarchy, went unchallenged, that dominance was only loosely imposed, so that the national state depended on local élites, delegating political functions, especially in the highlands, to *gamonales*.[41] The degree to which the Peruvian state existed outside Lima, apart from control of certain provincial capitals such as Trujillo, is questionable, since as we shall see below, in no way was the state 'the monopolist of violence in a given territory', which according to Weber's definition is its defining characteristic.

If the prevalence of 'ephemeral personal groupings' captained by caudillos instead of stable parties contributed to political 'anarchy', so too did the electoral system, which further weakened state legitimacy and instilled a strong element of violence and fraud into political competition. Although between 1900 and 1919 polling formally functioned in accordance with legislation passed in 1896, early twentieth century electoral attitudes and practices were greatly influenced by patterns of behaviour promoted by previous decrees. Of especial relevance was the 1861 electoral law. This act granted suffrage rights to men over twenty-one years of age and married males under that limit. Women and illiterates were disenfranchised, but unlettered master craftsmen and foremen qualified. If they owned property and paid taxes, male illiterates also enjoyed voting rights.[42] Theoretically this clause enfranchised the peasantry, but in practice suffrage stopped at the petty bourgeois trader and artisan. Voting rights also extended more to the highland towns than to the countryside. Rarely did the number of voters in a district exceed a few hundred.[43] As in Spain and Italy during this period, tiny electorates presented ample opportunity for manipulation and fraud. By influencing a relatively small number of votes an election could be decided. Bribery and corruption proved commonplace. When allied to mass exclusion and partisan interference by state functionaries on behalf of official candidates, all this acted to deprive the electoral process of legitimacy and lower Congress in popular estimation.

In addition to encouraging justifiable cynicism, the mechanism through which polling was organised bred political violence. The legislation of 1861 allowed a large degree of decentralisation. Electoral rolls were drawn up by district officials, usually a committee comprising the local mayor, governor and judge. Control over the register provided one key to electoral success, resulting in fierce rivalry to occupy these positions. Once in charge of drawing up the register opponents could be struck from the electoral list. Deceased persons and fictitious names were frequently added.[44]

Apart from gerrymandering, polling procedures frequently induced bloody clashes. On election day voters assembled in the district capital. After mass in the parish church, the ballot commenced with a show of hands to elect a *mesa permanente*, a small committee of citizens whose task was to administer the proceedings, issuing voting slips, supervising the ballot-box and counting the votes. When this body had been appointed, electors were then supposed to elect a group of local citizens mandated to attend an electoral college held in the provincial capital. Here votes were cast to select the president and members of Congress. Within this complicated system, the outcome of an election largely depended on which faction managed to control the *mesa permanente*. To achieve this it was standard practice for faction leaders to assemble their dependents in the district capitals on the eve of polling day. Hired gunmen might also be contracted. Early next morning the band would launch an assault to capture electoral rolls and ballot papers, enabling them to 'win' the election. This tactic was knows as *'el encierro y la toma de mesas'*, the encircling and seizing of voting tables. These events invariably led to pitched battles in the town square between rival factions using firearms, machetes, rocks and clubs.[45]

23

In an attempt to curb such excesses and dampen factional rivalry, the Piérola government promulgated a more centralist electoral law in 1896. Efforts were also made to democratise the process somewhat by abolishing electoral colleges so as to allow direct voting for candidates. A nine-member National Election Council, the *Junta Electoral Nacional*, was now given the task of organising elections.[46] This body was empowered to appoint members to departmental and provincial electoral committees, the *Junta Electoral Departamental*, and *Junta Electoral Provincial*. This latter organ was charged with supervising the election at a provincial level and its membership was supposed to be determined by a random draw to select five *mayores contribuyentes,* or leading taxpayers, living in the provincial capital. The provincial committee in turn appointed district level bodies and supervised the elaboration of an electoral register. Membership of these local committees and the voting roll could be examined and altered by the Lima-based National Election Council. The Council also had to select *Juntas Escrutadoras*, or Scrutinizing Committees, in each province. This was supposed to comprise five members, one from each of five occupational groups.[47]

The 1896 legislation failed to moderate electoral fraud and armed conflict. No widening of the franchise occurred, so the voting register remained small, local interest powerful and electoral chicanery rife. Nationally, control of the Nation Election Council became vital in determining electoral fortunes, while locally conflict centred on dominating provincial and district level meetings of *mayores contribuyentes.* Hustings to choose a president and members of Congress took place in theory every four years, but one-third of the senate and deputies was renewed every two years. After the death of Candamo in 1904 presidential and congressional elections were out of phase until 1919. Municipal elections were also held biennially. Frequent hustings gave added impetus to faction-based political turmoil. Despite attempts at reform, during the early decades of this century the route to electoral success still remained the violent seizure of voting urns and ballot slips.

V

From the above account it can be appreciated that a *mélange* of structural and superstructural developments occurring in Hualgayoc during the late nineteenth century contributed in different ways to the outbreak of endemic violence between 1900 and 1930. Of prime importance was the high degree of peasant freeholder involvement in off-farm pursuits. Tendencies towards pauperisation forced numerous smallholders into more frequent contact with local landowners and merchants, so encouraging the cementing of close patron-client ties and a concomitant heightening of peasant embroilment in factional conflicts. Semi-proletarianisation also stimulated freeholder nomadism, providing many male household heads with certain necessary qualities if the jump from peasant smallholder to proficient bandit or clan warrior was to be successfully accomplished. Migration to the coast or within the highlands widened horizons and peasant knowledge of the surrounding terrain. Muleteering and cattle droving likewise acquainted freeholders with trade routes, the business habits of merchants, the location of good ambuscades and hide-outs, as well as enabling peasants to establish a network of contacts over wide areas. Not surprisingly, the distinction between cattle drover or muleteer on the one hand, and part-time rustler or full-time brigand on the other, was frequently blurred.

On the political front, Hualgayoc had in the recent past undergone the traumatic experience of foreign invasion and civil war. These conflicts spelt economic ruin for many freeholders, who sought in banditry a solution to their material problems. This alternative was fomented by two other consequences of the war: arms were widely distributed among the population, who were also trained to shoot. The collapse of an already chronically weak state, devoid of coercive powers and moral authority, further encouraged the spread of lawlessness. Another development heralded by conflict with Chile and the ensuing civil war was an exacerbation of faction-based fratricidal strife that permeated all sections of society, from the salons of Hualgayoc's landed and mining élite down into the smallest cells of peasant society. After 1900 this conflict was to follow an unforseen path, one which would lead many of its participants to an untimely death.

# CHAPTER 3

# Commercial Rivalry and Factional Violence 1900–1913

## I

If conditions propitious to a generalised outbreak of vendetta politics intermingled with banditry arose out of late nineteenth century developments in Hualgayoc, then the catalyst bringing this potentially explosive situation to fruition was to appear around the turn of the century, paradoxically in the shape of a mild economic recovery. Rising silver production in the late 1890s and the early 1900s pumped more specie into Hualgayoc's battered economy, stimulating business activity. Commerce was further encouraged by a rapid expansion between 1890 and 1920 of agrarian capitalism in the neighbouring department of Lambayeque. During the agricultural year 1894-5 haciendas in the coastal Chancay and Zaña valleys produced 10,000 metric tons of sugar. Output steadily increased to average 29,724 metric tons over the period 1911-13, before growing sharply to a level of 60,698 metric tons in 1920. By the agricultural year 1914-15 approximately two-thirds of the cultivated land in Chancay and Zaña was under sugar cane.[1] These developments on the coast had a profound impact in Hualgayoc. Demographic increase among the coastal population allied to an absorption of cereal fields and pastures by the relentless advance of sugar cane, meant that Hualgayoc became a significant supplier of livestock and agricultural products to coastal markets. Nor was this growing regional trade confined to animals and foodstuffs, for an ever increasing number of migrant labourers also made their way down to the sugar estates of Cayaltí, Pucalá, Pátapo, Pomalca and Tumán in the years leading up to 1920.[2] Profits were also to be made from the retailing of basic commodities and manufactured goods among a highland population that had, through necessity, become more deeply integrated into the national economy. Hualgayoc's merchants and landowners fiercely competed among each other to control the largest possible share of this expanding commercial activity, naturally looking to the utilisation of factional political structures as a means through which they could further their entrepreneurial ambitions.

Nowhere were the tensions brought about by this growth in trade more visible than in the district of Santa Cruz, which straddles the Andes' western flank and thus occupied a key position on the trade routes linking the highlands with the Chancay and Zaña valleys. The most consequential business figure in Santa Cruz was Eleodoro Benel Zuloeta, the owner by inheritance of the hacienda El Triunfo, also called La Samana. This property occupied approximately 5,000 hectares in the parish of Samana twenty-five kilometres south-east of Santa Cruz town on the banks of the upper reaches of the Chancay river (see Map 2). Upon his marriage to Domitila Bernal, Eleodoro Benel was able to join his wife's adjacent *fundo* Santa Rosa de Achiramayo to El Triunfo, thus forming the most extensive agricultural enterprise in the district. In 1920 he increased his landholding interests still further with the acquisition of the haciendas Silugán and Sedamayo, estates sited in the northern part of Cuervo province which covered nearly 25,000 hectares adjacent to the Chamaya and Huajango rivers, tributaries of the Marañón.[3]

Nature had been kind to El Triunfo, its ecological diversity furnishing the landowner with a variety of vendible commodities. Nearly one-fifth of the estate lay in a sheltered inter-Andean valley at altitudes of 1,800 to 2,200 metres. On these lands Eleodoro Benel cultivated sugar cane for processing into *aguardiente* and *chancaca*, two products that always enjoyed a buoyant demand in Hualgayoc's mining camps, towns and villages. Soils in this ecological niche were also dedicated to the cultivation of maize, legumes and improved pastures. Most of the maize was destined for pig meal. Pig rearing and lard manufacture was a major business activity in El Triunfo, the estate's pens containing a herd of over two hundred improved stock.[4] After being fattened on cane pulp and cereals, the swine were slaughtered in the hacienda. Lard was tinned and sold in the highland towns, the coastal sugar estates, Chiclayo and Chepén. Most of the meat went at a nominal price to families settled on the hacienda and its environs, or was retailed in the local towns of Santa Cruz, Hualgayoc and Bambamarca. The lower slopes rising up from the valley floor were given over to wheat and root crops, as well as enclosed meadows, which provided pasture for large numbers of cattle, mules and horses. The main market for cattle was the coastal sugar estates and towns, whilst during times of peace the mules were used for moving Benel's goods to market. A limited amount of dairying was practised, butter being tinned and transported down to coastal markets or the highland mining camps. Extensive woodlands covered the surrounding mountains at elevations between 2,600 and 3,000 metres. Timber was sold to the mines at Hualgayoc for shoring galleries and smelting, as well as supplying the highland market with wood for construction purposes.[5] Eleodoro Benel was not an absentee landlord: he exploited El Triunfo, in the main employing quit-rent tenants and wage labourers who were recruited from minifundist zones adjacent to his estate.[6] He also installed carpenter's and blacksmith's shops on the estate, which apart from their normal tasks manufactured rudimentary agricultural implements such as spades, hoes, picks and machetes.[7]

Silugán and Sedemayo were never so intensively exploited as the El Triunfo complex. Here Benel largely eschewed wage labour and relied on quit-rent tenants and sharecroppers to produce coffee, tropical fruits, sugar cane and small quantities of coca.[8] Cattle rearing was the only branch of these estates' economic activity that involved the payment of cash wages. No doubt

27

this greater reliance on tenancy agreements was in part due to problems of administrative control, for these properties lay three days strenuous horse ride from El Triunfo, the nodal point of Benel's business operation. Fruit, coca and liquor produced on Silugán and Sedemayo were retailed in the highlands, while coffee was sold to the foreign-owned merchant houses based in Chiclayo. Livestock were mostly marketed in the coast.

In addition to his wide-ranging landowning interests, Eleodoro Benel was also heavily involved in mercantile pursuits, owning well-stocked shops in the *plazas* of Bambamarca, Chota, Hualgayoc and Santa Cruz, to add to that he possessed in the hacienda El Triunfo. These establishments retailed agricultural products provisioned from his estates as well as manufactures and luxury items imported from Europe and the USA. Purchased through the larger merchant houses located in Chiclayo and Pacasmayo, these latter commodities were transported up the winding trails into the highlands by the returning mule trains that had delivered the fruits of Benel's haciendas to his coastal clients.[9] Trusted dependents were hired to manage the stores in Bambamarca, Hualgayoc and Santa Cruz, with Benel closely monitoring his employees' behaviour by paying frequent unannounced visits for auditing and stocking purposes. The boss himself served in the El Triunfo outlet, while that in Silugán was staffed by his eldest son, Castinaldo Benel.[10]

Labour recruitment for the coastal sugar estates formed the third pillar in Eleodoro Benel's highly integrated business organisation. *Enganchador* activity was a thriving occupation and a useful source of capital accumulation, one which Benel had been engaged in since the 1900s when he began to supply Cayaltí and Tumán with migrant workers. In 1911 Benel's role as a trafficker in labour power was put on a more formal footing when he signed a contract with the administration in Cayaltí to provide labourers under the following terms:

'You will make the loans with your own capital and send the labourers to this hacienda with their respective chits up to a maximum value of S/.50 or S/.60. Whenever you so desire, accounts will be settled and we will reimburse all the money that you have invested in loans. You will be paid a commission or remuneration amounting to 25 per cent of the total value of your chits. The debts of runaway workers will be deducted from your account. We will make payments in bills of exchange 15 per cent above the Lima rate and drawable on our account.

For every fifty *peones* that you have working in this hacienda we will provide a foreman at a wage of S/.25, paid by us, to oversee your labourers'.[11]

Provided the number of *prófugos* could be kept to a minimum, resources diverted into the *enganche* business offered an attractive 25 per cent return on invested capital for each transaction undertaken, and had the added advantage of a rapid turn-over if accounts were drawn up at regular intervals.

Moreover, Benel did not only gain from the 25 per cent return on his advance, but also the profits that came from goods purchased by the *enganchado* labourers with the credit, for the peon normally took at least a proportion of the advance in goods rather than money. Given these circumstances it is not surprising that by 1915 Benel was one of the most important labour contractors in Hualgayoc province, especially as he possessed the necessary military muscle to force any recalcitrants quickly back into line.

Tax collection was another source of profit for Eleodoro Benel.[12] Apart from bringing economic benefits, this activity brought political advantages insofar as it enabled Benel to widen his network of dependents, and strengthen existing patron-client ties. Through a mixture of a wide network of contacts, ruthlessness, and an entrepreneurial skill that enabled him to integrate intelligently four different branches of business – agriculture, commerce, labour recruitment and tax collection – Eleodoro Benel was able to take good advantage of the favourable trade conjuncture between 1900 and 1920. In so doing he firmly established himself as the most powerful businessman in the eastern districts of Hualgayoc province and as an influential member of the provincial élite. But Benel was by no means the only enterprising individual in this zone with a determination to make material progress. Others strove to emulate Benel's success, with the result that the rise in inter-regional trade acted to strengthen the ranks of medium-scale merchant-farmers.

A descendent of one of the Basque families that founded Santa Cruz in the sixteenth century, Zenón Burga was a typical member of this middle-ranking provincial bourgeoisie. The owner of a store in the town of Santa Cruz that retailed local wares as well as foreign manufactures, in 1903 Zenón Burga widened his business activities when he bought the hacienda Litcán from his brother, Isidro Burga, for a price of S/.11,000.[13] Litcán had an extension of 3,400 hectares, of which less than fifty hectares was irrigated land apt for cereal cultivation, with most of the remainder being either natural pasture given over to extensive livestock rearing, or woodland. In 1920 Zenón Burga further expanded his holdings by purchasing two adjoining smallholdings.[14]

Although they came from very different origins, by 1910 the Alvarado brothers had risen to occupy a position akin to that of Zenón Burga in the local social structure. The father of Marcial, Fortunato, Gerónimo and Leopoldo Alvarado was a Chinese who found himself transported to Peru in the late 1860s to work as an indentured labourer on the Chancay hacienda. The intelligence and diligence of this migrant soon attracted the attention of the landowner, who upon the abolition of coolie status in 1874 was quick to promote the Asian to a responsible position within the estate administration. As was the custom, the Chinese adopted his employer's surname. He also began small-scale trading on his own account. In the 1890s the labourers of the Sociedad Agrícola San Antonio de Chancay rebelled, burnt down the estate's buildings and forced the landlord to relinquish control.[15] The hacienda was subsequently divided and sold to the former workers and tenants. Due to the accumulation of a reasonable capital as a result of his private commercial dealings, the former indentured labourer was able to purchase a decent holding carved out of some of the best land around the old *casa hacienda* on the banks of the Chancay river. From this base the Alvarado family expanded their operation into the commercial sphere, so that by 1910 they were well-established medium-scale merchant-farmers possessing a lucrative store in the town of Santa Cruz.[16]

Finding that their potential for accumulation was being undermined by the rapid proliferation of Eleodoro Benel's business network in the province of Hualgayoc, the Burga and the Alvarado families slowly emerged as the central figures in a political alliance whose main objective was to halt the advance of Benel. This coalition under the local tutelage of medium-scale entrepreneurs was gradually cemented between 1908 and 1912. Given the effect of late nineteenth century events already outlined, this new bout of commercial rivalry brought in its wake an exacerbation of social tension that went hand in hand with escalating faction-based political violence in Santa Cruz. Analogous developments were unfolding elsewhere in Hualgayoc during the first decade of this century, and it is to a discussion of their social consequences that we now turn.

## II

The dawn of the twentieth century coincided with a good measure of chaos and bloodshed. January 1900 witnessed the assassination of the governor of Niepos by a bandit gang under the leadership of Edilberto Vásquez, who, with his brothers had long been operating a twenty-strong well-armed band that was the scourge of the more peaceable citizens settled in Niepos and San Gregorio.[17] Cattle lifted in these districts were driven down to the Cayaltí hacienda for sale, a business encouraged by the landowners of the Oyotún and Culpón estates in the Zaña valley, who offered protection to the Vásquez family and their coterie of brigands.[18] The governor's untimely end, however, was not primarily caused by his efforts to control rustling. He was a loyal member of the faction led by the Correa and Palacios families, medium-scale farmers of a Cacerist persuasion who disputed local political hegemony with the Vásquez and their allies now affiliated to the *civilista* party. Later that year the whole of Hualgayoc province was thrown into turmoil due to the antics of a *montonera* column under the aegis of Leoncio Villacorta, a large landowner from the neighbouring province of Cutervo. This hastily assembled armed force swept through the province of Hualgayoc in October, before fizzling out as abruptly as it had erupted.[19] But commerce and life remained under threat, especially in Bambamarca and its environs, where a bandit group energetically plied their trade on the outskirts of the town from the latter months of 1900 through 1901.[20]

These and countless parallel incidents set the tone for future developments. In 1903 the frequently haphazard nature of bandit activity in Hualgayoc was placed on a more organised footing owing to the scheduling of presidential elections for that year. As usual, political quarrels unfolding at the national level jointed with local conflict to determine the contours of political and armed struggle. Since 1895 the dominant force in Peru had been a coalition of Nicolás Piérola's Partido Demócrata and the Partido Civil, a political alliance that had been forged by a common wish to oust General Andrés Cáceres and his Partido Constitucional from office.[21] By 1902 the *civilista*-Democrat pact was under severe strain, owing to personality clashes and a power struggle to control the National Election Council. In September 1902 the *civilistas* succeeded in manoeuvering their supporters into a majority position on the Council. This enabled them to regulate the appointment of local electoral officials at the departmental and provincial level and so exercise an important influence on the outcome of the forthcoming election. Amid an atmosphere charged with tension, the *civilista* party then felt strong enough to break with the Democrats, entering into an agreement with the Constitutionalists.[22] Swayed by the abstentionist views of Piérola and realising that they had been tricked into a minority position, the central committee of the Partido Demócrata decided not to participate in the elections of May 1903. These machinations in Lima had their impact in Hualgayoc. Individuals and factions excluded from local office-holding and official patronage since 1895 saw in this national political realignment an opportunity to turn the tables on their rivals, settle old scores and capture administrative positions. For their part, those in authority endeavoured to scheme astutely in order to maintain their station. Uncertainty made the 1903 election a particularly bitter contest.[23]

Although they were formally abstaining, an important section within the Pierolist camp intervened in the campaign by trying their utmost to disrupt the poll. In this they were assisted by the miniscule Liberal Party led by Augusto Durand. Other Democrats reacted in a more opportunistic fashion, joining the ranks of the *civilistas*, thus adding to the feelings of acrimony and confusion. By January 1903 the election campaign was already becoming somewhat fervid. That month found the governor of San Miguel complaining to the prefect about the 'scandalous, grave and criminal acts' perpetrated by José Félix Esguerra.[24] Esguerra was heading a group of Democrats and Liberals who were hunting down their *civilista* enemies. The door to a shop owned by Manuel Barrantes was blown to smithereens with dynamite. They also attacked Juan Quiroz as he was walking down the street, badly wounding him before he was able to flee pursued by a hail of bullets. Quiroz took refuge in his house, which during the ensuing skirmish was pockmarked with rifle fire. Frustrated by this failure to dispatch their adversary, Esguerra and his cronies publically burnt Quiroz's hastily jettisoned hat in the town square 'amid scenes of savagery'.[25] The governor proceeded to report that the Barrantes family and their allies were lying low in their houses and dared not venture out onto the street.

Commotion was likewise the order of the day in Niepos district. May 1903 found the local *civilista* schoolteacher, Alejandro Aurazo, addressing a letter

31

to the prefect in Cajamarca. His letter was prompted by the deeds of a 'bandit gang' organised by the locally influential Correa-Palacios faction. In early 1903 this group gave its support to the dissident minority of the Constitutional Party who backed the candidature of Fernando Seminario and his allies in the Liberal Party.[26] The schoolteacher claimed that this band were committing indiscriminate robbery and murder in the locality:

> 'a group of individuals armed with rifles belonging to the State have long been imposing their will in Niepos against the wishes of the population. They form a gang of delinquents whose actions have not been subjected to the legal sanctions appropriate to their dastardly crimes. They rob, kill and extort from those defenseless citizens who choose to remain aloof from local rivalries and refuse to follow their example of corruption and ignorance . . . A few days ago my father-in-law, Don Carlos S. Correa, was treacherously attacked without reason by these enemies of order and honourable citizens. In Niepos social respect and a public position do not provide any security, so it has become necessary for me to abandon my post and travel to this city to denounce the social and political disorder that the aforementioned rabble of brigands have created. They openly and criminally use arms belonging to the State and I request that they be immediately disarmed. This is the only efficient manner in which individual security and public order can be guaranteed.
>
> It is necessary that your Excellency is aware that the aforementioned group of bandits form a seed of revolution that totally lacks civic consciousness. These delinquents are desperate to attain office so that they can better accomplish the revenge and abuses that they feel irresistibly inclined towards, due to man's instinctive cruelty when law, education and punishment are absent.
>
> Not only do they covet office to satisfy their perverse passions, these villains also proclaim support for the Liberal Party day and night in the streets, cheering the name of candidate Fernando Seminario at the top of their voices.
>
> Among the numerous delinquents in Niepos who possess arms belonging to the State, and are the principle instigators of disorder, figure the following individuals: José Manuel Palacios, Simón Correa, Clemente Burga, José María Becerra (Justice of the Peace), Juan Palacios and Manuel Jesús Palacios'.[27]

Aurazo ended his letter by stressing that 'the citizens of Niepos are alarmed by these unnerving spectacles and the lamentable increase in bloodletting perpetrated by the accused', and requested that a police post be established in the district. He conveniently made no mention of the turbulent activities of the Vásquez gang who had placed their services at the disposal of the *civilista* cause.

In the district of Santa Cruz robbery, violence and politics were also infrangibly enlaced. Throughout the 1903 election campaign the *civilista* faction, jointly headed by the local priest and the justice of the peace, engaged in running street battles with their political opponents. During one of these affrays, the *civilistas* had two of their combatants shot dead, while several others were badly wounded. The Pierolist faction and the dissident Cacerists, led by the Aguinaga family and Neptalí Horna, had five of their followers injured.[28] Nor were all the disturbances provoked by inter-factional rivalry, for in the absence of any serious electoral opposition at the ballot box, the various alignments within the *civilista*-Constitutionalist alliance on occasions began to squabble among themselves as personal jealousies and ambitions came to the fore. In early April 1903 Hualgayoc's subprefect, in a brazenly misleading statement no doubt stimulated by an attempt to placate his superior's nerves and enhance his own reputation, informed the prefect that 'this Province does not support any political party other than the established government, the Constitution, the laws of the State and the maintenance of law and order'.[29] He then proceeded to report that Catalino Miranda, prominent *civilista*, wealthy mineowner and a member of an eminent landowning family, was easily the most popular candidate standing for the Senate. One month later, however, the subprefect was writing in a somewhat less enthusiastic vein:

'Today at 1 o'clock in the afternoon, a group of men supporting the candidature of Sr Catalino Miranda, led by Sr Matías Gallardo, used the pretext of a public meeting to instigate a public scandal. I am not mistaken when I qualify this as a subversive act aimed at overturning the established order. During the meeting Sr Gallardo, who is the secretary to this subprefecture, made a speech in which he publically declared opinions against the existing political regime. He also challenged and denounced my authority, as well as that of the Supreme Government, whose power I represent in this Province'.[30]

Gleeful at this dissention among the official ranks, opposition supporters took advantage of the situation to mount a riot that the local police detachment only contained by firing over the heads of the demonstrators.

Given the boycott by opposition forces, their control of most local returning officers and the support they received from the local bureaucracy, the Partido Civil comfortably won the 25 May 1903 elections. Abstentionism by parties outside the governing alliance nevertheless deprived the poll of all legitimacy in the eyes of an important sector of the populace. It was a particularly frustrating situation for the Pierolists and the dissident Cacerist minority: they won many of the street battles, but were unable to register any electoral successes, partly due to their own self-defeating political strategy. This situation helped maintain a high level of inter-factional rancour in the post-election period. Skirmishes involving firearms, machetes and clubs frequently erupted in all districts over the latter months of 1903 and the early part of 1904. When in November 1903 the *civilista* subprefect jailed a group of bandits in the pay of opposition politicians, Democrats, Cacerist followers of Seminario and Liberals attacked the prison in Hualgayoc town, dynamited one of its adobe walls and released all those interned.[31] *Civilista* appointees at the grass roots experienced great difficulty in imposing their authority on a large section of the population or maintaining public order, while complaints about their partisan behaviour inundated the prefect's office.[32] Post-election tensions in Santa Cruz were such that the five Aguinaga brothers and Neptalí Horna had to flee the town, their lives threatened by opponents who swore to avenge the assassination of their factional allies. The fugitives managed to evade capture and came to a business arrangement with the landlords of the Oyotún and Chumbenique haciendas, who offered them protection and took a percentage of the proceeds when they began working as highwaymen in the Zaña and Chancay valleys. Information about the movement of muleteers, waggoners, pedlars and ordinary wayfarers through these valleys was fed to the brigands by their clansman, Víctor Aguinaga, who lived in the town of Chongoyape.[33]

In addition to the absence of legitimacy attached to the 1903 poll, the flames of political rivalry were also fanned by the death of recently elected president Manuel Candamo on 7 May 1904. New elections were announced and on this occasion the Democrat-Liberal alliance decided to participate. Piérola and Durand were nominated as presidential and vice-presidential candidates respectively. José Pardo headed the official ticket. Short of funds and not dominating the bureaucracy or the electoral machinery, it soon became evident that the opposition was heading for certain defeat. Under these circumstances, Piérola thought it opportune to wire the provincial committees of his supporters announcing that they were to abstain from voting. This was argued on the grounds of widespread official favouritism on behalf of the Partido Civil and fraudulent behaviour in the selection of local returning officers. The outcome was that the *civilista*-Constitutionalist slate gained an overwhelming victory in the elections of August 1904, and José Pardo became president.[34]

Once again the passions roused by the elections ended up in fevered exchanges on the streets. During one of these clashes, Manuel Ramírez, the governor of San Miguel, was fatally gunned down by anti-*civilista* partisans in the town square before more than two thousand peasants and townspeople attending the hustings.[35] Faced with a succession of bloody clashes at Santa Cruz and San Miguel, the authorities declared a state of martial law in these districts and tried to curtail constitutional guarantees. Detachments of five *gendarmes* were stationed in each of the district capitals in an abortive attempt to control what the subprefect described as 'the abnormal situation of turmoil that exists in the towns of San Miguel and Santa Cruz'.[36] Considering that most of the adult male population possessed firearms of some description, the posting of five police did little to maintain the peace. In early 1905 even this token force proved too much of a strain on the departmental exchequer and was withdrawn, a move that gave the competing factions a free hand to settle their differences in the accustomed manner.

Given the near absence of any moderating or coercive state authority, inter-faction hostility and widespread lawlessness continued unabated in 1905 and 1906. From Santa Cruz the artisan Juan de la Cruz Cadena wrote to the prefect complaining that for some time:

> 'the authorities in my town of residence have unleashed a heinous persecution against me. This has reached such a pitch that I have been forced to abandon my humble home, leaving my wife and young children in the utmost misery so that they have to rely on public charity. I, fleeing from my tenacious persecutors, am forced to hide in the mountains and forests, often without food for two or three days at a stretch'.[37]

Cadena's plea for assistance met with no sympathetic response from the *civilista* prefect. Things were no less disorderly in San Miguel. After murdering the governor in 1904, José Gálvez, Juan Gálvez, Manuel Cubas, Carlos Tarro and other members of their faction fled the town and took refuge in the parish of Tongod, a wooded mountainous area some twenty-three kilometres to the north on the road to Santa Cruz. Having no legal means of support, the assassins turned to brigandage. Apart from robbing on country lanes, this band acquired sufficient confidence to enter the highland towns, where in addition to thievery they took the opportunity to harass Partido Civil supporters. Such activity prompted the nervous *civilista* governor of San Miguel to report that 'Almost every night they come here unchallenged. The bandits ride around the town firing shots and threatening certain families before hiding once again in their stronghold'.[38] Attempts to eradicate this band met with no success, as was also the case with the Aguinaga-Horna group operating in the Zaña and Chancay valleys. One outcome of the 1903 and 1904 elections, therefore, was to increase the prevalence of banditry with a political tinge.

Being an important member of Hualgayoc's provincial élite, Eleodoro Benel could not stand aloof from factional imbroglios. His first recorded involvement in gun-law politics occurred as a young man of twenty-two, when he enrolled in the ranks of a *montonera* organised by the Pierolist caudillo Teodoro Seminario against president Cáceres.[39] From late 1894 to 1895 this rebellious column rode through the department of Cajamarca, only fading away on Piérola's election to the presidency in August 1895. After this escapade Benel became clearly identified as an active member of the ruling Pierolist-*civilista* alliance who was not afraid to squeeze the trigger when the need arose. This affiliation marked the young landowner out as a prime target, and he quickly became embroiled in serious clashes. How far these had developed by the turn of the century is evident from the contents of a letter sent by one of Benel's clansmen, the subprefect of Hualgayoc, to the departmental prefect in Cajamarca:

'I have been notified by Don Eleodoro Benel that on the journey to his hacienda La Samana, he has not been attacked. However, as soon as his enemies found out about his arrival, they have been skirting the hacienda with the idea of provoking him and threatening him with death.

As my administration has no police force, nor any means of tracking down and capturing the individuals who are interrupting the tranquillity of the aforementioned Benel, I am writing to inform you so that you can take the necessary steps'.[40]

Swimming with the political tide, between 1903 and 1904 Benel dropped his earlier Pierolist sympathies and began to support the Partido Civil. This change in political loyalties embittered erstwhile factional associates, who determined to wreak maximum material and physical damage against their former ally.

Numbered amongst these was Tristán Cabrejo, landlord of Polulo, a medium-scale farm bordering on the hacienda El Triunfo. Commencing in late 1904, Cabrejo directed a group of brigands from the adjacent mountain retreat of Tumbacucho, who made several vain attempts to ambush and assassinate Benel. Benel responded in kind – assembling a pack of armed dependents, whose hard core was recruited from trusted employees settled on his lands. By 1906 mutual hatred had reached fever pitch. On 6 May 1906 Benel and his followers launched a full-scale attack on Cabrejo, who was pinned down in his *casa hacienda* by a hail of bullets while his livestock were herded onto El Triunfo.[41] Five days later Cabrejo mounted a reprisal raid with the help of the Tumbacucho bandits under the command of Máximo Moreno and Isaías Vargas. At midnight on 16 May the brigands and tenants from Polulo attacked Benel's estate, trying to break into his house and murder him. It was only when Benel's followers heard the ensuing exchange of rifle shots, and took up arms to defend their *patrón*, that the assault was beaten off. On their retreat the attackers from Polulo attempted to lift some livestock, but with the defenders counter-attacking fiercely, there was no time for this and the animals were shot on the spot instead. Three days after this incident, Benel was still complaining to the authorities that Cabrejo's bandit henchmen were prowling around the perimeter of his estate awaiting an opportunity to murder him.[42]

Tensions simmered on and minor clashes frequently erupted. In May 1907 Benel signed a contract with his *pariente*, subprefect Carlos Montoya Benel, to supply 700 planks for the construction of a state school in Hualgayoc town. In addition to felling his own trees, from June to August 1907 Benel proceeded to invade woodlands inside Polulo's boundaries and extract Cabrejo's timber. Knowing that the subprefect was Benel's man, a complaint was lodged directly to the prefect stating that:

'Don Eleodoro Benel, due to his position as a large landowner and because he possesses modern firearms belonging to the State, is

36

the most feared individual in this area. He has invaded our property, cutting more than a hundred trees in order to fulfil his contract with the authorities'.[43]

As the local judge, the lieutenant governor of Samana, the governor of Santa Cruz and the subprefect were either allies or officials in the pay of Benel, this protest was quietly shelved. But although Cabrejo could make little headway with the authorities, his influence with the Tumbacucho brigands caused Eleodoro Benel many headaches. The outlaws could not be eradicated, and throughout 1907 they committed scores of robberies in the district of Hualgayoc and its environs. Between 1906 and 1907 their numbers were swelled to around twenty-five as criminals from Cajamarca, Cajabamba, Bambamarca and La Encañada joined the band.[44] To avoid assassination and defend his business interests, Benel found himself compelled to strengthen his own armed following.

Vendettas in Hualgayoc acquired an added dimension in 1908 with the holding of elections for Congress and a new president. National political alliances remained unchanged. With the National Election Council still firmly in the grip of the Partido Civil, who had also consolidated their control over the bureaucratic machine since their 1904 electoral success, the Democrat-Liberal opposition had little chance of victory and staged a half-hearted campaign. On 1 May 1908 a putsch centred in the department of Lima and led by Augusto Durand attempted to overthrow the government, but ended in miserable failure and the jailing of many prominent opposition politicians.[45] According to Jorge Basadre, the election of 25–27 May passed without difficulties, and this, coupled with the easy supression of the rebellion, 'seemed to affirm the existence in the country of a feeling of hostility to upheavals, and a wish for order and progress'.[46] While this may well have been true of majority opinion in Lima, sentiments in Hualgayoc (and the rest of Cajamarca department) were very different.

During the first days of May it was reported that the Correa-Palacios directed bandit group supporting the opposition were poised to attack the town of Niepos, and were awaiting orders from contacts in Trujillo and Piura to launch a *montonera* uprising.[47] Following the *débâcle* of Durand's uprising in the central *sierra* on 1 May, the anticipated rebellion in the north never materialised. Instead, these anti-*civilistas* continued to unleash a series of violent skirmishes against the Vásquez gang and their allies. Confronted with a situation of generalised violence in Niepos, the authorities were compelled to establish a police post in the district and attempted to reconcile the warring factions. This initiative appeared to have met with success when on 11 June 1909 the leaders of the respective bands signed a non-aggression agreement and handed in some of their arms to the authorities. Two days later, however, this pact was torn asunder due to a crime of honour, when the brothers Juan del Carmen Vásquez and Agustín Vásquez were murdered on a country lane outside Niepos town by Alejandro Aurazo and the Palacios brothers. Acc-

37

ording to the daughter of Juan del Carmen Vásquez, her father had been having an 'illicit relationship with the daughter of Aurazo', who felt so strongly about the liaison that he sought aid from his factional rivals in order to ensure that the affair was terminated.[48]

Nearby in San Miguel faction-motivated violence was also commonplace, with the subprefect reporting that:

> 'As in all the districts of this Province, two clearly defined factions exist which compete for local mastery, and do not miss any opportunity to inflict damage on their rivals. One such incident occurred on the first of this month. Various enemies met in the street and began firing shots from revolvers. One of these killed a peasant called Marcelino Cerrano, who was not involved in the affray. The authorities, assisted by members of the public, managed to capture Manuel Cubas, who was cited as the perpetrator of the crime. But given the deep divisions within the population, a fight developed between the delinquent's friends, who wanted to save him from prison, and his enemies, who opposed this'.[49]

During the fracas Cubas managed to escape and abscond with his associates to Tongod. In contrast to most other districts in Hualgayoc, Bambamarca was relatively quiet due to the police force billeted in the town. But this was a deceptive calm and the subprefect warned that 'their withdrawal would result in grave disorder that the authorities would not be able to control'.[50]

If a tenuous peace momentarily reigned in Bambamarca, in Santa Cruz vendetta politics were becoming more acrimonious. As already mentioned, this development was partly stimulated by intensified commercial rivalry. Between 1908 and 1912 three medium-scale entrepreneurs – Marcial Alvarado, Zenón Burga and Tristán Cabrejo – united in order to combat the rapid expansion of Eleodoro Benel's business network. This local conflict unfolded to the back-drop of significant changes in national politics that worked to heighten discord locally, and were to exercise an important influence on future events. Since 1902 the ruling Partido Civil had been plagued by internal wrangling and splits. Although these healed somewhat during the administration of José Pardo, with the election of Augusto Leguía as president in 1908 the divisions accentuated. At first two major factions formed. One circled around Leguía. The second, led by José Matías Manzanilla and Luis Miró Quesada and known as *El Bloque*, represented the more traditionalist wing of the party.[51] Between 1908 and 1912 Eleodoro Benel backed the ruling faction within the Partido Civil, a position that enabled him to maintain his influence over Hualgayoc's subprefect, the governor of Santa Cruz and many of the parish level lieutenant governors. Meanwhile, his leverage was enhanced at the centre of power with the appointment of Rafael Villanueva as minister in charge of the cabinet office. Landowner of the Yanacancha hacienda, sited adjacent to Hualgayoc, Villanueva was an ex-*iglesista* who had fought alongside Benel's father during the civil war between 1882–5. As a result of the long-standing family friendship, Benel thus had the ear of a very astute politician who held a key position in the Lima government and enjoyed the president's confidence.

Benel's strong political ties both locally and nationally presented his enemies with certain problems. While he was favoured in his business activities, received state contracts, entered into commercial agreements with prominent *civilistas* on the coast, and could expand his armed following with impunity, the Alvarado-Burga faction found that their complaints to the authorities went unheeded. Their businesses were discriminated against, and any resort to armed action targeted at Benel or his allies was denounced before the prefect by the province's officials. Thus, when in November 1909 the private army formed by Benel attacked Burga's hacienda Litcán and the village of Pulan, where many of Burga's *pistoleros* lived, Benel ignored a request by the subprefect to explain his actions and no official sanction was forthcoming.[52]

Much to the chagrin of the clans led by Marcial Alvarado, Zenón Burga and Tristán Cabrejo, this political balance favourable to Benel was maintained throughout Leguía's first term in office. Despite certain minor successes they were never fully able to prise Benel's hands off the reins of local power. For example, in 1909 Benel's cousin was removed from his post of subprefect and replaced by a personal friend of the departmental prefect. After an initial period of tension, during which the subprefect began to question some of the activities undertaken by Benel's gunmen, a working arrangement was arrived at. At the same time Benel was using his contacts with the *civilista* hierarchy in Lima and the town of Cajamarca to get the potentially troublesome subprefect removed. In mid-1910 this lobbying bore fruit when the subprefect was fired and replaced by an official more to Benel's liking. Shortly afterwards Benel had to machinate once again in order to block another possible threat to his political control. In February 1910 the *benelista* governor of Santa Cruz, Conrado Ugaz, was shot dead by Manuel Burga and his allies. Following some artful intrigue involving the deposed subprefect and a local senator, in early 1910 the Alvarado faction in Santa Cruz succeeded in getting one of its members, José Orrego, nominated as the new governor. Again Benel proved able to nip this menace in the bud, organising the replacement of Orrego in October 1911 by one of his own supporters, Isidro Urraca.[53] Consequently the efforts of Alvarado, Burga and Cabrejo to undermine their enemy's position came to nought. They thus determined to exploit as best they could the opportunity presented by the 1912 national and municipal elections to wrest local power out of the hands of their sworn adversary.

## III

1911 and 1912 were years of considerable turmoil in Peruvian national politics, with all the major political groupings wracked by deep internal disagreements. As the dominant partner in the ruling coalition, divisions within the Partido Civil proved particularly important in deciding political fortunes. Among the *civilistas* the major bone of contention revolved around attitudes towards the maverick figure of Augusto Leguía. A sector of the party hierarchy organised around *El Bloque*, was determined to thwart Leguía's ambitions. When their plan to marginalise Leguía made little headway, this group split to form the Partido Civil Independiente. In 1912 they refused to back the official *civilista* candidate, Antero Aspíllaga. Instead they gave support to Guillermo Billinghurst, the nominee of the Democrats. The political waters were muddied still further by the fact that Aspíllaga was not a supporter of Leguía, he simply cherished a burning desire to wear the presidential sash. Nor did Leguía have much liking for Aspíllaga. Rather, the outgoing president was anticipating a hung parliament in which he could muster sufficient support to continue in power.[54]

Such a veritable cat's cradle of intrigue and hostility in Lima posed serious problems for faction leaders in Hualgayoc. Should they align with the official *civilista* candidate or support the dissidents, even if this meant backing the Democrats? Eleodoro Benel was placed in a particularly delicate situation: he maintained friendly business relations as a supplier of labour and foodstuffs with the Aspíllaga family of the Cayaltí hacienda and the Pardo family of Tumán. Yet while Aspíllaga was the official *civilista* candidate, the Pardos, as backers of the Partido Civil Independiente, gave their support to Billinghurst. Eventually, Benel, like many other *civilistas*, decided that Leguía presented a greater threat to his position than the declining Democrats, and came out in favour of Billinghurst for president. Simultaneously support was given to non-*leguiísta* members of the Partido Civil for parliament, so adding further intricacy to an already confused situation. The Alvarado faction, on the other hand, threw in their lot with Aspíllaga and pro-Leguía forces inside the Partido Civil.

Municipal elections in Santa Cruz were arranged for Sunday 14 April 1912. Benel and his factional supporters controlled the town council, the mayor, and the district governor. They could thus appoint their allies to the *mesa receptora de sufragios*, the committee of polling officers, who held the key to electoral success. In an attempt to overturn by intimidation what would otherwise have been a *fait accompli*, Benel's opponents assembled an armed band drawn from the Alvarado's Chancay hacienda, the parish of Uticyacu and the village of Lacas.[55] Under the command of Lizandro Orrego, 'groups of bandits' armed with rifles and pistols occupied the town hall and the upper storey of the house owned by Marcial Alvarado. From these vantage points they could dominate the town square.[56]

Numbered among the Alvarados' *guapos* was Manuel Santa Cruz Romero, alias *el carnero* ('the ram'), a peasant of fabled reputation as a rustler and hired assassin. On Saturday 13 April at 10 o'clock in the morning, Romero happened upon Adolfo Ugaz, one of Benel's key allies in Santa Cruz. He fell

40

upon Ugaz, stabbing him several times with a dagger. Attracted by the ensuing commotion, the *gendarmes* and municipal police managed to overpower Romero in the shop owned by Gerónimo Alvarado, and march him off to jail. The opposition, led by Marcial, Gerónimo and Leopoldo Alvarado, Benjamín Romero and José del Carmen Azula, quickly gathered their band and intercepted the police by the prison entrance. During the following fracas Romero managed to break away from his captors and flee to the house of Marcial Alvarado.[57]

According to the *benelista* governor, the occupation of Santa Cruz by Alvarado's militia:

> 'responded to a well-planned plot by the enemies of public order to obstruct or impede the work of the electoral officers and the wishes of the majority of voters, who gave their backing to the victorious list of councillors and political supporters of representative Don Demetrio Miranda, and the Supreme Government'.[58]

The governor then proceeded to inform this superiors that:

> 'the municipal elections passed without incident. Citizens supporting the Supreme Government were triumphant. Riled by their defeat, the opposition headed by the Alvarados and others . . . mortally wounded the minor Santiago Celis. A bullet from a Malinger rifle passed through his stomach. This took place when a volley of shots were discharged by the bandits at the municipal guard, who were patrolling the town under the command of the lieutenant governor Don Anacleto Vargas'.[59]

Isidro Urraca, the *benelista* governor, omitted to mention that on the afternoon before polling day Eleodoro Benel and Adolfo Ugaz entered the town at the head of 'a multitude of armed bandits' from Samana.[60] According to the parish priest, Reynaldo Rabanal, 'they began to commit all kinds of crimes', and engage the *pistoleros* of Alvarado in gun battles.[61] With Marcial Alvarado's men pinned in the town hall and violence on the streets, the electors were reluctant to venture out of their houses and polling could not proceed normally. In the words of sargeant Eliseo Vásquez, the officer in charge of the local detachment of *gendarmes*, 'the Alvarado band abstained from voting'.[62] To have attempted to vote would have been extremely foolhardy with Benel's personal militia surrounding the members of the *mesa receptora*. The electoral committee thus rubber-stamped a fraudulent poll that guaranteed a further period of *benelista* local predominance.

This outcome failed to lower political tempers and frequent clashes continued to erupt between the rival bands. One such incident involved governor Isidro Urraca and the priest Rabanal, the latter being a loyal follower of the Alvarado-Burga faction in local politics. Realising that the burial ceremony of Santiago Celis might spark off a serious engagement between the rival bands, Urraca ordered that the corpse be buried immediately without any

41

ceremony. The cleric deeply resented this infringement of his authority, and on the morning of Tuesday 16 April buttonholed the governor outside his presbytery. According to Urraca, the priest began to shout insults at him in the middle of the street and threatened him with a severe beating. When Rabanal ordered one of his friends to ring the church bells a crowd assembled, among whom were men belonging to the Alvarado-Burga faction with guns concealed beneath their *ponchos*. The governor claimed that 'if it had not been for the presence of the police they would probably have killed me and maybe a general massacre would have broken out'.[63] Rabanal gave the subprefect a different story, claiming that the governor, armed with a sword-stick and accompanied by his bodyguards, provoked the disturbance. When the clergyman approached the governor to complain about the non-Christian burial of the shot boy, the latter:

'summoned his soldiers and bandits. He ordered them to attack me, as well as some three individuals who happened to be passing by at the time and were shielding me. Observing their plan, I moved out into the middle of the street, accompanied by many citizens, who were crying and shouting, for they believed that the attackers were going to kill me. When the soldiers and bandits did not open fire, I immediately tried to calm the assembled populace. Increasing numbers of my parishioners came to my defence in an attempt to prevent an unfortunate incident'.[64]

These conflicting accounts were passed on to the prefect in Cajamarca by subprefect Wenceslao Mori, a *benelista*, who advised his superior that the claims of *cura* Rabanal 'are completely unfounded and motivated by factional passions'.[65] Having successfully attained the desired election result, Eleodoro Benel withdrew most of his men from Santa Cruz on 17 April. The following day, the Alvarado band retired to the Chancay hacienda, stopping to fire many rifle shots down on the town from a ridge on the outskirts of the settlement.[66]

Understandably the poll had no legitimacy in the eyes of the opposition. They therefore decided to appoint their own mayor and town council parallel to those recently installed by Benel and his associates. This total lack of agreement between the factions created conditions propitious to instability and violence. Numerous gun fights occurred, forcing the subprefect to move his residence from Hualgayoc to Santa Cruz in July 1912. Extra police were drafted into the district, but all efforts to restore peace and reconcile the rival factions came to nothing. The subprefect analysed the problem in the following terms:

'Each faction controls and protects a group of criminals. They thus become accomplices to crime and unfortunately make the task of the authorities impossible. So long as the leading figures in this district continue to aid these delinquents and do not come to some common agreement to persecute them, it will be very difficult to establish the rule of law and public tranquillity in Santa Cruz'.[67]

As if to highlight the subprefect's preoccupations, two days after this letter was written a serious incident developed in the town involving the Vargas brothers, who were *capos* in Eleodoro Benel's private army. According to the subprefect:

'A lamentable situation is to be found here. Two completely opposed factions exist, and from what I can gather these are only divided on local issues. There are even two mayors, each one claiming to be the legitimate office-holder . . . The events of the 15th originated and developed in the following manner: Misael Vargas, a criminal who has been sentenced to prison, is accustomed to go into the street armed with a pistol in his belt and a sword, which when in its case, he uses as a club. A man with a bad record, and clearly identified as a member of one faction, he had the idea of provoking a bloody clash with some men from the opposing band, who also have a disreputable past. These individuals form the nucleus of a group of dangerous people who carry out the revenge killings that have occurred due to the situation of hatred between the rival political and economic interests which are found in this district.

On the afternoon of the 15th, Misael Vargas, completely drunk, shot five bullets from his revolver in the street near his house. Overcoming the opposition of his brothers Práxedes and Aurelio, Misael went down into the *plaza*, where he began to provoke various individuals belonging to the rival band, and threaten them with his empty revolver. The rival's numbers gradually rose to between twenty and thirty, whereupon they attacked Vargas to shouts of 'Throw him in jail'. Pulling out revolvers and Mauser pistols, they began to shoot. Arming themselves with the thick ropes that are used to protect some of the trees in the *plaza*, they furiously attacked Misael Vargas and his two brothers. Misael was felled and lay prostrate on the ground. Judging him to be already dead, they left him. Práxedes Vargas, already wounded by bullet and knife wounds, was dragged to the jail under a torrent of clubs on the orders of lieutenant governor Don Fernando Orrego. Aurelio Vargas, the youngest brother, fled and in his flight was wounded by pistol shots in the knee and his left foot. Collected by his parents, Misael was taken to his house, where at present he and his brother are being treated.

Práxedes Vargas, badly wounded, died in the jail at 10 o'clock at night on the 17th . . . During the fracas, a bullet fired from the middle of the *plaza* wounded the minor Romulo Castro. He was on the balcony of the house belonging to senior alderman Don Elías Calderón, which is sited on a corner of the town square. Already

43

wounded, the youth in question descended the stairs and went out into the street, where he ran crazily for two blocks before dropping dead . . . The rifts found in this district are deep. Their main cause dates from nine years ago, when Mercedes González was assassinated by Martín and Bautista Aguinaga, and Neptalí Horna, who since that day have not dared live here. This division was accentuated with the assassination of Conrado Ugaz two years ago by Manuel Jesús Burga, Mateo Fernández and Noé Aguinaga, who frequently visit this town and who have not yet been sentenced by the courts, because nobody has issued an order for their detention.

To these grave crimes need to be added the murders of Ruperto Vásquez, Santiago Celis (a minor), and most recently that of Práxedes Vargas. All these deaths have been inspired by the hatred and division that reigns in Santa Cruz'.[68]

Incensed by this attack on three of his most trustworthy gunmen, Eleodoro Benel led his private militia into Santa Cruz, determined to annihilate the leaders of the rival faction. On his arrival in the town, Benel discovered that the Alvarados and Orregos had prudently bolted. They fled to the city of Cajamarca, where through their *compadre* the lawyer Manuel Antonio Burga, a plead for protection was lodged with the prefect.[69]

Clashes such as these continued to undermine the subprefect's attempts at mollification, even though he later reported that reconciliation 'has been accepted by everybody in principle and is considered necessary if order and peace are to be attained in the district'.[70] He noted that despite the drafting of extra *gendarmes* into Santa Cruz the governor's authority was not recognised by many citizens. Indeed, on occasions police indiscipline provoked disturbances. August 1912 found the lieutenant governor reporting that:

'the *gendarmes* Baltazar Aguirre and Esposorio Torres were found drunk firing their revolvers in the street. I ordered that they be escorted to their billet. But they came to my office in an insolent manner, swearing at me, and refusing to obey my orders. They then ran to collect their rifles, no doubt with the intention of attacking me in my own office'.[71]

Humiliated, the lieutenant governor was thus forced to flee from his own police force. This anarchic situation bred a psychology of uncertainty, fear and violence. Factional partisans like Elías Calderón and Marcial Alvarado began to fortify their town houses, 'preparing for an armed conflict between the rival bands of this district'.[72] Meanwhile, in the countryside, Adolfo Ugaz was forming a new armed band in his *fundo* Limac. Equipped with modern weapons, they threatened to invade Santa Cruz to engage the Alvarado-Burga faction in combat. Eleodoro Benel in El Triunfo and the Alvarados in Chancay likewise began to further strengthen their military capabilities. In addition to arming agriculturalists settled on their properties, they also recruited roving proletarians, seasoned bandits and fugitives from the law elsewhere in highland Cajamarca.[73]

Acrimonious sentiments were so entrenched by 1912 that even close relatives became enmeshed in mutual vendetta struggles. One notable example was the feud that developed between Dolores Benel and her brother. In January 1910 Eleodoro Benel leased the Santa Rosa de Achiramayo farm to Raimundo Ramos, the elder of five brothers. By 1911 the Ramos brothers, aided by their half-brothers, cousins, in addition to Apolinar Vargas, Joaquin Díaz, Alfonso Vargas, and Genove and Bernabe Fernández, formed the nucleus of a much-feared bandit gang.[74] These individuals began to earn a living as highwaymen, robbing travellers on the country lanes, as well as plundering livestock and crops from the local peasantry. When in November 1911 peasants settled in the vicinity of Samana complained to Eleodoro Benel about their exactions, the landlord tore up his contract with the Ramos clan and forcefully evicted them from the farm.[75] Dolores Benel opposed this act, swayed by the liason of her daughter with Dionicio Ramos.

Upon their eviction the Ramos family settled in the Llaucán hacienda, adjacent to Bambamarca. They maintained their group of brigands intact and swore vengeance on Eleodoro Benel. Word of this reached Benel's ears, and as his sister was supporting some of his most dangerous enemies, she too became a rival to be crushed. This quarrel between sister and brother was accentuated in January 1912, when Dolores Benel and the Ramos gang conspired to assassinate Ruperto Vásquez, a *pistolero* who worked a small farm nearby Chugur and was one of Eleodoro Benel's more proficient hired guns.[76] In reprisal for this attack, Benel started to strike at his sister, who was soon forced to seek refuge in the town of Cajamarca and to appeal to the prefect for protection:

> 'Last 14 February my house was attacked by gunfire and became the scene of a bloodbath. This was instigated by a rabble of delinquents led by the ex-governor of Santa Cruz, don Isidro Urraca, and my own brother, don Eleodoro Benel. Since then I have been insulted and threatened, without receiving any of the guarantees that the authorities in my district are legally required to offer me'.[77]

During the gun-fight one person was killed. Dolores Benel went on to complain that in addition to Urraca, the lieutenant governors of Samana and Polulo also participated in the raid. So did the three Galarreta brothers, peasant gunmen in the pay of Eleodoro Benel. She concluded by informing the prefect that 'my principal enemies are powerful personages in Santa Cruz. They generally have the support of the authorities and are backed up by sentenced criminals'.[78] Her brother's influence with local officialdom, especially the subprefect, was such that Dolores Benel was jailed soon after writing this letter. Even though she was accused of serious crimes (homicide and being the leader of a thirty-strong bandit group), she managed to arrange her release in early October 1912. This discharge was facilitated by the appoint-

45

ment of Augusto Montoya y Batanero as *gobernador militar* (military governor) of Santa Cruz in late September 1912. Faced with escalating violence in the district (on 24 September Eleodoro Benel and Adolfo Ugaz once more militarily occupied the town of Santa Cruz, seeking out those who gave succour to the Ramos gang), and pressurised by Cajamarca's elected representatives to control the situation, the prefect Carlos Edwards ordered Montoya y Batanero to pacify the area.[79] To accomplish this he was allocated the derisory force of eight *gendarmes*. Independent or impartial policing had no history in Hualgayoc, with the result that soon after Montoya y Batanero took up his post he was bought by one of the competing factions. On this occasion it was the Alvarados, who having come to an arrangement with the officer requested that Dolores Benel be set free.[80]

Within weeks of regaining her liberty, Dolores Benel became involved in another serious incident, one that witnessed the murder of Catalino Galarreta. The victim's mother described her son's demise in the following manner:

'Last Friday, 25 October, my unfortunate son Catalino was on his way to the Ninabamba hacienda to buy a bullock, with about one hundred *soles* in his pockets. Failing to buy an animal, he set out on the return journey to La Samana. At three in the afternoon, he had almost reached the house of Don Eleodoro Benel, and climbed a tree to gather *lúcumas* (a pear-shaped fruit – LT). He was spotted by second lieutenant Don Augusto Montoya y Batanero, who was in the house of Doña Dolores Benel which faces the aforementioned tree. Montoya came forward with his rifle and shot at my son from point-blank range. He was instantly killed and flopped onto the branches, which prevented him from falling to the ground.

Without extracting the corpse from the tree, second lieutenant Montoya and the *gendarmes* who accompanied him, as well as Ignacio, Eloy Francisco and José Isabel Ramos, Dionisio and Isabel Ventura and other individuals, advanced in the direction of the house of Don Eleodoro Benel firing their guns. They expected to find my other sons, Manuel, Eulogio and Rómulo Galarreta, with the aim of killing them as well. They failed in this as my sons were in my own house, located a league away from the scene of these events.

Seeing that he was threatened in this way, Don Eleodoro Benel fled to a safe place, so that no resistance whatsoever was offered to the *gendarmes* and the other attackers, the only person remaining in the house being Doña Domitila Bernal, wife of Benel. Questioned by the aforementioned officer, Sra Benel replied that her husband was absent, and when she asked the reason for his inquiry, Montoya y Batanero said that it was to personally give him the news that the young Galarreta had just died. Sra Benel retorted that Montoya should know of this as he was the assassin. At this the second lieutenant replied: 'Yes, it was I who killed him'.

46

Frustrated in their criminal intentions, the murderers returned to the house of Doña Dolores Benel. Here the *gendarmes'* officer sent his men to retrieve the corpse from the tree . . . After desecrating the body, stealing all the money found in the pockets, a gold ring, a watch with silver chain, two gold cufflinks, a belt and a notebook containing documents, they stuffed the corpse into a sack and brought it to the town of Santa Cruz by muleback during the night of the 25th.

Before proceeding further, I should mention a few facts to Your Excellency so that these events can be better understood. A strong animosity exists between Doña Dolores Benel and her brother Don Eleodoro Benel due to family matters, to the extent that they consider each other capital enemies. The latter of these was a friend of my son Catalino, and is friendly with my other sons. In their capacity as law abiding citizens and upholders of the public peace, they worked determinedly in favour of the current of opinion that has carried to power His Excellency Don Guillermo E. Billinghurst. This brought my sons into open conflict with the other party headed by Ezequiel Orrego, Don Fortunato Alvarado and others, who promoted the official candidature of Señor Aspíllaga. This latter group was wholeheartedly supported by the police force stationed in Santa Cruz. Doña Dolores Benel is very much in league with the Alvarado and Orrego families. She took advantage of their friendship with second lieutenant Montoya y Batanero to persuade him to take the *gendarmes* to La Samana with the criminal intention that the said leaders Alvarados and Orregos would do away with my sons, killing them off one by one. Moreover, it is public knowledge here that these individuals and the Benel woman have paid the officer and his troops a substantial sum of money. This then, has been the real motive behind the murder of my son Catalino, and it is also the reason why the authors of the crime are trying to put the blame on Don Eleodoro Benel, when in truth he was earmarked to be another of their victims.

This also provides the key to understanding the barbarity shown by the assassins towards my son's corpse. His body was handed over to his political enemies by the chief of the *gendarmes*. They stripped it in the town square and committed the savage act of whipping his corpse, dragging it around and shooting at the most noble part of the body. Upon the appeals of charitable individuals, only then did they reluctantly consent to place the corpse naked and without a shroud into a coffin to be buried.

Events so horrible as that which I have just denounced are very frequent in Santa Cruz. Only three months ago Don Práxedes Vargas died of fourteen stab wounds and his corpse was mutilated in the public jail. Once again the perpetuator of this crime was the band led by the Alvarados and Orregos, with the reason behind the assassination being that the victim was a political supporter of His Excellency Sr Billinghurst'.[81]

Fearing her brother's vengeance, shortly after this murder Dolores Benel fled from her farm and sought refuge in the coastal town of Chiclayo.[82]

Much to Eleodoro Benel's annoyance, the Ramos brothers did not follow his sister's example and abandon the province. Instead from their redoubt in Llaucán they earnestly began a campaign of harassment against the landlord of El Triunfo, attempting to lift his livestock and assault his followers. Skirmishes between the factions occurred with portentous regularity. One such clash took place in January 1913, when the Ramos gang launched a marauding expedition against *benelista* peasants in Samana parish. Miguel Mego and his brother were wounded by rifle bullets when they sought to defend their possessions against the bandits. In revenge the third Mego brother, Raúl, ambushed the attackers in the forest above the *fundo* Santa Rosa, killing Nicolás Ramos with a well directed rifle shot.[83] Persuaded by Benel, the subprefect posted an officer and four *gendarmes* in El Triunfo, but this stationary and uncommitted force proved unable to shackle the Ramos gang.

Likewise in the town of Santa Cruz post-election passions refused to wane. Conditions were deemed sufficiently explosive in late November 1912 to require the residence of the subprefect in the town yet again. Within days of his arrival he was informing the prefect in Cajamarca on the local political situation:

'After my arrival here I have made meticulous efforts to discover the roots of the deep divisions that exist in this district. I clearly see that the murders perpetrated at various times by the Alvarado band have sparked off unfortunate incidents that are constantly being repeated. Thus the seeds of intense blood feuds have been sown. Because of this both groups are armed and have converted this noble district into a gladiatorial arena. These hatreds have reached such an extreme that not even the honour of the most distinguished families is respected'.[84]

In the same communication the subprefect went on to inform the prefect about the latest attack to have taken place in Santa Cruz. On 30 November 1912 the local postmaster, Juan Orrego, entered the house of prominent *benelista* Adolfo Ugaz. He made his way to the bedroom of Ugaz's wife, Carolina, who was sick and resting in bed. Completely drunk, Orrego drew a revolver and tried to assassinate Carolina Ugaz. Intoxication spoiled his aim and the ensuing commotion caused by her cries when Orrego threw himself upon the sick woman in an attempt to strangle her, roused the servants. They succeeded in overpowering the befuddled attacker and called the authorities, who had Orrego thrown in jail.[85] Events such as these provoked the subprefect to complain to his superior about 'the complete demoralisation found in the province under my authority'.[86] This situation, nevertheless, was not improved by the subprefect's clear affinity with the local *benelista* forces, a partisanship that was to embroil him in skirmishes. On one occasion in January 1913 when he was drinking in a bar with six members of the ruling Benel faction, Daniel Orrego, a leading figure in the opposition ranks, happened upon him. Inebriated, Orrego began to insult and threaten the subprefect and his cronies, 'claiming that he had fifty men, armed with rifles belonging to the State, who were ready to sweep aside myself and the police force at any moment'.[87] Pursued, Orrego managed to slip away from his rivals through the back door to his house. Once inside, he grabbed his rifle and revolver, and engaged the subprefect's group in a fierce gun battle.[88]

Although factional conflicts were most intense in Santa Cruz, Hualgayoc's other districts also experienced heightened political strife in the months following the 1912 election. In Llapa a gun-fight between rival political factions erupted on the town's main thoroughfare, leaving one man shot.[89] By May 1913 the subprefect had been forced to leave Santa Cruz and take up residence in Bambamarca in an attempt to control an increasingly tense situation. 'Vagabonds, drunks and rabble-rousers' were firing guns in the streets.[90] To make matters worse, the officer in command of the *gendarmes* billeted in the town was in the pay of the opposition faction, who were threatening their rivals and 'even the district governor'.[91] Shortly afterwards a local notable was gunned down by factional rivals, an aggressive act that unleashed yet another round of vendetta bloodshed in Bambamarca:

> 'Owing to the death of don Juan de la Rosa Tello, a campaign of vengeance and crime has broken out. Bands rob and assassinate those who they believe were the authors of Tello's murder. Last October fourteen or more individuals attacked don Amadeo Fernández during the night, badly beating him. He died a few days later in the hospital of Hualgayoc as a result of his injuries. Many citizens find themselves threatened and almost every night countless rifle and pistol shots are fired. Many of the inhabitants are very anxious indeed'.[92]

With only nine *gendarmes* policing the whole of Hualgayoc province over most of 1913 and 1914, the daily round of feuding was allowed to progress unchecked. This was partly brought about by officialdom's unwillingness to cross local power brokers by infringing on their activities. Inaction was also the result of an incompetent and financially impoverished state machine. The outcome was a neo-Hobbesian environment that was shortly to spawn a bloodbath of lamentable proportions.

# CHAPTER 4

# The Llaucán massacre

## I

In May 1861 the hacienda Llaucán was bequeathed by government decree to the recently founded Colegio San Juan, a school located in Chota town. Llaucán was organised along *grundherrschaft* lines, whereby the landowner did not directly cultivate any of the estate's soil. Instead the entire hacienda was rented out to a *conductor*, or lessee, who in turn collected rent from subinfeudates called *arrendatarios*. Every five years the property was put up for public auction, with the highest bidder obtaining the right to exploit the estate. This ensured that the rent paid by the lessee was ever rising, which in turn forced the *conductor* to increase the rent obligations of the tenants. Without resorting to this measure, the lessee could not obtain enough cash with which to pay the Colegio San Juan and make a profit. In response to the pressures for ever greater exactions, the tenants mounted a succession of rent strikes.[1] Over the five decades 1870-1920 Llaucán's rugged terrain also offered a haven for brigands and other malefactors. Simultaneously, tenants settled in Llaucán frequently became embroiled in the province's fierce factional battles. Life on the hacienda turned particularly convulsive once the bandits led by the Ramos brothers took up residence after being evicted from the *fundo* Santa Rosa by Eleodoro Benel in late 1911. Rustling, incursions by armed bands, and the incidence of violent crime all increased with the presence of Raimundo Ramos and his fellow criminals.[2]

The lease on the Llaucán hacienda came up for auction on 27 September 1914. Commercial rivals from the provinces of Chota and Hualgayoc were keen to control the property, among them Eleodoro Benel. In order to conceal his interest and prevent politically-motivated bidding against him, Benel resorted to the frequently adopted tactic of hiring a substitute to represent him in the roup. Thus on the morning of the auction he ceded legal power to his associate Bernardino Guerrero Gayoso, who was instructed to tend on his behalf.[3] During that afternoon Benel's bid was successful, but at a cost. He only obtained the five-year lease on Llaucán by offering an annual rent of S/.16,500, more than double the existing sum of S/.6,800.[4] Although no documents record his intentions, one assumes that Benel expected that this capital investment would yield a satisfactory return. Opportunity for money-getting presented itself on five fronts. First, Llaucán was the most densely populated hacienda in the province, by 1914 supporting over three thousand peasants. As an *enganchador* Benel was undoubtedly keen to attain direct access to this source of contractable labour. Second, in addition to collecting rents in cash, the lessee also had the option of receiving payment in kind. Livestock and crops could thus be acquired from tenants settled on the estate. Holding the lease would consequently enable Benel to expand his business as a supplier of these agricultural commodities to coastal sugar estates or Andean markets. Third, the lessee would have the possibility of extending his mercantile activities by establishing a store in the estate. Fourth, profits could accrue from rents collected from the tenants. Although higher rents would have to be levied in order to meet commitments to the landlord as well as make a profit in addition to the S/.16,500 due to San Juan college, such an imposition could be forced on the peasantry, as the coercive capacity of Benel's private army could be used to guarantee rent payment if persuasion failed. Political influence wielded at a provincial and departmental level could also be employed towards the same end. Finally, acquiring an interest in Llaucán could bring political dividends. Being the most populous hacienda in Hualgayoc province meant that the number of Benel's dependants would be increased, as could his band of armed followers. This in turn would augment Benel's political clout regionally and enable him to defend his business network more effectively.

On a number of fronts, therefore, Eleodoro Benel's success in the auction for the lease on Llaucán hacienda represented a significant potential growth in his landholding and commercial activities. Such a development was viewed with trepidation by mercantile and political enemies of Benel, who quickly moved to scupper his expansionist plans. The ringleaders of this counter-offensive were the Alvarado brothers, who enlisted the support of Oswaldo Hoyos Osores and Régulo Regulado, prominent citizens based in the town of Chota, and commercial rivals of Benel who had hoped to win the lease on Llaucán. They thus had ample grounds on which to make common cause with the faction led by Marcial Alvarado. Pivotal to the plan was Raimundo Ramos and his band of brigands. Their tool was to be the peasantry settled on the estate. Ramos was summoned to the house of Regulado in Chota, paid, and given instructions to foment anti-Benel sentiment among Llaucán's tenants, a task he readily accepted in order to further his vendetta against the new lessee.[5] Accordingly, upon returning to the hacienda, Ramos and his fellow brigands proceeded to agitate on the rent question, always a conflictive issue with the tenants. Rumours were also spread to the effect that Benel intended to evict non-compliant tenants and burn down their homes. Anyone who did not fall in with his orders was going to be shot.[6]

Gossip quickly circulated around the estate, for the task facing the Ramos bandits was greatly facilitated by the unusual social structure found on the hacienda Llaucán. Not only was the property the sole *grundherrshaft* hacienda in Hualgayoc province, but also within the peasant ranks large wealth differentials existed. This provided the material basis for the establishment of clientelistic ties. Fifteen well-to-do peasant households controlled a disproportionate share of Llaucán's land and livestock resources.[7] These wealthy tenants had more land at their disposal than they could farm, and so sub-let plots to less prosperous peasant families. Strong patron-client relationships existed between the *arrendatarios* and the *subarrendatarios*.

51

Clearly then, the aims of the plotters would be best served by winning the support of the wealthier tenants, who in turn could use their influence among the sub-tenants to promote anti-Benel sentiments throughout the estate. Playing on legitimate fears about future rent increases, and by issuing thinly veiled threats, the Ramos gang first converted prosperous tenant Emilio Torrillo to their cause. Torrillo then met with his peers, whipping up anti-Benel feeling among them.[8] Similar views were then transmitted to their subinfeudates. Owing to these efforts, two months after the auction the mood among peasants farming on the hacienda Llaucán was extremely hostile to Eleodoro Benel.[9]

Ill-will towards the new lessee was further fuelled by simmering peasant unrest throughout 1913 and 1914. In mid-1913 the existing lessee, Luis Prado, energetically assisted by his son Edilberto, embarked on a number of attempts to exact higher rents from the *arrendatarios* of Llaucán. The probable motive behind this initiative was a desire to appropriate as much as possible from the estate and its inhabitants before their lease expired in the third quarter of 1914. This aggression evoked various responses from the peasants. Violent clashes erupted when a sector of the tenantry declared a rent strike. Others reacted more cautiously, and decided to pay no more than the mutually agreed rent levels. When this latter group went to settle their accounts with Prado in June 1914, he refused to accept the payment, insisting that they should hand over the higher amounts demanded. The Prados threatened the *arrendatarios*, who then decided not to risk another face-to-face encounter with the lessee and his son. Instead they deposited their rents with lawyer Manuel Santolalla, who agreed to intervene on the peasants' behalf. Confronted with this situation, Andrés Díaz Bustamante and other tenants farming on Llaucán made written complaints to the prefect about the 'large number of cruel acts and extortions' committed by their 'enemy', who 'has increased hatreds' and 'threatened them with death'.[10]

Other tenants were not so defensive when faced with the demands made by the Prados. July 1914 found Aurelio Zaldívar, director of San Juan college, writing to the prefect in a different vein to the letters originating from the peasantry. He expressed great concern about:

> 'the threats against the lessee made by a group of individuals led by Sr Francisco Besnard. Armed with rifles belonging to the State, on various occasions they have attacked the *casa hacienda* with the aim of murdering Prado or expelling him from the estate. Their other objective is to avoid paying rents. They already owe two quarters and have declared themselves the owners of these lands'.[11]

Amenable to Zaldívar's request, the prefect sent troops to try and restore landlord authority in Llaucán, but the *gendarmes* failed to act resolutely and were soon withdrawn to another province. This ineffectual intervention by the authorities left both parties dissatisfied, but had the effect of heightening animosity between Prado and the tenants.

Peasant discontent was augmented on another score, one that was hinted at in the letter of Aurelio Zaldívar quoted above. Shortly prior to the auction for the lease on Llaucán, the tenants lodged a plea with the governing body of the Colegio San Juan stating that they collectively wanted to become the new lessees and would pay their rents directly to the school. This was a demand that came from some tenants every time the lease was up for renewal, and as usual it was rejected by the governors. Such a response caused added bitterness among a sector of Llaucán's inhabitants.

Another group of peasants held a less conciliatory position on the issues of rents and ownership. Instead of offering to pay rent direct to the Colegio San Juan, they aspired to the complete dissolution of Llaucán as a hacienda, arguing that each *arrendatario* should be allowed to purchase the holding she or he cultivated. This faction was supported by the Lima based Asociación Pro-Indígena, or Indian Association. They were also backed by large numbers of citizens living in the town of Hualgayoc, who due to considerations of inter-town rivalry, were in disagreement with the handing over of Llaucán to '*intereses chotanos*'.[12] One of the most active peasant leaders on the estate, Lorenzo Guadaña, was a fervent advocate of fragmentation through private sale. Guadaña's agitational activities on this question, as well as his outspoken opposition to Benel taking up the lease under conditions that obviously spelt more onerous rent exactions, soon brought him into a new round of conflict with the Prados and the representatives of the Colegio San Juan. Efforts were made to capture Guadaña and threats were made against his physical safety. This induced Guadaña to appeal to the prefect for 'personal guarantees', as well as to protest that:

'For eight years the authorities have known about the most cruel acts committed against my person and my interests by the lessee of Llaucán, Don Luis Prado and his son Edilberto Prado. They robbed all my animals, whose value amounted to S/.8,000. After reducing me to abject poverty, they used the judicial system to accuse me maliciously and falsely of arson, burglary and other crimes. Due to the influence they enjoyed among the judiciary, the Prados got me jailed in Hualgayoc for seven years. After an appeal, a higher court found me innocent and wrongly accused. The Prados were discovered to have accused me in order to cover up crimes that they themselves committed. Consequently, my release was ordered. The court also decreed that my property should be restored to me. Unfortunately, Sr Prefect, this has not occurred, and I am living like a beggar'.[13]

Guadaña proceeded to ask the prefect to intervene against 'the evil people who carry out the terrible atrocities against me and the other Indians of Llaucán'.[14] Not surprisingly, the authorities failed to act on behalf of the 'dangerous troublemaker' and 'escaped criminal' Lorenzo Guadaña.[15]

## II

Multifarious issues, therefore, contributed towards creating the turbulent social environment that existed in Llaucán over the months of October and November 1914. Events began to accelerate when on 17 November the Colegio San Juan administrators decided to hand over the lease on Llaucán to Eleodoro Benel for a trial period of one quarter. This was agreed on receipt of S/.4,200 channelled through three associates of Benel in Chota, Gerónimo Saldaña, Juan Fernández Zuloeta and Bernardino Guerrero Gayoso.[16] When details of this development quickly filtered back to Llaucán's inhabitants via anti-*benelistas* in Chota and the Ramos brigands, the rent strike spread and more tenants adhered to the position that the new lessee should not be permitted to take charge of the property.

Faced with growing opposition, Benel and the representatives of San Juan college attempted to manoeuvre Belisario Ravines, the prefect of Cajamarca, into a situation whereby he would be forced to intervene more vigorously on their behalf. A telegram was sent by the governors in Chota to the *Director de Gobierno*, or permanent secretary to the cabinet, in Lima. The governors claimed that 200 armed tenants had stormed the *casa hacienda* with the aim of thwarting the collection of overdue rents and the entry of the new lessee onto the estate.[17] It was reported that the treasurer of San Juan college, Manuel Cadenillas, and his assistants were pinned in Bambamarca town along with Eleodoro Benel. A group of 300 tenants, the cable stated, had fired on them and impeded their journey to the estate. In addition, the rebels had assassinated two peasants and burned down a number of shacks belonging to those opposed to them. After mentioning these incidents, the governors suggested that the *Director de Gobierno* should command Ravines to send fifty troops to disperse the troublemakers.[18] A copy of this cable, along with an instruction to restore public order, was wired to the prefect in Cajamarca on 20 November.

That very day the prefect received a second telegram from the *Director de Gobierno* in Lima. It relayed to Ravines the contents of another cable they had received, this time from Cadenillas in the town of Bambamarca. The school treasurer maintained that disorder and banditry were sweeping Llaucán. An individual named Martín Fuentes had been killed the previous night, and many people had suffered injury as a result of the disorders.[19] The looting of homes was occurring unchecked. Rape, and the robbery of livestock, were commonplace. Law and order had completely broken down. To underline the point, it was claimed that César Miranda, landowner of the adjacent hacienda Chala, had been shot at by the rioters. Moreover, 'bandits' were making the roads impossible to travel and were in danger of cutting off the town. The telegram ended by stating that the Llaucán 'bandits were a real danger to travellers and townspeople', and pleaded for the re-establishment of order by outside forces, because 'the subprefect has no troops'.[20] The contents of this telegram indicate a conscious attempt by Benel and Cadenil-

54

las to label the Llaucán rent strikers as 'bandits', so creating an additional excuse for implementing a policy of severe repression. In this respect, the involvement of the Ramos brigands adequately served their ends.

The following day a cable carrying a different message landed on the desk of the *Director de Gobierno* in Lima. This time it originated from Andrés Díaz Bustamante, who, as has been mentioned, was a peasant leader from Llaucán of pro-Alvarado persuasion. It stated that Eleodoro Benel, 'backed by fifty armed criminals' from the parish of Samana, was encamped in Bambamarca town and poised to 'attack the inhabitants of Llaucán'.[21] Among his gunmen figured the son of the ex-lessee Edilberto Prado. Díaz proceeded to 'implore the government to save Indian lives and property' by giving them protection.[22]

In an attempt to contain what was a rapidly deteriorating situation as far as the custodians of law and order were concerned, on 23 November a captain Prada at the head of twenty-five troops was despatched to the hacienda 'with the objective of putting a stop to the riotous behaviour of the Indians of Llaucán'.[23] The subprefect of Hualgayoc was instructed by Belisario Ravines to accompany the soldiers 'and take whatever action is necessary to bring about conciliation and tranquillity, so as to prevent unfortunate developments'.[24] The stated good intentions failed to produce any positive results. Yet again the presence of poorly trained, badly disciplined and uncommitted troops failed to cow the peasantry or bring about any reconciliation. The rent strike and the negation of landlord authority persisted unchecked. It was clear that through his own resources alone, Eleodoro Benel did not yet have sufficient military strength to impose his will on Llaucán's rebellious peasantry.

Meanwhile, news of the anarchic situation in Llaucán spread throughout the province and beyond. Such a state of affairs could do no other than perturb Hualgayoc's landowning élite, owing to the threat that discontent might spread onto their own hitherto relatively trouble-free properties. After the failure of the detachment led by captain Prada to restore peace, lobbying by influential parliamentarians Rafael Villanueva and Demetrio Miranda — whose estates happened to border on the hacienda Llaucán — produced a further cable from the *Director de Gobierno* in Lima to prefect Ravines, ordering him to pacify the estate.[25] Accordingly, on 30 November the prefect rode out of the town of Cajamarca for Hualgayoc. Accompanied by all the troops he could muster, Ravines wrote that his intention was to 'settle the differences that exist between the lessee of Llaucán and the Indians of that estate'.[26]

After stop-overs to rest their mounts in the hacienda Yanacancha and the town of Hualgayoc, on the morning of 3 December 1914 the force commanded by Ravines commenced the 16.5 kilometre ride from the provincial capital to Llaucán. Upon their arrival at the estate, the prefect and his 150 supporting troops found the large majority of Llaucán's inhabitants assembled in and around the occupied *casa hacienda*. The soldiers halted a hundred metres distant from the *llaucaneros* on an expansive meadow adjacent to the estate buildings. They formed a double line and spread out into a semi-circle.[27] Several thousand strong, and armed with clubs, rocks and sticks of dynamite obtained from the mines in Hualgayoc, the peasants were in an aggressive mood. They shouted threats and insults at the increasingly nervous troops. Prefect Ravines advanced towards the tenants and appealed for calm. This only further angered the peasants, who began to slowly advance on the government forces and surround them. This manoeuvre added apprehension within the ranks. In response, Ravines threatened to open fire. A peasant woman, Casimira Huamán, ran towards the prefect shouting that he should not hand over the hacienda Llaucán to 'the bandit Benel'.[28] She tried to drag Ravines from his mount and lashed him with a rope. The prefect's son, who was a captain in the government force, rode up to assist his father. He drew a pistol, and fired three shots into Casimira Huamán, who collapsed to the ground. Incensed by her murder, the peasants let out a roar of anger and proceeded to run at the troops. Ravines ordered his men to fire a volley over their heads, but this failed to halt the *llaucaneros'* advance, who replied with a hail of rocks and ignited sticks of dynamite. Having completely lost control of the situation and seeing the resolve of his troops faltering, Ravines gave the order to open fire directly at the peasants. Several dozen crumpled to the ground during the first volley. Two additional rounds were discharged at the *llaucaneros*, leaving the field strewn with dead and wounded. Overcoming their initial state of shock, the survivors started to flee, seeking refuge in their shacks and the surrounding countryside. Amid the carnage, Ravines lost his head and commanded the troops to hunt the retreating peasants down. The soldiers first bayoneted the wounded littered over the meadow and then dispersed throughout the estate. Children, women and men were dragged from their homes and murdered. Others were cut down as they scurried along the country lanes or hid in the fields. At the end of the day more then 150 peasants had perished, while the troops suffered one man slightly injured.[29]

Not surprisingly, the central protagonists failed to show their faces. Eleodoro Benel remained in the town of Bambamarca throughout the massacre. Friends had advised him that his presence on the estate would be provocative, which given the turn of events was somewhat ironic. Manuel Cadenillas and other governors representing San Juan college stayed with Benel, as did Edilberto Prado.[30] The non-appearance of their factional rivals, who also played an important role in provoking the bloodbath, was equally conspicuous. Marcial Alvarado, the intellectual author behind the tragedy, lodged with factional allies in the town of Bambamarca, and like Benel, did not venture onto the estate. Oswaldo Hoyos and Régulo Regulado remained in Chota. Likewise, their *agents provocateurs*, bandit Raimundo Ramos and his brothers, wisely kept well away from the government forces.

The murder of civilians on such a large scale created a national scandal. Shortly after the massacre four peasants from Llaucán set off for Lima

56

'carrying a few heads of murdered children to show the government'.[31] Newspapers in Lima gave over their front pages to the Llaucán events and the incident was debated in parliament. The vociferous *indigenista* movement also devoted much publicity to the affair. Amid the furore, all those officials who had played a part in the massacre moved to cover their tracks and absolve themselves of blame. Prefect Ravines destroyed documents. He also attempted to minimise the death toll and place all the responsibility for the murders on the shoulders of the peasants. Instructions went out for the capture of tenants identified with the rent protest. Félix Huamán, Aniceto Ramírez, Catalina Atalaya, Manuel Palma and others had to go into hiding to avoid being arrested and charged with attacking Ravines and his troops.[32] Misinformative cables were fed to the Lima press stating that only thirty *llaucaneros* had died, while an additional fifteen had been wounded with seventeen taken prisoner.[33] A doctor, Hermógenes Coronado, *chotano* and ally of Benel, was commissioned by the prefect to undertake the post-mortem examinations. He made every effort to downgrade the role played by the authorities, stating that 'most of the deaths have been caused by the Indians' own dynamite and bullets. They were all intoxicated after drinking *aguardiente* with gunpowder mixed into it. In their drunkeness they killed their own people'.[34]

Not everyone was prepared to go along with the official interpretation of events or attempts to bury the affair. Some made efforts to proportion blame and sanction those responsible. In the opinion of *El Ferrocarril*, a newspaper published in Cajamarca town, 'the Llaucán massacre was a barbaric crime'.[35] The editor of the paper highlighted the rent question as the root cause behind the bloodshed:

> 'To meet the high rent, the new lessee of Llaucán has had to triple the *arriendos* levied on the tenants, who have been born and lived all their lives on the estate as if it was their own property'.[36]

The article went on to argue that the new level of rents that Eleodoro Benel was trying to impose on the peasantry was excessive. It was also implied that Benel was ultimately responsible for the tragedy.

Dissenting voices were also raised in Lima. Fed with information by the Asociación Pro-Indígena, certain members of Congress criticised the inaction of officialdom and the moves to protect those directly involved in the slaughter. At the end of a speech during the sitting held on 30 December 1914, senator Rojas Loaysa declared:

> 'I cannot emphasise too strongly the serious nature of these events due to the fact that they were carried out by the very people who are supposed to protect citizens' lives and uphold public order. In the first place, your honour, more than a hundred Indians have been murdered *en masse* by the police force, with the prefect at their head. Although they have used modern weapons, they have acted as if we

57

were primitives. Among the victims figure women, old people and children, who were massacred because they stood up for their rights. Secondly, the so-called defenders of law and order claim that they were attacked. However, they only registered one soldier wounded, in addition to four mules. Two of these were injured and two killed'.[37]

The senator went on:

'Your honour, the minister concerned has moved very slowly on this question. He has not dismissed the prefect or the commander of the troops and begun judicial proceedings against them. One presumes that they are to blame for these crimes. Neither has he ordered the withdrawal of the police force that committed the murders. Such steps are necessary if justice is to be done, if the enquiry into the incident is not to be distorted by the political influence of those who wish to escape blame . . . those who are directly compromised in this shameful, deplorable incident, cannot remain a minute longer in their posts. They should be dismissed and handed over to the courts so that they can be impartially tried'.[38]

This demand that the authorities involved should be removed from their positions and brought before the courts received unanimous backing from the Senate. So too did a motion censuring the *Director de Gobierno* for his lack of vigour in investigating the matter. As a result, *Director de Gobierno* Fernando Fuchs resigned.[39] During the session held on the following afternoon, another call for the dismissal of prefect Belisario Ravines and the officer in charge of the troops was put before the Senate and approved.[40] Pressure from these sources led to the removal of the prefect in February 1915. Second lieutenant Enrique Rodríguez and twelve soldiers were discharged.[41] Legal proceedings were opened against them, but the court moved with extreme slowness. Public interest in the massacre naturally subsided with time, so that in late 1915 the investigations were quietly shelved and no further sanctions against Ravines or his troops were invoked. A similar fate befell an attempt to prosecute Eleodoro Benel.

Undeterred by the large loss of life brought about by the desire to expand his commercial ventures, Eleodoro Benel still determined to take up the lease. Two weeks after the clash he again requested the prefect to billet twenty-five troops in Llaucán. His declared aim was to 'uphold my legal guarantees and normalise the situation . . . so to prevent the repetition of new disorders on the part of the Indians of Llaucán'.[42] Given the public outcry following the massacre, this request was ignored by functionaries who felt that involvement would be too risky. Widespread opposition to Benel becoming lessee of the estate under the terms of the November 1914 contract also weakened his position. Dora Mayer and Pedro Zulén, leading figures in the Asociación Pro-Indígena, lobbied congressmen and the executive arguing that the only manner in which the conflict could be peacefully resolved was through parcellation. The *arrendatarios* and *subarrendatarios* should be allowed to purchase their plots, thus leading to the dissolution of the estate.[43] Despite vigorous lobbying in parliament, articles in the national press and continued trouble in the estate, this option did not gain wide support among parliamentarians.[44] Many were landowners themselves and perhaps thought that a law decreeing the fragmentation of Llaucán would set a dangerous precedent. Instead, the contract agreed between the Colegio San Juan and Eleodoro Benel was anulled. Rents were to remain at their old levels. Responsibility for administering the estate was temporarily put in the hands of the Ministry of Education in Lima, who appointed an official named Pedro Ureña to oversee the property. Essentially a compromise worked out with regard to political expendiency in Lima, this 'solution' failed to impress the tenants so that in 1916 a new round of rent protests developed.[45]

In April 1918, four years after the massacre, Aurelio Zaldívar made a public statement giving his version of how the incident developed. The ex-director of the Colegio San Juan first noted that 'a group of armed Indians seized the *casa hacienda*' and 'began to commit monstrous crimes'.[46] This forced Zaldívar to seek intervention by the authorities in order to evict the tenants and collect unpaid rents. Being the lawyer of Eleodoro Benel, Zaldívar placed responsibility for the tragedy firmly on the shoulders of the Alvarado family, Hoyos and Regulado in Chota and the Ramos gang:

> 'Over one thousand Indians participated in the Llaucán insurrection. They possessed more than two hundred rifles of various makes, as several travellers witnessed during the month of November. The rebellion was concocted and instigated by the personal enemies of Benel as well as several rivals in the auction, who had hoped to win the lease at a very low rent'.[47]

Aurelio Zaldívar's interpretation of the Llaucán affair reflected the views of his client. The machinations of Marcial Alvarado and his friends had succeeded in blocking Eleodoro Benel's plans for business expansion. This infuriated the landlord of El Triunfo hacienda and gave added impetus to the factional struggle in Hualgayoc province. Another important outcome of the Llaucán massacre was to deepen acrimony between the hegemonic Osores *parentela* in Chota province and the pro-Benel faction who dominated neighbouring Hualgayoc, a situation of mutual hostility that was to last until 1922–3, when common opposition to president Leguía spawned a wholesale realignment of political forces in the two provinces.[48]

# CHAPTER 5

# Bandits and governors

## I

Cajoled by Aurelio Zaldívar and Eleodoro Benel, prefect Ravines ordered the capture of Marcial Alvarado, who was apprehended in Santa Cruz shortly after the Llaucán massacre, transferred to jail in the town of Cajamarca and accused of incitement to riot.[1] Nevertheless, the goaling of Marcial Alvarado did not have the dampening impact desired by the authorities or his personal enemies. Having efficaciously frustrated the threatened expansion of Benel's business interests, the opposition faction were gleeful and in no mood to lie low. Rather than sitting back and savouring their success, over the early part of 1915 the Alvarados and their allies became increasingly belligerent and determined to press home additional attacks against their rivals.

Taking advantage of Benel's absence — for a time he was in Cajamarca trying to persuade the authorities to allow him to take up the lease on Llaucán — Gerónimo Alvarado, Zenón Burga and Tristán Cabrejo embarked on a campaign of hounding *benelista* supporters. Once again the brigands led by Raimundo Ramos were central to their plans. Immediately following the bloody incident in Llaucán, the Ramos bandits temporarily abandoned their homes on the hacienda and sought refuge with the Alvarado family in Santa Cruz. Due to these developments, by January 1915 the epicentre of factional conflict in Hualgayoc switched from the district of Bambamarca to Santa Cruz. Gun fights were provoked on the street and robberies in the surrounding countryside were everyday occurrences. The district governor was helpless to contain the violence. This induced him to write a series of desperate letters to the subprefect stationed in the town of Hualgayoc:

'once again I inform you that at approximately six o'clock on Sunday evening, after the new lieutenant governors of this district had been sworn in, the insurrectionists fired rifle shots and provoked a number of scandalous incidents. Among them figure Idiasar Fernández, Abel Leyva, Juan Aguinaga, Herminio Santa Cruz, three of the Ramos family and others who are unknown to me. The latter group have come from Llaucán. Undoubtedly they have fled from there. They are all billeted in the house of Gerónimo Alvarado, who gives them protection and maintains this bandit group. His aim is to intimidate the townspeople and threaten the lives of peaceful citizens in Santa Cruz'.[2]

Unwilling to remain in office because of the death threats made against him, the governor attached his resignation to this communication and suggested that police reinforcements be sent to capture the lawbreakers.[3]

A fortnight later the situation in Santa Cruz became more critical. Clear-cut evidence against Marcial Alvarado was not unearthed, for instructions to Raimundo Ramos and the other plotters had been issued orally. This enabled lawyer Manuel Burga to lodge a successful petition requesting the release of Alvarado on 25 January 1915. His client was freed that same day.[4] When Alvarado walked out of jail the opposition received an important boost to their morale, as it became obvious that the ringleaders behind the Llaucán peasant agitation would escape official sanction. Evidence of this was soon forthcoming in the shape of escalated aggression against the dominant *benelista* faction in Santa Cruz. Marcial Alvarado hired several new gunmen among criminal elements in Cajamarca town. On the march back across the moors to Santa Cruz, this band met with a group of clansmen who were marauding on the *jalca* after having been forced to flee the hacienda Llaucán.[5] Entering Santa Cruz on 26 January, Alvarado and his *condottieri* started to terrorise the town. Shots were fired at those citizens foolhardy enought to venture onto the streets. Several houses owned by adherents of the *benelista* faction were looted and burnt, while 'the shopkeepers do not open their stores out of fear of being killed by a stray bullet or having their businesses ransacked'.[6] During the ensuing weeks of disorder a number of people were assassinated. In a typical incident, Pedro Burgos was gunned down by Francisco Ramos and Hermógenes Pérez as he sat in a drinking club.[7]

Permission to relinquish his office was not granted to the jittery governor. His pleas for the posting of *gendarmes* were echoed by the subprefect in various letters to the departmental prefect. But with memories of the Llaucán massacre still fresh in their minds, the authorities in Cajamarca failed to respond.[8] Official inaction allowed the Alvarados and their followers a near free hand in Santa Cruz. Repeating earlier complaints about his predicament, the hapless governor argued that the situation:

> 'becomes more alarming with every day that passes. We are in a desperate position. The Alvarados have more than thirty armed men quartered in the houses mentioned to you in previous despatches. They hold the population in a state of siege. My family, myself, and the majority of other households are dispersed in the countryside out of fear that our children and relatives will be killed by these criminals. Since they have arrived here they have subverted public order and given a free reign to their bloodthirsty vendettas'.[9]

The governor ended his letter by repeating that 'I have no force with which to contain them'.[10]

If Eleodoro Benel was to maintain his position as local caudillo, he could not allow the Alvarados to act with impunity in Santa Cruz for long. Inaction would undermine his personal authority, encourage internal dissension, thereby placing stress on the ever fragile clientele network. In March 1915, once it became obvious that attempts to possess the lease on Llaucán had foundered, Benel started to devote more energy to strengthening his local political dominance. The surest way to achieve this and restore the confidence of his *clientela* was by attacking the opposition. *Pistoleros* from the parishes of Ninabamba and Samana joined up with gunmen resident on the hacienda El Triunfo under the command of Misael Vargas, and marched on Santa Cruz. Following a series of street battles, the Ramos brothers and their fellow brigands were driven out of town. In addition to scoring this military success, Benel reinforced his hand politically by supporting the candidature of his business associate José Pardo — landowner of the Tumán sugar estate — who became president of the republic in August 1915.[11] Thus the Alvarado-Burga faction proved unable to wrest local supremacy out of the hands of their rival, and found themselves pushed back onto the defensive. This process culminated in November 1915 with an assault on the hacienda Litcán. Zenón Burga maintained a band of armed men on the property, which was also a frequent place of refuge for bandits operating on the surrounding moors. Transversing the *jalca* dividing Samana from Litcán at night, the *benelistas* led by Misael Vargas launched a surprise dawn attack. Several gunmen in the pay of Burga were killed, buildings were looted and razed to the ground, but the landowner was away in Santa Cruz sleeping in his town house, and so escaped assassination.[12]

Threatened by armed aggression and unable to break Benel's influence with the subprefect and other members of Hualgayoc's state bureaucracy, Alvarado and Burga were in desperate need of political allies. They thus started to build ties with anti-Benel elements in neighbouring Chota, using the contact established with Oswaldo Hoyos Osores and Régulo Regulado during their combined efforts to stir up trouble in the hacienda Llaucán. These moves soon bore fruit when they enlisted the support of Daniel Touset, the subprefect of Chota. By good fortune, shortly after the raid on Litcán, prefect Iglesias ordered Touset to hunt down bandits in Santa Cruz and Bambamarca. A citizens' militia was formed in Chota under the command of Fernando Díaz, a personal enemy of Benel resident in Lajas.[13] This force, assisted by ten *gendarmes* stationed in Chota, failed to disperse the 'gang of criminals armed by Benel for vendetta and business reasons'.[14] Advised of the *chotanos* approach, Misael Vargas led his men onto the densely wooded mountain of Ushushque adjacent to El Triunfo. Fearful of being ambushed, their pursuers dared not follow, so Díaz and his men returned to Chota without accomplishing their mission.[15] Benel's private army was thus kept intact, and with it his local predominance.

The struggle for supremacy in Santa Cruz waged throughout 1915, cost many lives and produced panic among the population. After several months of uncontrolled factional feuding, the district capital was 'nearly de-populated, for the majority of its inhabitants have fled to other localities, abandoning their affairs in order to save their families'.[16] Numbered among them was Marcial Alvarado and his family. Elsewhere the situation was not quite as tense, but nevertheless outbreaks of factional violence frequently occurred. From March to July 1915 the district of Bambamarca was the scene of considerable turmoil motivated by the proximity of municipal elections. In March the band led by Alejandro Verástegui, which allied itself with the subprefect and Benel in local politics, fell upon Francisco Alva in the town square. Alva was badly beaten up and then kneecapped.[17] The same group tried to force their way into the home of the Vargas family, intent on raping the daughters of the household. When their mother resisted the attackers, she was clubbed and kicked.[18] Verástegui and his associates also engaged in gun fights. On 4 April they assembled at the house of Mariano Lara and climbed onto the roof. From this vantage point they opened fire on the house of Santiago Salazar and opponents who happened to be walking in the street.[19] Incidents like these became commonplace in the run-up to the July elections and all the evidence pointed to a fiercely contended gun fight to control the voting tables on polling day. In an effort to avoid additional bloodshed, the authorities arranged a meeting of local notables representing the two competing factions. It was agreed that twenty names, ten from each side, be written on slips of paper and placed in a hat. Ten slips were to be drawn, and these individuals would be 'elected' to sit on the town council.[20] Things went smoothly until the lottery designated Reinaldo Salazar for the position of mayor. The rival band could not agree with Salazar's 'election', denounced the whole procedure as a fraud and refused to participate further. This ended the tenuous truce, and sparked off a new round of armed clashes.

In his *Memoria* for 1915 subprefect Egusquiza highlighted some of the features of political life in Hualgayoc. The report started by noting that several zones 'have been the scene of murders and disorders due to deep divisions between the inhabitants, as well as the large number of modern firearms that the townspeople and rural population possess'.[21] The subprefect then stressed the contrast in firepower between the state and private individuals:

'The seven *gendarmes* that comprise the permanent policing force in this province, cannot begin the task of disarming the hundreds of men in the valleys of Santa Cruz district, especially those in the parishes of Samana, Ninabamba and Polulo, not to mention various localities in other districts. Still less can they pursue and apprehend the criminals that live in these zones, for they would almost certainly lose their lives at the hands of these felons. Furthermore, the few troops at my disposal have to guard the growing number of prisoners held in the public jail'.[22]

To emphasise the lack of *gendarmes* to police Hualgayoc, Egusquiza mentioned that when Francisco Ramos shot dead Pedro Silva in Bambamarca town in August 1915, the assassin was captured by a posse of townsfolk, 'because there was a complete absence of a police force'.[23] The predicament confronting the subprefect was underlined in the following month, when even the seven *gendarmes* vigilating the goal in Hualgayoc did not prove up to their task. On the night of 17 October 1915 one of the guards fell asleep on duty, so allowing Máximo Puerta, Abraham Ramos, Tobías Ramos and Benigno Vásquez to make a hole in the tiled roof and escape. In spite of being chased, the prisoners were able to avoid recapture due to the darkness and the heavy mist that hung over the bleak mining town.[24]

If 1915 proved a riotus year, then 1916 witnessed a slight abatement in the intensity of factional conflict in Hualgayoc. No elections were held, while tempers that had been raised by the Llaucán massacre gradually subsided. Yet within this slightly more peaceful environment, Santa Cruz was to be a nodal point of tension. In January 1916 the authorities in Cajamarca made a half-hearted attempt to pacify Santa Cruz by drafting a column of *gendarmes* into the district. These troops received instructions and information from the *benelista* district governor, with predictable consequences. At this juncture Benel and his followers were striving to take advantage of disarray within the ranks of the opposition faction caused by the enforced absence of Marcial and Gerónimo Alvarado. Logically they used the *gendarmes* to pursue this end. Middle-ranking and grass roots supporters of the Alvarado band were disarmed and interned in Chota jail.[25] In order to ingratiate himself with the prefect by giving an appearance of compliance with official goals, Benel voluntarily offered to hand over ten rifles to the subprefect of Chota, a superficial gesture considering that the landlord of El Triunfo could call on a personal militia of more than sixty gunmen.[26]

The *gendarmes* retired from Santa Cruz in early April 1916. Hearing that the troops had departed, the Alvarado brothers made plans to return to their homes and restart trading. Rumours circulated around the town, and the *benelista* faction threatened to organise armed resistance to the re-entry of the Alvarado family. On being informed of this, the prefect ordered a new detachment of *gendarmes* into Santa Cruz to prevent violence.[27] Although the Alvarados were able to take up residence in the town once again, their political faction had been much weakened during the course of the previous six months. Not until 1917 did the minority band feel confident or strong enough to mount attacks on Benel and his allies.

Even though faction-motivated violence diminished, armed robbery continued to plague the province. Niepos was among the districts most afflicted by bandits. Ramón Caruatanta, Frederico Suárez and Vidal Suárez led bands of armed men who engaged in the long-established practice of rustling cattle in the highlands for sale to landlords and livestock traders in the Zaña valley. The brigands also assaulted muletrains and individual travellers at will. According to the governor, 'they daily commit every kind of abuse and crime against defenceless citizens'.[28] In September 1916, when membership of these bandit groups had swollen to over sixty, they threatened to occupy the town of Niepos and kill the mayor, the priest and a number of prominent citizens. A ransom of S/.1,000 was demanded from the mayor, S/.2,000 from the priest

and S/.1,000 from merchant Guillermo Díaz. A further S/.3,500 was requested from various other townspeople, making a total ransom of S/.7,500.[29]
This particular attempt at extortion was instigated by the brigands' thirst for
revenge after one of their lieutenants had been assassinated in Chepén by the
authorities. The ransom notes were signed 'The avengers of Millones', in
reference to their fallen comrade, and emphasis was made that failure to pay
would result in death.[30] Flustered by this threat, the governor organised an
urban militia to protect the town. A request for ten to fifteen troops was
heeded by the prefect, but the *gendarmes* rarely ventured outside the vicinity
of the district capital, thus allowing the brigands a free hand to terrorise the
rural population and passing wayfarers.[31]

Hand in hand with endemic banditry went high levels of violence. Nearly
all rural and urban households possessed firearms, local élites fomented
rather than clamped down on bloodletting, while the judiciary often proved
unable or unwilling to convict lawbreakers. In addition they were highly
bribable. Under these circumstances, vendettas were allowed to progress
unchecked, with the result that a bellicose environment pervaded town and
country. People were murdered or seriously wounded on the slightest pretext.
For example, when Daniel Guardia went to retrieve two young oxen that had
accidently strayed into a meadow belonging to the hacienda Casmalca, the
estate foreman attacked him without warning, hitting the unfortunate Guardia around the head with a machete. When the peasant fell to the ground, the
foreman pounced on him, stabbing the wounded man several times in the face
and neck.[32] Family feuds also led to many deaths. In October 1916 Eloy
Vásquez was shot dead by Bonifacio Medina in a vendetta killing. Several
years previously 'the former murdered the latter's wife. When Medina fled,
members of the Vásquez family, undoubtedly aided by the Coronel clan,
burnt down his house'.[33] With these kinds of incidents recurrent, throughout
1916 a weekly average of two homicides, in addition to numerous attempted
homicides, took place in the provinces of Hualgayoc and Chota.[34] As in
previous years, the population lived in a Hobbesian social climate, which
nevertheless lacked the restraining presence of Leviathan itself.


## II

Above all else, two factors helped make 1917 a particularly turbulent year.
Municipal elections were scheduled for April and May, an event guaranteed
to arouse passions as rival bands battled for local dominance. Additionally,
the launching of a new offensive by the Alvarado-Burga faction led to serious
ructions in Santa Cruz. This wave of violence in the most trouble-ridden
region of Hualgayoc spilled over into other districts of the province.

Undeterred by the return of Marcial Alvarado in June 1916, Eleodoro
Benel felt secure enough to make a business and holiday trip to Lima. This
lasted from December 1916 to early February 1917. Before departing Benel
left instructions with Misael Vargas to drive opponents out of Samana,

Ninabamba, Polulo, Uticyacu and Chancay. Dependents of established enemies such as Tristán Cabrejo and Domitila Benel who lived in Polulo and
Samana parishes were particularly vulnerable, given their proximity to the
hacienda El Triunfo. For example, in December 1916 a homestead in Samana
parish farmed by the family of Eulogio García was attacked. Thirteen-year-
old Moises García was shot dead and his younger brother incurred serious
bullet wounds as their father fought to repel the assailants.[35] On 17 February
1917, shortly after the return of Benel from Lima, a group of *pistoleros* led
by Misael Vargas and Eduardo Mego again assaulted the García family.
Their house was looted, and the smallholding presented to Eduardo Mego in
payment for loyal service.[36] As she tried to flee Francisca Sánchez, the
*compañera* of Eulogio García, was seized by the *benelistas* and taken to El
Triunfo hacienda. There she was badly beaten and suffered a miscarriage as
a result of her rough treatment.[37] Within a few days of this incident the cane
fields belonging to José Ventura and the farm of Heriberto Sánchez were
similarly attacked. The owners were driven away, their homes sacked and
livestock slaughtered or lifted.[38]

With an eye to containing the mounting violence in Samana and surrounding parishes, in February 1917 the prefect sent a detachment of seven *gendarmes* to police the area. The commander of this force, *comisario*, or law
officer, Augusto Durand, was almost immediately regarded by the minority
faction as a puppet in the pay of Eleodoro Benel.[39] Durand and his force were
housed in El Triunfo, and even though at first he accepted versions offered
by Benel to explain various crimes, the *comisario* soon began to display
anti-*benelista* sentiments. He took up residence in the town of Santa Cruz.
Then a succession of reports written by Durand in April produced a prefectural order dated 1 May instructing Benel 'to abstain from committing
crimes. To leave the people of Samana in peace, and not endanger their lives
or property'.[40] By May 1917 the *comisario* was remitting dispatches to the
subprefect and the prefect denouncing offences committed by 'the gang of
bandits who obey the orders of Eleodoro Benel'.[41] These detailed incidents
arising from the continued implementation by Benel of the policy of driving
opponents out of Samana and surrounding parishes. In one case, Durand
described how on 10 May fifteen armed men shot down three peasants. The
victims were 'peacefully harvesting maize in their field, when they were
attacked by surprise and riddled with bullets. I am told that the killers were
sent by don Eleodoro Benel Zuloeta, for these individuals are in his service
and are protected by him'.[42] The lawman continued by stating that this
bloody act was an 'open flouting of the order commanding Benel to respect
the lives of citizens in this locality'.[43] He called on the prefect and the
*Ministerio de Gobierno* to place extra and better equipped troops in Santa
Cruz, as 'the only way to stamp out banditry'.[44] Without determined action
from above, the lawman argued, 'my efforts will be in vain, because these
individuals are impossible to capture. Every time the troops approach, they
look on them with indifference'.[45]

While clashes caused by the expulsion of non-*benelistas* from parishes adjacent to the hacienda El Triunfo continued during the first half of 1917, April and May witnessed serious conflicts throughout Hualgayoc motivated by municipal hustings. In Santa Cruz, rival bands twenty or thirty strong fought to control the streets and so determine who would be victorious at the poll.[46] Complaints were lodged about the partisan behaviour of the *benelista* governor, who was hounding oppositionists. After noting that 'bloody and deplorable scenes' had characterised the election campaign, *alvaradista* merchant Santiago Celis alleged that Zenón Flores, the local tax collector, had falsely accused him of smuggling fifteen bottles of *aguardiente* into Santa Cruz.[47] Celis claimed that this charge formed part of a plot concocted by the governor and the tax collector, who were both *benelistas*, to hamper their rivals: Celis was fined and jailed so that he was unable to participate in the campaign or the poll.[48] Given these methods and the superior firepower of the dominant faction, no change in local control materialised in Santa Cruz, despite determined efforts by Marcial Alvarado and his allies.

The election campaign in Bambamarca mirrored that taking place in Santa Cruz. Official partisanship and armed skirmishes proved the order of the day. Ten *mayores contribuyentes* led by Manuel Santolalla addressed a letter to the courts and the prefect protesting about the activities of Juan Hernández, governor of Bambamarca, and Alcibiades Contreras, the governor of San Miguel. They complained that the governors had 'unlawfully interferred' in the meeting of the *mayores contribuyentes* called to nominate the polling officers. This intervention was 'in favour of a particular political band'.[49] Such moves to decide the election developed as follows:

> 'governor Juan Hernández arrived in the town on Sunday 4 March riding at the head of fifty men armed with rifles belonging to the State. Firing shots, they rode into the *plaza* causing a scandal and threatening the population, for among their ranks figured criminal elements who have been sentenced to prison. Their objective was to prevent the *mayores contribuyentes* attending their meeting. This was to be presided over by the first signatory to this petition [Manuel Santolalla — LT], who has legal powers from the Finance Ministry. Governor Alcibiades Contreras, accompanied by don Ciro Novoa and twenty-five armed men, stationed himself on the road between Bambamarca and San Miguel, in order to prevent the arrival of the *mayores contribuyentes*. Shots were fired to frighten them off'.[50]

During the election campaign three people were assassinated, included among them the local president of the Partido Civil, but despite demands that 'these bad authorities be immediately suspended', no action was forthcoming and the faction associated with governor Hernández was not ousted.[51] Elsewhere, tactics similar to those employed in Bambamarca and Santa Cruz ensured that opposition bands were successfully prevented from seizing local hegemony.

As on previous occasions, the elections lacked legitimacy and municipal office holders governed through force rather than on the basis of moral authority or consensus. Equally predictable was the absence of post-electoral peace. Misael Vargas and his fellow gunmen continued a scorched earth policy against opponents of their *patrón*, looting and killing at will over the summer of 1917.[52] Riled by their inability to overturn the political status quo in Santa Cruz, while constantly seeing their followers harassed by *pistoleros* loyal to Benel, Marcial Alvarado and Zenón Burga devised an audacious scheme aimed at assassinating their principal enemy. On 21 November the four Alvarado brothers secretly met with Zenón Burga and his four brothers in the hacienda Litcán. At this meeting plans were laid for an assault on the hacienda El Triunfo. The objective was to murder Eleodoro Benel, his family, and the maximum number of *benelista* gunmen.[53] Word went out to Raimundo Ramos and his brothers at Llaucán that they should present themselves in Litcán as soon as possible. They were informed of the planned raid and agreed to lead it. In addition to Raimundo, Ramón and Domingo Ramos, Dionisio Ventura, Isabel Ventura and Manuel Llalli were also hired. The latter three individuals were tenants employed on the hacienda Quilcate, who combined pastoral activities with banditry.[54] Artemio García, Gonzalo García and Rosendo Mondragón, tenants and gunmen kept by Zenón Burga on the hacienda Litcán agreed to participate, the former two no doubt intent on avenging the murder on 2 June of their relation Eulogio García by the *benelistas*.[55] An escaped prisoner from the jail in Cajamarca who had integrated himself into the Ramos gang, José Villa Uriarte, also enlisted in the raiding party. These hardened criminals were joined by two members of the Vásquez clan from Chugur. The group was completed with the inclusion of three tenants from the hacienda Llaucán, who also supplemented their farming income through brigandage. All together, the force assembled by Burga and Alvarado numbered fifteen experienced gunmen.[56]

Manuel Goicochea, a carpenter employed in the hacienda Yanacancha, was a fringe member of the Ramos clan. He was sent to El Triunfo on a spying mission. Under the pretext of buying goods in the estate store, for thirty minutes he was able to observe the lay out of buildings and the placement of sentries.[57] Undetected, Goicochea returned safely to Litcán. After hearing his report, it was decided to press ahead with a suprise attack against Benel's estate. The date was fixed for Thursday 29 November. Arms and ammunition were supplied to Raimundo Ramos and his band by their backers.[58]

By a fateful coincidence, during the afternoon of 28 November two acquaintances of Eleodoro Benel arrived at the hacienda El Triunfo. They were Herminio Segura, local president of the Partido Civil and the legal representative of Benel in Hualgayoc town, and Eladio Estela. The two travellers, who were on their way from Hualgayoc to Santa Cruz on business, accepted an offer to dine and spend the night in the hacienda. That evening Benel and his invitees passed the time drinking, talking and playing games.

At one o'clock in the morning the guests retired to their rooms situated on the ground floor of the *casa hacienda*.[59] Five hours later the band led by Raimundo Ramos silently crossed the meadows leading to El Triunfo. With firearms concealed beneath their *ponchos*, they infiltrated the hacienda buildings. Once in position around the *casa hacienda* they opened fire and began to break down the door with an axe.[60] The assailants quickly gained entrance and started to search the ground floor rooms. Rudely awakened by the rumpus, Eladio Estela opened the door to his bedroom and almost immediately was shot through the heart. Herminio Segura received a bullet in the head as he struggled out of bed.[61] Meanwhile, in their bedrooms on the first floor, Benel and his family realised that they were under attack and leapt out of bed. The landlord grabbed what firearms lay to hand and started to snipe at the assailants. These replied by trying to tumble the house with sticks of dynamite. Efforts were also made to throw dynamite through the first floor windows.[62] Although the sons of Benel were away on the coast, his daughter Lucila had been trained to shoot by the lawman Augusto Durand. While her father concentrated fire on those members of the Ramos gang who were occupying the lower section of the house, Lucila Benel directed bullets at the second group of raiders who had broken into the hacienda store and were looting it.[63] When the bandits inside the house managed to break down the door at the bottom of the stairway leading to the upper floor and started to ascend, Lucila Benel joined her father and commenced shooting at the approaching assailants. One of her bullets pierced the throat of Isabel Ventura, who started to pour blood. Seeing their accomplice wounded, the other attackers faltered and carried Ventura below out of the firing line.[64] In the meantime Misael Vargas and his fellow *pistoleros* had been alerted by the sound of gunfire, and during this lull in the battle, they began to surround the estate buildings. One group of attackers thus became trapped in the lower section of the *casa hacienda*, with the second pinned down in the estate store and the adjoining carpentry workshop.[65] Those inside the house managed to break down a door leading to the workshop and unite with their associates. A drawn out siege then commenced. Shots were interchanged, but even though Raimundo Ramos and his colleagues were heavily outnumbered, they were well entrenched and had restocked their arsenal with firearms and ammunition looted from the estate store. Several attacks were launched against the intruders, with *benelista* gunman Daniel Cotrina losing his life in the course of one assault.[66] Two other dependents of Benel, José Goicochea and Rómulo Barrantes, were seriously wounded.[67]

Stalemate ensued. Messengers were dispatched to Santa Cruz and Hualgayoc requesting the presence of the *gendarmes* and the local justice of the peace. Neither appeared until the following day. Throughout the afternoon no change in the fortunes of either side occurred. Raimundo Ramos and his fellow raiders could not break out, while the *benelistas* proved unable to overrun them. In late afternoon a heavy rain commenced and mist began to roll down off the adjacent hills. When night fell thick clouds blotted out the moonlight. Taking advantage of the darkness, the beseiged brigands used dynamite to blow a narrow tunnel in the adobe wall separating the carpentry workshop from the estate pig pens. They then crawled among the pigs and through the piggeries to the perimeter of the hacienda complex, before breaking out and escaping to the shelter of the wooded mountains.[68] Raimundo Ramos and his friends did not flee empty handed. It was claimed that the bandits stole money and gold watches from the corpses of Segura and Estela, along with S/.2,000 in cash and S/.3,000 in jewelry belonging to the Benel family.[69]

On 30 November the subprefect and *comisario* Julio Vargas visited the hacienda El Triunfo. Their reports to the prefect stated that the attack had been led by the Ramos brigands, who were also responsible for the murder of Segura and Estela.[70] Meanwhile, news of the incident quickly spread throughout the department. Rumours circulated by enemies of Benel suggested that the victims had been murdered by their host. Gossip alleged that the landlord of El Triunfo had dynamited his own home and pock-marked it with rifle fire in order to put the blame for the killings on the Burgas, Alvarados and Ramos. By no means all the judiciary in Cajamarca were well disposed towards Benel, among them criminal judge José del Carmen Gallardo. On 3 January 1918, subprefect Jorge Rivasplata and judge Gallardo, accompanied by three officers and twenty-five troops, arrived in El Triunfo to investigate the crime.[71] Confident in his innocence, Benel cordially greeted the arrivals and willingly agreed to collaborate with their interpellation. Judge Gallardo started to question the landlord in an aggressive manner, but Benel remained calm and could not be baited. This exasperated the judge, who ended his interrogation by declaring that Benel had not cleared himself of suspicion and should therefore be detained.[72] The landowner offered no resistance and was taken to jail in Hualgayoc without incident.[73] Shortly after the suspect was transferred to the public gaol in the town of Cajamarca.

Gallardo justified his actions on the grounds that 'the alleged attackers have left no evidence of their stay in the hacienda, which lasted for more than twelve hours'.[74] Moreover, it had 'not been fully proved that the deaths (of Segura and Estela — LT) were caused by outsiders. It is Benel Zuloeta who has to account for these lives, as he has already admitted that he was talking with them well into the night'.[75] Until the investigation was completed, the judge decreed, 'Benel should remain in detention'.[76]

The Peruvian legal system has never been renowned for its speed or efficiency, and Eleodoro Benel was to languish in jail for twelve months. But bureaucratic incompetence was not the prime cause of his lengthy incarceration. Not only were a number of key officials such as Gallardo hostile to his release because of traditional rivalries, political developments unfolding at the national level also conspired against the release of the landlord of El Triunfo. By late 1917 the *civilista* government of José Pardo was facing grave

70

difficulties and becoming increasingly unpopular. This was partly due to the disruptive impact of war in Europe on the Peruvian economy and its social repercussions.[77] These externally generated sources of tension coalesced with intense personal antagonisms between leading figures inside the Partido Civil, to produce a growing split within the governing political party.[78] The divisions accentuated during 1918 as various factions inside the Partido Civil jockeyed for hegemony, becoming particularly acute once José Pardo patronised Antero Aspíllaga for the position of party head and presidential candidate for the forthcoming 1919 election.[79]

These trends in national politics had their local impact. A majority of large-scale landowners in Cajamarca gave their support to the conservative wing of the Partido Civil, as represented by Antero Aspíllaga.[80] Eleodoro Benel was clearly identified as a member of this tendency among the *civilistas*. As on previous occasions, the main opposition to Aspíllaga gathered around Augusto Leguía, who presented himself as the leader of a progressive current within the *civilista* tradition, calling for a mild reform of the system through measures that would undermine the appeal of revolution by bringing benefit to the middle and working classes.[81] In Cajamarca this reformist stance gained Leguía support among urban artisans, middle class professionals and small-scale merchants, all of whom were experiencing economic hardship due to wartime inflation. One of the occupational groups most attracted to the growing ranks of *leguiístas* in Cajamarca was the legal profession.[82] *Leguiísta* lawyers and judges had no interest in releasing Eleodoro Benel from prison.

As with the imprisonment of Marcial Alvarado in December 1914, the incarceration of Eleodoro Benel failed to bring tranquillity to Hualgayoc. Misael Vargas and his fellow gunmen sought revenge for the jailing of their *patrón*. A new wave of violent attacks was launched against opponents in and around Samana. The unfortunate Francisca Sánchez was once again captured after being chased through the fields, beaten and then carried off to the El Triunfo hacienda, where she endured further harsh treatment.[83] According to the lieutenant governor of Samana, over the early part of 1918 armed clashes were daily occurrences. In one of these, his own smallholding had been beseiged by the band led by Misael Vargas. The bandits surrounded the house belonging to the lieutenant governor and peppered it with two hundred rifle shots in a skirmish lasting several hours.[84] This act was motivated by suspicion that the lieutenant governor had clandestinely assisted in the arrest of Benel. Not all the criminal acts perpetrated at this juncture were the work of *benelista* gunmen seeking vengeance. Although the raid on El Triunfo had not attained its prime objective, namely the assassination of Eleodoro Benel, the enterprise could not be judged infructuous from the perspective of Alvarado and Burga. The internment of their hated enemy presented the Alvarado-Burga faction with an opportunity to wreak economic damage on Benel. Similarly, if they could take advantage from the removal of the linchpin in the opposing faction, then possibilities existed to erode its dominant position. Perspectives in this direction were enhanced due to the growing state of flux in national political alignments. Moreover, the recently appointed *comisario rural* had not been bought by the *benelista* faction. Consequently, the Alvarados determined to press home what might be only a temporary advantage. Fresh raids were mounted against property owned by Benel, as well as individuals allied to the landowner. These induced the landlord of El Triunfo to write a number of letters from his prison cell to the authorities requesting constitutional guarantees. In the first of these, it was claimed that an armed band, twenty-five to thirty strong, was billeted in the hacienda Litcán. It was led by the Alvarado and Ramos brothers, who were poised 'to murder my family and expropriate my possessions, taking advantage of my unjust detention. The *comisario rural*, Don Julio García Vargas, who is my enemy, instead of giving me the protection that is my constitutional right, is in continuous cohorts with the aforementioned criminals'.[85] After a second appeal in February 1918, the prefect ordered that the Benel family be given protection.[86] This time, however, the weakness of the state worked against Eleodoro Benel. Despite their good intentions, the prefect and the subprefect did not possess sufficient troops to be able to offer Benel adequate protection, with the result that the armed band formed by Marcial Alvarado and Zenón Burga were able to undertake several successful raids against the property of their foe.

Frustration produced by continued internment and a feeling of helplessness in the face of these attacks, prompted a new flow of letters from Benel to the prefect. In the first of these, he began by noting that after months in jail no charges had been brought. Also, the relatives of Segura and Estela knew who the real culprits were and had opened proceedings against Alvarado, Burga, Ramos et. al.[87] Over the past months 'this group of bandits have been causing terror' in Santa Cruz, and are:

'now carrying their perfidy to the extreme of trying to assassinate my defenceless family, including my young children. During my stay in prison on several occasions these bandits have invaded my estate, robbing cattle and firing rifles as if we were in a revolutionary situation. They have not respected life or property that has been honourably acquired through hard work.

The enclosed telegram, Mr Prefect, has been sent to me by my son Fernando Benel. It illustrates the state of siege endured by my family, who are in danger of being assaulted and killed. My hacienda is also under threat of being sacked. Last Friday night they stole another batch of eight cattle. There is no way to prevent this, for they number thirty men dressed up in military uniform'.[88]

Benel concluded this letter by naming the Alvarado, Ramos, Díaz and García brothers as the principal members of this bandit group, all of whom were his 'mortal enemies'.[89] Allegation was also made that another of his enemies, the *comisario rural* of Santa Cruz, was 'allied to this group of bandits'.[90] In response to this request for protection, the prefect stationed three *gendarmes* in El Triunfo. Unfortunately for Benel, the troops did not prove an effective deterrent. Raids against the properties of *benelistas* and El Triunfo itself continued over the following months. In July 1918 the holding owned by María Santos Romero in Ushushque parish was attacked. Romero was a first cousin of Benel, and during this assault his cousin, Antenor Vargas, was killed by the Ramos brigands. According to the landlord of El Triunfo, these acts had as their objective 'the elimination of all my family in order to take over our possessions'.[91] Mention was also made of the fact that the subprefect of Chota, *enganchador* and merchant Catalino Coronado, who was also a bitter commercial rival of Eleodoro Benel, maintained clientage ties with the bandits and turned a blind eye to their activities.[92]

## III

In Hualgayoc subprefect Rivasplata was a political ally of Benel. He believed that Raimundo Ramos and his gang were responsible for the events of 29 November 1917. The prefect in Cajamarca shared these views, and in contrast to Coronado in Chota, both he and Rivasplata regarded Raimundo Ramos as a tool of the opposition and were anxious to eradicate his band. Since 1910 hardly a month had passed without someone being assassinated by the Ramos outlaws, and the raid on El Triunfo was the last straw as far as Rivasplata and the prefect were concerned.[93] While many of these killings were undertaken for factional motives, most victims were shot during the consummation of petty robberies. One typical incident occurred on 16 September 1914. Manuel and Wenceslao Uriarte were sat in the *tambo*, or store-cum-tavern, situated on the moorlands overlooking the Quilcate hacienda. The brothers happened to be travelling back to their home parish of Lajas after attending the annual fair at San Pablo. They had halted at the *tambo* to drink a few glasses of *aguardiente* when up rode fifteen to twenty members of the Ramos gang, accompanied by several tenants from Quilcate who also engaged in brigandage. The bandits ordered Manuel Uriarte to hand over the revolver stuck in his belt. When Uriarte refused, the two brothers were gunned down and their corpses fleeced.[94]

Over the intervening three years Raimundo Ramos and his associates participated in scores of similar scenes. One week after the assault on El Triunfo, they killed Domingo Llamoctanta, who was peacefully harvesting potatoes with three other peasants on his plot in the Llaucán hacienda, when the Ramos band fell on them. The unfortunate peasant was shot down without warning. Wounded, he lay writhing in a furrow, only to be finished off with a *machetazo*, or machete blow.[95] A measure of the assassins' confidence in their ability to evade retribution can be gleaned from the fact that they never even bothered to murder the witnesses.

As a result of this kind of behaviour, the Ramos gang became the most feared brigand *foco* operating in northern Cajamarca. Being the most prolific killers in the province, their activities had also greatly contributed towards creating a Hobbesian social climate in Hualgayoc. In order to stop their butchery and also prevent the opposition faction from employing the gang as its *brazo armado*, or military wing, fresh attempts were made to destroy them. A surprise raid on Ramos property in the Llaucán hacienda was planned for 20 December 1917. Its aim was 'to capture the culprits for the crimes in La Samana'.[96] One group of *gendarmes* left the town of Hualgayoc at midnight for the Llaucán hacienda. Travelling by foot, they arrived at the home of Ramón Ramos at three o'clock in the morning, but when the door was broken down, the outlaw was absent.[97] The mission was not completely in vain, as the troops managed to capture another brigand called José Vicente Azánero. Azánero, whose alias was 'Rache', had 'co-operated in the assassinations at La Samana'.[98] Synchronised with this raid was a strike at the main Ramos stronghold sited at the place called El Enterador in the Llaucán hacienda. At ten o'clock at night on 19 December, the governor of Bambamarca, accompanied by the lieutenant governor and eight *gendarmes*, set out of the town on foot and followed a roundabout route to El Enterador. Arriving at their destination at four o'clock in the morning, the troops attempted to surround the dwellings of Raimundo Ramos and Calixto Uriarte:

'but this was impossible, on the one hand due to the strategic position in which the buildings are placed, and on the other because of the fierce resistance offered by the bandits. They put us under merciless fire. I am informed that they number more than twenty. The brigands are well-armed and possess lots of ammunition. The *gendarmes* fired over 150 rounds of shot at them in order to defend ourselves'.[99]

When the sun rose, the troops were forced to retreat. Once back in Bambamarca, an extremely apprehensive governor informed the subprefect that, 'I have been told that as a consequence of this attack, the outlaws are preparing to invade the town with the aim of finishing off the authorities'.[100]

Undeterred by this failure, over the early months of 1918 the authorities kept up their attempts to capture the Ramos band. Given the brigands' superior knowledge of terrain and their elaborate network of informants, these efforts proved largely unsuccessful. Harassment by the *gendarmes* nevertheless caused the outlaws a degree of inconvenience, and they frequently gave vent to their feelings of persecution by committing particularly barbaric crimes. On 8 March 1918 the Ramos gang were trying to evade government troops. At ten o'clock that morning Raimundo Ramos and seven other members of his band rode into the hamlet of Chadín, located in the parish of Paccha approximately ten kilometres outside the town of Bambamarca on the Chota road. Two of the bandits were dressed in black, a mode of livery probably chosen to convey a sinister image and strike fear

74

in the minds of ordinary citizens. As they entered the hamlet, rifle shots were aimed at the shacks occupied by the local peasants. When lieutenant governor Silvestre Apaéstegui asked the brigands to cease firing, one of them replied 'now you will pay with your life for the bull you impounded'.[101] Two bandits grabbed Apaéstegui and started to force him to the ground. During the struggle the lieutenant governor managed to let off two revolver shots at his attackers, but once pinned down he was dispatched with a bullet in the head.[102] Esteban Rodríguez came out of his home to protest and was threatened with similar treatment. His daughter, Margarita, tried to plea for her father's life, but to no avail, as both of them fell riddled with bullets. The bandits then started to break into and sack the peasants' shacks, in the process killing three more men with machetes and firearms.[103] Before they rode off, the witnesses Pedro Figueroa and Anastasio Guevara were forced to gulp down half a bottle of *aguardiente* each. The pockets of the survivors and victims alike were emptied, while the brigands also robbed a sack of coca.[104]

Maintaining pressure on the Ramos gang gradually brought results, for its members started to disperse in an attempt to avoid detention. In May 1918 the subprefect scored a major success when Ramón Ramos was apprehended. Word got out that the Ramos brothers were visiting a smallholding nearby the *casa hacienda* in Llaucán. Troops were sent and they managed to surround the house unobserved. When the *gendarmes* burst in they found Ramón Ramos 'drinking in the company of several associates and women'.[105] The bandit tried to break out, but was overpowered, bound and transferred to jail in Hualgayoc town. Keen to keep him there, the subprefect requested five extra men to guard 'the famous brigand'.[106] Soon after, Domingo Ramos also fell into the subprefect's net and was locked up alongside his brother. Thus two serious blows were delivered to the Ramos band during mid-1918. These developments helped foment dissension within the bandit ranks. Simultaneously, the outlaws were forced to take greater precautions through increasing their mobility and plying their trade in more remote areas. For example, on 1 October 1918 a fire burnt down the Ramos house in El Enterador when a drunk Raimundo Ramos started to squabble with the equally inebriated Antonio and Canuto Vásquez over the division of booty. Other members of the gang joined in, and during the mayhem the house caught fire.[107] Until then challenges to the authority of Raimundo Ramos had been unheard of. Over the latter half of 1918 the harassed band also tried to avoid capture by carrying out a greater portion of its rustling in more inaccessible zones closer to the Marañón, with the hacienda Pallán in Celendín province being especially hit.[108]

While efforts to wipe out the Ramos gang continued throughout 1918, Eleodoro Benel remained behind bars. As the months passed and the legal proceedings advanced with more than customary slowness, it became increasingly obvious that the lengthy detention of the landlord of El Triunfo owed more to politics than crime. No verifiable charges were brought against

Benel, but opponents allied to the *leguiísta* faction continued to block his release. Moreover, the political aspect of the case came more to the fore as the 1919 presidential elections loomed on the horizon.

After talking with lawyer Aurelio Zaldívar, Castinaldo Benel felt that the only way his father would ever get out of jail was through a break out. He therefore devised an escape plan. Armed with legal documents containing examples of handwriting, signatures and seals, Castinaldo Benel journeyed to Chiclayo. On arrival in the coastal city, he paid forgers to concoct a court order authorising the release of Eleodoro Benel in the calligraphy of judge Gallardo and other magistrates. Official stamps of the court in Cajamarca were also reproduced by the counterfeiters. Documents granting the provisional discharge of Eleodoro Benel purporting to originate from the prefecture in Cajamarca were similarly manufactured. After a month in Chiclayo, Castinaldo Benel returned to Cajamarca to consummate his plan.[109] Early on the morning of 1 February 1919 Castinaldo Benel, accompanied by lawyer Aurelio Zaldívar and a group of friends, went to the Cajamarca goal and presented the fake documents to the head jailer. Their authenticity was accepted and Eleodoro Benel was allowed to walk out of the prison gates. Elated, the landowner invited the welcoming party to join him in a celebratory drink, so they walked to a nearby tavern and consumed a bottle of champagne. Thirty minutes after being released, Benel and his son briskly rode to the outskirts of Cajamarca, where a posse of men were anxiously awaiting to escort their *patrón* back over the moors to El Triunfo.[110]

News that Benel had been sprung from jail quickly spread, and the prefect wired telegrams ordering his recapture. Nevertheless the journey to El Triunfo passed without incident. The escapee and his party stopped to spend the night in Llapa. The following morning Manuel Cieza, the district governor, showed Benel the telegrams he had received from the prefect. A friend of Benel, governor Cieza ignored his instructions, and even provided the landlord with an escort of two *gendarmes*, who were told to travel with the fugitive and see him safely to the boundary of his estate.[111]

## IV

A new subprefect was sent to Hualgayoc in autumn 1918. Although he was not on as good terms with Eleodoro Benel as his predecessor, on returning to Santa Cruz the landlord of El Triunfo discovered that the Alvarado faction had not been able to overturn *benelista* local hegemony during his sojourn in prison. No doubt this was in part due to the difficulties besetting the Ramos gang over the latter half of 1918. While Raimundo Ramos and his followers were being hunted by the authorities, the band captained by Misael Vargas enjoyed a measure of official tolerance and had been able to maintain itself intact. So in February 1919 Benel still possessed the largest private army in Hualgayoc province. This was important, for in that month the campaign to elect a new president and one third of Congress commenced.

76

As on previous occasions, Benel backed the official *civilista* candidate, Antero Aspíllaga, in preference to Augusto Leguía. The rival Alvarado band opted for Leguía. Aided by votes and guns loyal to Benel, in the May 1919 elections the pro-Aspíllaga faction in Hualgayoc garnered 345 votes, compared to eight in favour of Leguía.[112] In the neighbouring provinces of Chota and Cutervo, Aspíllaga also romped home, obtaining 619 and 1,135 votes respectively, while Leguía only managed fifty-two in Chota and none in Cutervo.[113] These returns gave adequate testimony to the local dominance of the conservative *civilista* faction, as well as the influence of *oficialismo* and the tight control exercised by the subprefects over the electoral process.

Even though the hustings in Hualgayoc were fiercely contested in all districts, producing the usual armed clashes, events in the province were overshadowed by grave disturbances in Chota and Cutervo. In neighbouring Chota two hated rivals of Eleodoro Benel, Oswaldo Hoyos Osores and Cecilio Montoya, were standing for election as deputies on the *civilista* slate. Régulo Regulado, another enemy of Benel who played a part in the Llaucán massacre, was also pushing for the election of Hoyos and Montoya. Faced with this situation the participation of Benel in the hustings could not be consistent. Keen to block the ambitions of Hoyos and Montoya, Benel decided to support Leoncio Villacorta, the *leguiísta* candidate for the House of Deputies in Chota. Villacorta owned the hacienda Chetilla, and like Benel, commanded a powerful armed following.

Subprefect Merino blatantly supported the candidature of Aspíllaga and the Chota *civilistas*. This induced a stream of telegrams complaining to prefect García in Cajamarca about his behaviour, while an appeal to a *leguiísta* judge succeeded in getting Merino removed from the subprefecture on the grounds of electoral favouritism.[114] But the subprefect refused to give up his post and continued to work in favour of Hoyos and Montoya, jailing citizens allied to the opposing faction on fabricated charges. This incensed the *leguiístas*, who in retaliation employed the private militias of Villacorta and Benel to occupy the town square of Chota on 1 March 1919. Simultaneously, detachments of armed men were stationed on the trails leading to the town with orders to impede the arrival of *mayores contribuyentes* hostile to Villacorta.[115] Undeterred the ex-subprefect decided to press ahead with the meeting of the *mayores contribuyentes*, thus provoking a gun battle through the streets on 3 March. Merino and three gunmen loyal to Villacorta were shot dead during the fracas. Many other participants and bystanders received bullet wounds.[116] Similar scenes characterised the poll in Cutervo, but nowhere was the faction supporting Leguía allowed to register success. Wherever parallel meetings of *mayores contribuyentes* occurred, as in the provinces of Cajamarca, Celendín and Chota, the prefect accepted the pro-Aspíllaga *asamblea*.

Aspíllaga consequently garnered a clear majority of votes in Cajamarca, due to the support he received from most influential landowners and assistance from the state machine. But nationally, Leguía won the poll. This result

77

created multifarious problems. Despite a clear popular mandate to assume the presidency, Leguía realised that he would be faced with a hostile Congress: in the provinces sufficient Aspíllaga leaning senators and deputies were returned to reinforce mainstream *civilista* control of parliament. Moreover, in the immediate post-election period rumours abounded alleging that outgoing president Pardo, aided by the *civilista* dominated executive and legislative branches of government, were plotting to annul the presidential election result and declare Aspíllaga the winner. To forestall this, on 4 July 1919 Leguía staged a successful coup and proclaimed himself president.[117] Intent on avoiding difficulties in parliament, Leguía then dissolved Congress.

This unexpected turn of events immediately created complications for the anti-Leguía faction that had hitherto wielded political hegemony in Hualgayoc and elsewhere in Cajamarca. As in 1903 the choice had to be made between maintaining current loyalties or accommodating to the incumbent regime. These decisions had to be taken hurriedly, for the new president wisely wasted no time in appointing confidants to the office of prefect in the departments of Peru. To these key officials fell the important task of constructing local clientelage networks able to challenge mainstream *civilismo* and provide the nascent government with a solid political base. Consequently, over the latter half of 1919 *civilista* subprefects, governors, lieutenant governors and mayors throughout the department of Cajamarca were dismissed and replaced with supporters of Leguía. For example, in Santa Cruz the local web of patronage and control built up by Benel and his allies was quickly excluded from office. The minority Alvarado faction, who had suffered a resounding defeat at the polls, now obtained backing from the prefect and were given official positions. In September 1919 Gerónimo Alvarado became governor of Santa Cruz, while his brother Fortunato, assumed the post of *comisario rural*. The key figure in the anti-*civilista* faction, Marcial Alvarado, was appointed mayor of Santa Cruz.[118]

These changes were not forced through without opposition. Shoot-outs between *leguiístas* and *aspillaguistas* frequently erupted in the three months following the July coup.[119] Even so, the ousted supporters of the Partido Civil found it impossible to hold their ground as the new government took control of leading positions in the state bureaucracy and strove to expand its *clientela*. The process of marginalising former dominant groups accelerated during the latter months of 1919, when Leguía convoked elections for a national assembly that was to redraft the constitution. In preparation for this, a new electoral law was decreed on 2 September 1919, shortly followed by the poll. Only men identified with the president were allowed to stand as candidates, a restriction that naturally led to widespread abstention. Once 'elected', the national assembly passed changes in the constitution devised to curtail the influence of parliament and strengthen the position of the executive.[120] These moves by Leguía also worked to consolidate this regime and weaken the opposition, for Congress had traditionally been one of the power bases of the Partido Civil. Finally, the elections of autumn 1919 can be interpreted as an attempt by Leguía to enhance the degree of legitimacy attached to his administration. Initially this objective met with a modicum of success, but before long opposition to Leguía hardened. This development, when fused with the continuance of fierce local vendetta feuding, was eventually to usher in open rebellion and generalised civil war in the northern provinces of Cajamarca.

# CHAPTER 6

# From Vendetta to Civil War

## I

The shifting sands of national politics brought important changes in the socio-political situation of Eleodoro Benel. From being a respected member of the regional élite, the landlord of El Triunfo was now officially branded as a bandit leader and an escaped prisoner wanted for crimes of murder. Additionally, with the ascension of the hated Alvarado faction to public office, his role as leading local caudillo faced its most serious challenge yet. Never one to meet adversity with passivity, Benel reacted to these unfavourable developments in an aggressive fashion. Attacks on his enemies in Santa Cruz were stepped up. With Marcial Alvarado and Zenón Burga responding in kind, over the turbulent months of 1920 life for many innocents and participants alike came to a bloody end. Hardly a day passed without some report of robbery, homicide or armed confrontation in Hualgayoc entering the flow of documents addressed to the prefect.

Some indication of the level of violence pervading Santa Cruz at this juncture can be gleaned from the following, not untypical, dispatch filed by the district *comisario rural* in early 1920. In this document the law man relates a number of incidents, one of them a vendetta attack involving the Díaz gang, deadly enemies of Benel, against the Vargas clan, gunmen and brigands loyal to the landlord of El Triunfo:

'The other day I passed the hacienda La Samana, where various crimes have taken place. On Wednesday 31 March at approximately 3 p.m., Jorge and Antonio Quispe, armed with revolvers, in the company of Evaristo Meléndez, armed with a club, assassinated don Evaristo Reguego and Fidel Meléndez. After committing these murders, the aforementioned individuals went to another house about a block away from where they had murdered Reguego and Meléndez. Here they killed Lorenzo Infante and Melchora Alva, father and mother of Carmen, Clotilde and Otila Infante. They also wounded the right leg of Emilia Cotrina, the grand-daughter of Infante . . . On Friday 2 April, Policarpo Hurtado used a machete to assassinate the Chinese Toribio Vera, who was working in his field seventy metres from his house . . . when the felon was captured, Hurtado admitted the crime, stating that he killed Vera because the Chinese had refused to let him walk across his field. Hurtado was drunk when he committed the homicide, and is now in the public jail. On 4 April at seven o'clock in the morning, a band of fifty assaulted the Ramos Vargas family house at Yucaspampa. Their first move was to rob cattle belonging to the Ramos Vargas. When the Ramos Vargas went to recover these animals, they were fired upon and could not attain their objective. Then the assailants surrounded and attacked the house of the Ramos Vargas family. The leaders of this gang are Tomás Díaz, Gervasio, Aniseto, Anselmo and Agustín Díaz . . (list of 25 other names — LT) . . the ensuing gun battle lasted from seven in the morning until four in the afternoon, with the assailants' objective being the eradication of the Ramos Vargas family and their allies. The attackers killed Bonifacio Medina and Román Hurtado. Misael Vargas, Francisco, Juan and Santos Reguego, as well as Natividad Montenegro, were wounded. When the raiders returned they murdered Francisco Fernández, an uninvolved person, and burned down the house of Manuel Silva. Tomás Díaz, a ringleader, and Telésforo Guanca were shot dead on the attackers side'.[1]

Factional feuding of this genre acknowledged no constraining conventions. Anybody possessing a blood tie with an enemy was considered a legitimate target for attack. For example, six weeks prior to the events mentioned above, the young daughter of Inés Rojas was shot in both legs at point-blank range.[2] Her assailant was Vidal Collantes, who happened to be seeking out her father with the intention of shooting him. Finding that his intended victim was absent from the family homestead, Collantes vented his ire on the unfortunate girl.

If in Santa Cruz vendetta-motivated killing was now out of control, elsewhere in Hualgayoc the socio-political climate, although tense and mar- ked by frequent bouts of bloodletting, was less critical. One event that momentarily helped reduce vengeance assassination and other causes of violent crime was the arrest of Raimundo Ramos, the 'Famous bandit leader . . . the scourge of this province', who was apprehended in Bambamarca on 19 April 1920.[3] Although Ramos and his fellow brigands had in the past been hired by factional militants who now occupied middle- and low-ranking positions in the state bureaucracy, throughout 1919 pressure on the authori- ties in Cajamarca to eradicate the Ramos gang had been growing. Calls for determined action in this direction were voiced by the landlords of Udima, Jerez, Pallán and Combayo, haciendas that had suffered as the Ramos brigands expanded their operations over an area extending from San Pablo to the province of Celendín. After noting that Raimundo Ramos could call on fifty bandits, thirty of whom possessed modern weapons, the subprefect reported that on his holding in the hacienda Llaucán, the outlaw grazed:

'two hundred cattle, the product of the robberies that this crimi- nal has been committing almost daily. He stole livestock before the very eyes of their owners, who gave their consent due to the great terror he inspired in them. Ramos sold these animals on the coast, on many occasions personally driving the cattle. With the proceeds raised from these sales, Ramos purchased improved livestock. Through these methods he is the owner of a herd two hundred strong'.[4]

81

Having finally captured the most infamous bandit in northern Peru, the subprefect was keen to prevent his escape. Nine *gendarmes* were sent from Chota to reinforce the company of troops charged with transferring Raimundo Ramos to jail in the town of Cajamarca. The column also took the added precaution of travelling to the departmental capital by a roundabout route.[5]

Plans were also made to recapture Benel, but these proved unsuccessful.[6] Aware of the intentions of *leguiísta* officialdom, Benel rarely ventured outside his estates and adopted certain other precautionary measures. Trenches and fortifications were built on the *pampa* surrounding the hacienda complex at El Triunfo, as well as on the adjacent forested mountains. Following the 1919 election Benel also increased the size of his private army by recruiting peasants and artisans.[7] Given Benel's ability to call on the services of approximately a hundred gunmen 'who blindly follow his orders', it became extremely dangerous for Marcial Alvarado and his allies to venture outside the town of Santa Cruz.[8] Opponents were assaulted and raids launched against the town itself, as happened on 25 February 1920, when members of the *benelista* militia invaded Santa Cruz and vainly attempted to provoke the Alvarados into an open confrontation.[9] In addition to the advantage accruing from superior local military strength, Benel's ability to avoid recapture was facilitated by divisions within the *leguiísta* camp. Leading local caudillos Wenceslao Villacorta and Arturo Osores Cabrera, along with their *clientela* in the state bureaucracy in Chota, were by early 1921 becoming increasingly disgruntled with Leguía. They therefore forewarned Benel when moves were afoot to apprehend him, encouraged his attacks on Alvarado supporters and allowed the landlord to enter the town of Chota whenever he pleased.[10] As a result, even though Marcial Alvarado and his factional allies had strengthened their position by mid-1920, they remained inferior to Benel in terms of firepower.[11] They also proved unable to obstruct a significant expansion in their rival's business interests when in 1920 Benel acquired the haciendas Silugán and Sedamayo in Cutervo.

But for all his military muscle, Eleodoro Benel proved unable to dislodge the Alvarados from their occupancy of posts inside the bureaucratic machine, with the result that a period of stalemate ensued in Santa Cruz's factional struggle. Neither band was able to gain undisputed hegemony. This situation of unstable equilibrium in turn helped sustain the intense level of clan feuding that developed during and after the 1919 election. Homes owned by supporters of the rival group were looted and razed to the ground. Calculated, as well as random, assassination also worked to 'sow general panic' among the population, especially in the countryside.[12] Encouraged by increasing peasant poverty, the total breakdown in order and the insecurity of everyday life, in 1921 new bandit groups emerged to augment the violence successfully spread by their already established peers. The most important of these new gangs was that led by Pedro Zuloeta, which operated in the valleys and hills surrounding the town of Santa Cruz. According to a petition sent by the local district council to the subprefect, Zuloeta's men 'are ruining the already poor inhabitants of these parishes, for they impose ransoms, rob all species of animals, burn houses, rape young girls and do whatever takes their fancy'.[13] Elsewhere in the province, similar trends were in evidence. Rich peasant Emilio Torrillo, who had played a role in the events leading up to the Llaucán massacre, took advantage of the dissolution of the Ramos gang to form a new band of brigands on the estate.[14] Another recently established outlaw group organised by Eloy Marchena specialised in the rustling business. Beginning operations in 1921, the cattle they stole were hidden on the moors linking Hualgayoc, Llapa and San Miguel before being driven down to the coast for sale to slaughterhouses located in the sugar estates.[15] Efforts by the authorities to control this proliferation in lawlessness in 1921 and the following year met with no success. On several occasions columns of *gendarmes* thirty-five strong were sent into Hualgayoc from Cajamarca and Chiclayo, but their attempts to control brigandage and pacify the countryside came to nought. This was especially true of Santa Cruz district, where most of the populace was armed and linked to one or other of the factions that gave succour to bandits for political and business purposes.[16] Indeed, the level of lawlessness in Santa Cruz and surrounding districts was so adversely affecting trade that coastal merchants and parliamentarians lodged vociferous complaints to the authorities.[17]

Ineffective policing enabled Eleodoro Benel to continue unhindered his offensive against *alvaradista* life and property. As on previous occasions, non-combatants fell victim to this uncontrolled vendetta war. One such incident occurred in January 1923, when a group of gunmen led by Misael Vargas descended on the homestead of Rosendo Mondragón and Estanislada Ugaz. A *pistolero* in the pay of Zenón Burga, Mondragón had participated in the fateful raid on El Triunfo and was thus a targeted man. Having surrounded the Mondragón house, Vargas and his fellow outlaws discovered that their enemy was absent, so they fell upon his defenceless family:

'On 14 January the Vargas bandits and their gang burned down the house of Estanislada Ugaz in El Choro, four leagues distant from this town. They wanted to rape her daughter, the minor Dorila Mondragón. Dorila's elder sister, Ursula Mondragón, placed herself in the doorway, armed with a club to prevent the assailants from entering. One of the Vargas brothers shot his rifle twice, killing her instantly. They then carried off the aforementioned Dorila. I have been informed that the murdered woman was in an interesting condition and was about to give birth. For this reason, Estanislada Ugaz had left the house in search of a midwife. After committing this crime, the bandits passed on to the house of Guzmán Avellaneda, with the intention of raping a daughter of his named Tadea. Seeing them approach the girl managed to flee and hide'.[18]

Seven days later Vargas and his men shot another pregnant woman whose husband rode with Zenón Burga. On this occasion it was alleged that they slit open her belly and pulled out the unborn child.[19] This atrocity was followed by the murder of a couple and their ten-year-old son in the hamlet of Andabamba. The next day fifty of Benel's *condottieri* presented themselves at a feast taking place in Yauyucán. Shots were fired in the air, men badly beaten up and houses looted.[20] In addition to the physical annihilation of opponents and their kin, Benel also recommenced his policy of usurping their property and handing it over to his henchmen. During the early months of 1923 lands belonging to peasants in the parish of Yauyucán were invaded by the *benelistas* 'under the pretext that they belonged to his tenants'.[21] Then in July 1923 the *benelistas* struck directly at Marcial Alvarado. Misael Vargas launched an assault on the hacienda Chancay, ransacking the property, killing Alvarado's dependents and committing several rapes.[22]

While Hualgayoc's internecine factional conflicts continued unchecked, on the wider terrain of national politics significant developments were in motion. During the first period of the *oncenio*, the 'populist' phase that lasted from 1919 to 1924, president Leguía hounded key representatives of the Peruvian oligarchy with the intention of rendering them politically impotent. Due to their social standing and influence inside the Partido Civil, the Aspíllaga and Pardo families were amongst those most affected in this respect. Egged on by the *leguiístas*, an angry mob ransacked and burnt the Lima residence of Antero Aspíllaga. Shortly afterwards, Antero's brother, Ramón, suffered the indignity of imprisonment.[23] Such inconveniences persuaded members of these élite families to go into exile. Inside the country, meanwhile, several plots to oust Leguía were hatched by the conservatives, but none of them bore fruit.[24] With putschism proving unsuccessful, the hopes of the opposition came to centre on the removal of Leguía from office in 1924, the year his presidential term came to an end. Such expectations suffered a severe jolt in 1923, when through the opportunistic politician Mariano Cornejo, Leguía started to moot the possibility in parliament of annulling the article in the constitution prohibiting the reelection of a president.[25] By late 1923 it was clear that this constitutional change was acceptable to a majority in a largely amenable Congress. Most *leguiístas* readily acceded to their patron's desire to remain in office. Support for the reelection of Leguía was also forthcoming from the Partido Demócrata and the faction in the Partido Constitucional previously led by Andrés Cáceres.[26]

Now that hopes for a constitutional removal of Leguía were dashed, the thoughts of his *civilista* opponents once again turned to rebellion.[27] Rumours had been circulating from as early as January 1923 that Eleodoro Benel, with the support of a majority of leading citizens from Chota, was 'planning a revolution against president Leguía'.[28] But these intrigues do not appear to have advanced very far by mid-1923. Nevertheless, local and national events during the latter half of 1923 soon coalesced to give fresh impetus to the insurrectionary option. The manoeuvres aimed at securing Leguía a second term in office acted to widen and stiffen opposition, for it was felt in some circles that he had violated the constitution. Leguía's blatant use of the state machine to build up a political base also proved increasingly unpopular, while his attempts to reform the banking system brought the government additional enemies. Already in 1921 the faction of the Partido Constitucional led by experienced conspirator Arturo Osores Cabrera, who had been Minister of Justice and Education in the first Leguía cabinet, had withdrawn its support and adopted a posture increasingly hostile to the president. With Leguía now regarded by many as a dictator, the Osores position gained credence. To this background, from exile in Ecuador Osores and general Oscar Benavides began to plot the overthrow of Leguía.

A native of Chota, Osores had had many dealings with Eleodoro Benel, not all of them amicable, and now the *chotano* moved to enlist Benel's backing for an armed uprising. At first Benel acted cautiously, merely being content to engage the local *leguiístas* in combat. Then in September 1923 a fortuitous incident occurred that brought important repercussions. Traditionally, the most important festival in Santa Cruz, the *Señor del Costado*, is celebrated each year during the last week of September. Having been cooped up in El Triunfo for several weeks administering the hacienda, Castinaldo Benel was keen to visit Santa Cruz and participate in the merry-making. The young man was also making eyes at one of the town's local beauties, Margarita Ugaz y Ugaz. As his father was away working in the hacienda Silugán, Castinaldo and his mother, accompanied by four gunmen, journeyed to Santa Cruz on the morning of 26 September 1923.[29] Upon their arrival at approximately one o'clock in the afternoon, they proceeded to the house of Vicenta Perales. Perales was a relative of the Benel family and the sister of Narciso Perales, a *capo* in the *benelista* militia. After a leisurely stroll around the streets inspecting the fun-fair and the merchandise displayed by the many visiting traders, Castinaldo Benel ended up in the store owned by José Olivera. There he began to drink *aguardiente* with the local priest and other acquaintances.[30] Around seven o'clock Benel left the store. Accompanied by several other youths, he went to the home of Margarita Ugaz y Ugaz to invite the young woman to a dance scheduled for that evening in the house of Vicenta Perales. The door was opened by a maid. The servant informed Benel that her mistress was in church, whereupon the party sauntered down to the *plaza*. While climbing the church steps Castinaldo Benel was ordered to halt and state his name by a figure hidden in the shadows. After obeying the order, the youth was shot with a rifle at point-blank range and crumpled to the ground as he tried to draw his revolver.[31] On the following day Castinaldo Benel died of his wounds. Juan Aguinaga, the assassin, fled the town.

A messenger was dispatched to El Triunfo immediately following the shooting, and shortly after dawn the slumbers of the drunks in the streets were disturbed by Segundo Benel and Misael Vargas as they rode into Santa Cruz at the head of forty-five gunmen. The *benelistas* quickly took over the town. Perched on roofs and balconies, they laid siege to homes belonging to the Alvarados and Aguinagas. With the Alvarado faction defending themselves resolutely, a fierce gun battle raged for several hours. During the exchanges, Manuel Galarreta, a cousin of Eleodoro Benel, was also shot dead by the *alvaradistas*. The clash only came to an end when a dying Castinaldo Benel requested his brother to cease the attack in order to avoid further bloodshed.[32] Fearing that the siege might be only momentarily lifted, governor Alvarado, along with his family and factional allies, took advantage of the lull in the fighting to flee Santa Cruz. They hid in the hacienda Limac, from where pleas were made to the subprefect for troops to be sent to pacify the district.[33] According to Marcial Alvarado, Benel was poised to attack the town yet again, and to this end was press-ganging peasants settled in parishes around Samana into joining his private army. Those that refused were threatened with having their smallholdings expropriated. Allegedly Benel had also sent his son to the province of Pacasmayo to buy arms and ammunition.[34] But with Benel deeply shocked by Castinaldo's death, this anticipated attack on Santa Cruz failed to materialise.

News of this potentially explosive incident was rapidly relayed to the prefect in Cajamarca, who dispatched telegrams demanding information from his subordinates. Giving his version of events, governor Marcial Alvarado stated that Fortunato Alvarado was standing at the church entrance hearing mass when he was approached by Anacleto Vargas, 'an individual with an appalling record, who habitually commits bloody crimes'.[35] Vargas drew a pistol and fired five shots at the *comisario* from point-blank range. Two bullets passed through the left hand of Alvarado and a third lodged in his right leg. The assailant then ran off to join a group of his cronies who had congregated in a corner of the town square. This band used their firearms to cover Vargas's retreat. The rifle fire:

> 'sowed panic among the hundreds of faithful who were attending the mass said by Father Francisco Mori. The priest made great efforts to calm the multitude in church, who also included many visitors and merchants from neighbouring provinces as well as the departments of Lambayeque and Piura . . . Soon after the shooting, relatives and friends carried *comisario* Alvarado to his house. For over an hour sporadic gunfire could be heard around the *plaza*. Then news filtered through that Fernando Benel had been wounded. I do not know who shot him'.[36]

The governor's account amounted to a smokescreen aimed at deflecting responsibility away from his associates. Fortunato Alvarado was attacked, but this had taken place approximately two hours before the assassination of Castinaldo Benel. In late afternoon the *comisario* had beaten a son of Anacleto Vargas who was playing noisily in the *plaza* with a group of children. Enraged, Vargas went to confront the *comisario*, and after exchanging insults the boy's father drew a pistol and fired three times at his enemy. Alvarado fell to the ground, but only received superficial wounds and was carried to his house. This clash incensed the Alvarado faction, who decided

86

to even scores by shooting a member of the opposing band.[37] As luck would have it, their victim happened to be the eldest son of arch rival Eleodoro Benel.

The murder of Castinaldo Benel, who was being groomed to take over the family business, greatly bereaved his father. Requests that those implicated in the assassination be brought to justice were made to the court in Cajamarca and directly to the authorities in Lima.[38] Originating as they did from an escaped prisoner and a known opponent of the Leguía regime, these pleas fell on deaf ears. An embittered Benel thus became more amenable to the ideas of Osores and others who advocated that rebellion was the only way to topple Leguía. Consequently, by early 1924 a regular flow of letters started to pass between the landlord of El Triunfo and the plotters based in Ecuador. Most of these messages were channelled via the Pardos' Tumán sugar estate, where Alfredo Ferreyros and colonel Beingolea, the administrator and deputy administrator respectively, co-ordinated anti-government intrigues in northern Peru. Two other prominent employees in the labour contracting office at Tumán, Hermenegildo Ruiz and Pedro Coronado, were also involved in the plot. Correspondence was hidden in false bottoms built into the tins of lard Benel retailed in Tumán, or was delivered to the hacienda by trustworthy muleteers transporting *chancaca* and *aguardiente* to the coast. Loyal *peones* travelling from El Triunfo to fulfil seasonal work contracts in Tumán also carried coded messages for their *patrón*. From there, the dispatches went by ship from Pimentel, the port serving Chiclayo, to Guayaquil.[39] Alternatively, very important messages arrived in El Triunfo overland via the department of Piura. The couriers passed through the hacienda San Pablo located in Ayabaca province, a property owned by Eduardo Merino, another political opponent of Leguía.[40] From there, the carriers proceeded to the second staging post, the hacienda Sillangate in Cutervo province. This estate was administered by Arturo Osores Gálvez, the son of Arturo Osores Cabrera.

While entering into secret discussions with anti-Leguía politicians, Eleodoro Benel furthered his preparations for an eventual uprising. Strikes were launched against individuals allied to his son's assassins. On 27 November, fifteen gunmen led by Misael Vargas raided the smallholding of Juan Vargas in Mitapampa. The property was ransacked and then put to flame. Juan Vargas was forced to watch the destruction of his holding and then shot.[41] Six days later, the home belonging to the deputy lieutenant governor of Mitapampa, Nolasco Santa Cruz, received similar treatment. Having committed this crime, the *benelistas*:

'looted the house of don Fernando Mendoza and raped his daughter. Two oxen belonging to Tristán Zuloeta and a cow of Rosendo Correa were stolen. Then the bandits sacked the house of don Delfín Flores and violated his daughter. Finally, they raped the daughter of don Juan Germán, Hermelinda Germán, who is under thirteen years of age'.[42]

87

When being informed of these incidents, the prefect was told that the Vargas brothers and their fellow outlaws received protection from the authorities in Chota.[43] Shortly following these attacks, on 20 January 1924 the Vargas gang ambushed and assassinated one of the hated Díaz clan, Aniceto, in the parish of Ninabamba. After the shooting, his corpse was carried off to El Triunfo, where it was exhibited as a trophy.[44] Along with the elimination of factional opponents, the *benelistas* also adopted steps to strengthen their military position. Additional trenches and hill fortifications were constructed around Samana parish. Misael Vargas and his fellow gunmen started forcibly to extort contributions of S/.200 from those inhabitants of Samana and surrounding parishes who refused to purchase new rifles provided by the local caudillo or swear loyalty to Benel.[45] Through these measures Benel added to his fighting force and attained funds for the purchase of extra firearms. Cash and munitions were also forthcoming from Osores and his allies in Ecuador.

Aware of these machinations, the *leguiistas* tried to intercept messages between Ecuador and the plotters in northern Peru. On occasions the subversives were indiscreet enough to communicate via the postal and telegraph system. The Alvarados had naturally placed a relative in the telegraph office which enabled them to intercept some messages and relay their contents to Lima.[46] Government spies were also successfully infiltrated into the hacienda El Triunfo posing as brigands on the run, and these fed information to the authorities.

Although they knew that an uprising was being contemplated by Benel and his allies, at this stage the *leguiistas* failed to move resolutely to nip the threat in the bud. Columns of *gendarmes* were drafted into Hualgayoc during the first six months of 1924 with orders to hunt down bandits, but never in sufficient numbers to have a lasting effect. Consequently the government forces suffered some humiliating reverses, as happened on 12 April 1924 when Marcial Alvarado, accompanied by twenty-five troops, tried to capture prominent *benelista* fighters. As the *gendarmes* approached Samana, they were ambushed:

'by two hundred bandits led by Eleodoro Benel, Misael Vargas and Narciso Perales. Seeing that resistance was useless due to the large number of outlaws, I ordered the retreat. This produced the dispersion of my troops and panic when they saw some of their comrades fall. Several were killed, others wounded, as were a number of mounts. Second lieutenant Ezquivel, eight other soldiers and myself were able to save ourselves miraculously by fording a river. The remaining sixteen men tried to escape by another route, and at first I thought that they were all dead, because the rifle fire raining down on us was so intense. On the following day several of the soldiers arrived back in Santa Cruz on foot. Many were naked, others wounded, and all had been stripped of their rifles'.[47]

Three soldiers were taken prisoner by the *benelistas*. Alvarado also claimed that the government troops had been lured into a trap by their guides, who were in the pay of Benel. *Chotano* landowner Wenceslao Villacorta had also sent his men to waylay the soldiers, 'surely with the objective of forming a revolutionary force in this province'.[48] After suggesting that his enemies had attacked the troops with insurrectionary motives, Alvarado then named some of the plotters' contacts living in Santa Cruz:

> 'the bandits have their agitators and protectors in this town. They
> are Nardoqueo Calderón, Enrique Caballero, Julio Aguinaga and
> Carmen Azula. These individuals are hand in glove with the revolu-
> tionary leaders based in Lambayeque, and openly claim that a
> change in government will shortly occur. It is they who pass on all
> kinds of information to the rebels when a foray against them is
> planned, thus preventing its success. Moreover, these factionists are
> in contact with Dr Arturo Osores, for we know perfectly well that
> they constantly receive messages from that gentleman'.[49]

In order to curb subversive activities, Alvarado requested that one hundred soldiers be sent into the zone. 'Assisted by sixty private volunteers that could be easily recruited in this district', a force of such strength, the governor argued, would be able to thwart opposition plans.[50] As the Leguía regime was confronted with problems of social control in Puno and elsewhere, it was reluctant to devote such a large detachment of *gendarmes* to Hualgayoc and Chota. Consequently, the inferiority of the local *leguiístas* in terms of firepower continued.

Alvarado's ability to contain subversive activity was further weakened by the hostile attitude of the Osores faction who dominated neighbouring Chota, and gave protection to enemies of the *alvaradistas*. This was highlight-ed by the case of César Asenjo, a peasant gunman integrated into the *clientela* of Benel. Asenjo was arrested in early April 1924 and locked in the Santa Cruz jail. Shortly afterwards a raid on the prison led by Misael Vargas freed the brigand. Much to the annoyance of the Alvarado faction, Asenjo was then appointed governor of the district of Llama by the authorities in Chota. This induced Marcial Alvarado to register a complaint to the prefect:

> 'Recently César Asenjo has been named governor of Llama in the
> province of Chota. Asenjo has pursued a career as a bandit for ten
> years in the gang led by Eleodoro Benel, which has its headquarters
> in Samana. Asenjo is guilty of murdering Justo Huanca, Nazario
> and Francisco Díaz, Bartola Cabrejos and another person from the
> hacienda Chancay. He has also killed Zenón and Wenceslao Flores,
> Higinio and Nicolás Milian, Reinaldo Torres and many others from
> this district. In addition, he has committed countless robberies,
> violent assaults and rapes. He was among the group that attacked
> the government troops last 12 April.

89

This individual is assisted by his brothers Antonio and Desidero Asenjo, Antero Villalobos, the three Farro brothers and other delinquents from Samana and Ushushque. In all they total twenty-five. On 17 May this band went to take over the governorship of Llama. Then they proceeded to my hacienda Chancay, and robbed seven cows belonging to my gardener Domingo Peralta. These animals have been taken to the hacienda Huarimarca, which is owned by Matías Díaz, who protects these outlaws'.[51]

Indeed, in Chota the *leguiísta* subprefect sent by Lima to govern the province found himself almost completely isolated and politically impotent, to the extent that he rarely ventured onto the street out of fear of being murdered. Upon withdrawing their support from Leguía in 1921, Osores and his local allies organised in the Partido Constitucional moved closer to their traditional rivals in the Partido Civil. Combined, these two political forces dominated Chota. Broad opposition to Leguía consequently produced unlikely bedfellows. Merchant and *enganchador* Régulo Regulado, who had clashed with Benel during the contest to gain the lease on Llaucán, now found himself allied to his traditional rival. Another past enemy of Benel, Benjamín Hoyos, who like Regulado was a merchant and labour contractor, also became a political associate of the landlord of El Triunfo at this juncture.[52]

Preparations for an uprising took on new urgency in summer 1924. On 10 June Leguía's long expected nomination for a second term was finally approved by the House of Deputies. Then on 3 July the president publically accepted the 'request' that he should remain in office. With reelection now a reality, Osores, Benavides and their contacts inside Peru began to lay definite plans. According to the scheme devised by Osores, local caudillos in northern Peru would rise up and take part of Cajamarca in the name of restoring democracy and constitutional legality against the dictatorial usurper Leguía. This would spark off the second phase of the revolt, proclamations of support for the rebels by garrisons in the key coastal cities of Chiclayo, Trujillo, Lima and Arequipa.[53] Establishing contact with sympathetic officers and gaining pledges of adhesion to the rebellion was a task entrusted to the clandestine 'revolutionary committees' formed in Lima and elsewhere. If the combination of rebellion in Cajamarca and *pronunciamientos* from the barracks proved insufficient to unseat Leguía, then it was envisaged that the plotters would conquer large areas of northern Peru, before marching on the capital.

# II

To achieve success, it was vital that the crucial first stage of the uprising should proceed smoothly. As a local man, Osores was aware that deeply entrenched factional rivalries could jeopardise his ambitions. Therefore, he wisely sought to gain a minimum level of agreement between the various armed bands operating in Hualgayoc, Chota and Cutervo. If traditional enemies could not be brought together behind the rebellion, Osores hoped that at least they might be politically neutralised. This delicate mission was at first consigned to his son and colonel Samuel del Alcázar, a military officer who had sided with Pardo and tried to block the Leguía coup of July 1919.[54] Then Osores clandestinely entered Peru from Ecuador in October 1924 to personally supervise the delicate task of reconciling old hatreds in Hualgayoc. With Benel, most of Chota and the Terán gang in neighbouring San Pablo already committed to rebellion, their attention focused on the Alvarado faction in Santa Cruz and the bandits led by Anselmo Díaz based in the parish of Uticyacu.

Conflicts between Hualgayoc's various factional armies continued unabated over the summer of 1924. During one expedition in Ninabamba to exact money from the local peasantry for the purchase of arms, the *benelistas* shot dead Nicolás Díaz, who was unwise enough to resist their demands.[55] Indeed, at this juncture Benel's military dominance in the countryside was such that governor Marcial Alvarado and the town of Santa Cruz were placed 'under a state of siege'.[56] This environment, dominated as it was by hatred and bloodshed, made the task facing del Alcázar and Osores all but impossible. Nevertheless, feelers were put out to the Alvarados and Anselmo Díaz and despite all the odds, they appeared to achieve some progress. A tentative non-aggression pact was first negotiated with Anselmo Díaz. Then Osores attempted to arrive at some arrangement with Fortunato Alvarado, as the following letter illustrates:

'Dear Fortunato,
This letter is absolutely personal and confidential. I am here as the representative of all the parties with the special mission of saving the country from the harsh tyranny that is currently suffocating Peru. You have always offered to be at my service, and I expect your full and energetic assistance in this task of national regeneration. I am in complete agreement vis-à-vis our pact with Anselmo Díaz. If some prior compromise does not permit you to act alongside me, that is, on the side of good, then I hope that you will lend all your arms to our friend Anselmo. I await your reply. I trust that it will be clear and unfudged so that I know where I stand'.[57]

Almost immediately after this letter was sent to Alvarado, the apparent success in winning over Anselmo Díaz to the rebel cause came under stress due to an untimely armed clash between forces captained by Misael Vargas and the rival Díaz band. This caused Osores to rush off a conciliatory letter from his base in the hacienda El Triunfo to Anselmo Díaz:

'Dear Anselmo,
I was absent and therefore unable to prevent the fateful incident that started during the night and ended this morning. Fortunately, none of your friends have been killed.

91

This terrible situation has to end. I think this can be achieved via
the compromise I have offered you. According to the terms of the
pact, the Vargas clan and yourselves will sign, and then this agreement will be rigorously applied.
Please sign and return the enclosed pact.
Your dear friend and servant,
Arturo Osores'.[58]

Although Díaz put his signature to the non-aggression pact, his acquiescence
was a complete charade. Both Alvarado and the brigand were attempting to
extract information about the rebels' intentions by giving the impression that
some agreement might be reached. In fact Alvarado and Díaz were passing
copies of their correspondence with the insurgents to the authorities and
simultaneously planning to frustrate the armed rebellion. This is evident from
secret letters sent by Fortunato Alvarado to the subprefect in Hualgayoc,
who in turn forwarded them to the prefect in Cajamarca. From Santa Cruz
Alvarado informed his superiors of the latest moves in the rebel camp:

'I am writing this letter very hurriedly. Anselmo has just arrived
at 7 o'clock this evening from Utigiaco. He tells me that Dr Osores,
accompanied by a colonel, whose name he does not know, has
arrived from La Samana. They have written to me, but unfortunately the letter has not yet arrived. It is possible that Osores will
personally try and persuade me to join in his plot. The revolution is
planned for 20 November and he awaits me in Utigiaco so that we
can come to an agreement face to face. Osores says that he will make
no move until we have reached an agreement. I have ordered the
immediate arrest of the two individuals mentioned above, and it will
be prudent for you to lay similar plans forthwith. Anselmo is returning at this very moment with men who have been instructed to carry
out my order. The colonel has remained in Utigiaco, and Osores has
returned to Benel in La Samana. The forces in Chota, Cutervo and
this zone are already committed to the revolution. The colonel is
described as a tall man, with a maimed right arm and many bullet
scars over his body. You should take great care and adopt all the
necessary precautions'.[59]

Four days later, on 16 November 1924, Fortunato Alvarado dispatched
another message to the subprefect which revealed the extent of preparedness
attained by the local *leguiístas*:

'I have just received an express letter from La Samana informing
me that Benel, Osores and the colonel that I told you about in my
last dispatch, are still in La Samana. But Misael and Aurelio Vargas
have gone with seven men to Cochán. Rosario and Hermógenes
Vargas, with three others, have ridden to see the Terán brothers in
Tumbadén, who are also in the plot. These moves are to assemble

additional men. The messengers all carry arms, munition and money, and are obeying the instructions of Dr Osores. Meanwhile, Osores, colonel del Alcázar and Benel remain in La Samana constructing trenches so that they can confront the troops. At present they have 150 armed men. This information comes from trusted persons who have an intimate knowledge about what is happening in La Samana, for they are two men secreted into Benel's band and are actually among his personal bodyguard. This information can therefore be regarded as accurate.

The men I have ready number thirty-five in Ninabamba, thirty in Utigiaco, while I am here with twenty, plus four *gendarmes*. These groups have been ordered to prevent the movement of those in La Samana and are situated in the only places where the rebels can break out. In Polulo we also have approximately twenty-five men briefed, ready for action and close to the *montoneros* (rebels). I await the arrival of the troops from Lambayeque, and know from my own sources that eighty are already in Chongoyape. When they arrive I will immediately attack La Samana. I have also just received an express letter from Chongoyape which informs me that the troops have routed the Vásquez gang, causing twenty-five deaths. I enclose copies of the documents that I obtained from a courier who was carrying them from Osores to the colonel. It was impossible to capture Osores and the colonel, because when we arrived in Utigiaco they had already left for La Samana, which could not be penetrated due to their superior force'.[60]

Alvarado's assessment of the containing capabilities of his pistoleers proved optimistic. Concealed by heavy rain and mist, on the night of 19 November Benel and Osores led their *montoneros* across the Samana valley up onto the moors and struck out in the direction of Chota. The long predicted attempt to oust president Leguía was under way.

At dawn the rebel column came within sight of the town. Approaching from the south, they were met by María Bardales, a factional ally of Osores, who informed the rebel commander that the previous evening thirty government troops led by Zenón Noriega had entered Chota to reinforce the local detachment of twenty *gendarmes*. They had taken up defensive positions in key public buildings around the town square and were preparing for action.[61] Undeterred, but now aware that their circle of plotters was infiltrated, Osores and Benel decided to press ahead with the attack. Detachments of men under the command of colonel del Alcázar and another disaffected military man, lieutenant Carlos Barrera, were instructed to mount a multi-directional assault on the main concentration of troops housed in the Chota police building. Different groups were allocated the task of capturing other strategic points. Watches were synchronized for the assault to commence at six-thirty. Easy targets like the telegraph office and the subprefecture were overrun without difficulty, so that within minutes the battle came to focus on the town

93

hall and adjoining barracks opening onto the *plaza*. The government troops soon found themselves encircled and under heavy fire, as their assailants occupied sniping positions in the facing church tower and adjacent rooftops. With the soldiers offering resolute resistance, a protracted siege commenced that dragged on for several hours. Impatient, the *benelistas* resorted to military improvisation in an effort to break the stalemate. Tins of evaporated milk stuffed with dynamite were hurled at the doors and balconies of the town hall complex.[62] Finally a large opening was blown in the rear wall of the barracks and the assailants prepared to mount an offensive. Hungry, low on ammunition, suffering from falling morale and seeing that further resistance was futile, early in the afternoon the surviving defenders hoisted the white flag.[63]

After disarming the government troops, the *benelistas* called on the defeated conscripts to switch sides. Several joined the rebels, with the remainder being turned loose on the outskirts of town. Prominent *leguiístas* trapped in Chota, including wealthy *enganchador* Catalino Coronado, were forced to hand over a 'revolutionary contribution' to the rebels. Officially appointed authorities were also stripped of their positions and replaced with townsmen loyal to Arturo Osores.[64] Discrepancies then arose within the leadership over the treatment of the captured officers. Benel argued that they should be placed before a firing squad forthwith, an attitude coloured by the presence of captain Benigno Alvarez among the captives.[65] Sticking to military protocol, colonel Samuel del Alcázar opposed such behaviour and succeeded in curbing Benel's natural instincts. After being held for several hours, Noriega, Alvarez and their fellow officers were allowed to abandon the town. A week later, however, the leniency of del Alcázar was not reciprocated.

Meanwhile, the question of maintaining the uprising's political momentum loomed large. If the 'revolution' was to have any chance of success – a remote possibility given that the hoped-for army revolt failed to materialise – it was essential that the rebels move swiftly to capitalise on their initial gains. Quick raids on Bambamarca and Hualgayoc would enable them to capture neighbouring provinces and open up the way for an assault on the weakly garrisoned departmental capital. From Cajamarca a substantial anti-*leguiísta* force could then march on the important coastal city of Trujillo, a move that might initiate a political crisis in Lima and stir the barracks into action. But the constitution of 56-year-old Arturo Osores was no longer able to withstand the strenuous side of factional politics. Shortly after the fall of Chota, the caudillo fell ill with a recurrent stomach ailment.[66] Despite the forceful interventions of Benel, who urged an immediate march on Cajamarca, it was decided that the rebel force should remain in Chota until Osores was fit to ride.

Infected by the insurrectionary fervour that swept the town, many *chotanos* from all walks of life, from artisans to merchants, and labourers to lawyers, enrolled in the anti-Leguía militia. The rebels were also strengthened by the arrival of the Vásquez brothers and forty of their *clientela* from the district of Lanche in Cutervo province.[67] While recruiting was under way in Chota, fifty *montoneros* led by *benelista* gunman César Asenjo were sent to reconnoitre Bambamarca. Asenjo entered the town on 22 November and encountered no resistance, the *gendarmes* posted there having fled to Hualgayoc. After collecting arms and cash 'contributions' from a number of well-to-do citizens, including the landlord of the hacienda Chala, the rebels returned to Chota. Three hours after Asenjo rode out of Bambamarca, a column of troops directed by subprefect Angel Macciotta entered the town. A net was beginning to close around the rebels.

In addition to the force approaching Chota from the south, a second column was making its way up into the highlands from Lambayeque. Under the command of Raúl Zavala, the 1st Artillery Regiment and the 11th Infantry Regiment passed through Chongoyape in the Chancay valley and headed for Santa Cruz. They then marched on the hacienda El Triunfo, along the way reinforced by the bandit gangs led by Marcial Alvarado, Anselmo Díaz and Pedro Zuloeta. At dawn on 25 November the soldiers began their attack on the estate. Fearful that Benel might have left a strong guard in his property, the hacienda buildings were first sprayed with machine gun fire, but as the landlord had taken all his gunmen to Chota the troops met with no opposition. Several hacienda labourers and tenants who tried to flee were gunned down by the troops, who occupied the estate buildings. Alvarado and his cronies then proceeded to loot the hacienda store. Cattle in the adjacent meadows were turned loose, along with several hundred pigs. After ransacking the *casa hacienda*, Benel's house was burnt.[68] Following a night of drunkenness and indiscipline, the next day Zavala marched his men through Uticyacu in the direction of Chota. Sleeping in the hamlet of Lajas on the 26 November, at eleven o'clock the following morning the government troops occupied the hacienda Churucancha, sited four kilometres to the north-west of Chota.

Osores lay ill for six days. Although his *montonera* had grown to over four hundred men during this period, all chances of victory also evaporated. Informed about the arrival of Zavala in Churucancha, the insurrectionists marched out of Chota to confront the government troops. Twenty minutes later the hacienda came into sight. Colonel del Alcázar divided the rebels into three groups. Avelino Vásquez and his men were instructed to circle the estate, cut the coast road and attack from the north-west. Benel and his *pistoleros* skirted leftwards and stationed themselves to the south-west, thus blocking any retreat in the direction of Santa Cruz. Osores and del Alcázar led the main column, largely comprised of volunteers from Chota, and began to advance on the opposition from the south-east across the meadows facing the estate buildings. Zavala attempted to break out of the cordon by abandoning the *casa hacienda* and managed to withdraw as far as the Condorcaga escarpment, where he was hemmed in by the anti-Leguía militia.

Faced by defensive machine gun fire, the attackers dug in and engaged the government troops. Firing continued for several hours and the battle finally turned against the soldiers when *benelista* gunmen and Vásquez's *lanchinos* simultaneously began to penetrate their right and left flanks.[69] Encircled and unable to break out, the troops started to suffer casualties and were forced to retreat into an ever decreasing area. Morale slumped and as nightfall approached a meeting of officers was called to discuss the situation. A single officer disagreed with the decision to surrender, and with one soldier waving a white flag on his own initiative, the assailants held their fire. Again an argument blew up among the rebel leadership. Benel advocated a decisive attack with the objective of wiping out the troops, while del Alcázar was equally adamant that there should be no unnecessary loss of life. The rebels should keep the soldiers penned in and wait until daybreak to receive a formal surrender from Zavala. With the resolve of Osores waivering, much to Benel's disgust, the position of del Alcázar, who was formally the military commander of the 'revolution', won the day.[70]

At dawn the following morning expectations of an incident-free surrender were rudely shattered. A second column of troops had been dispatched from Lambayeque into the highlands. Commanded by major Elías Rosas, these soldiers passed through Cutervo and the district of Lanche in pursuit of the Vásquez brigands.[71] En route Rosas' force linked up with Wenceslao Villacorta and his band of armed retainers settled on the hacienda Chetilla. Together they headed for Chota. Picking up further reinforcements along the way, their numbers increased to approximately three hundred well-armed civilians and troopers.[72] Approaching Churucancha under the cover of darkness, Rosas launched a surprise dawn attack on the rebels. The group of *chotano* volunteers led by del Alcázar was caught completely unawares. Panic rapidly spread among the ranks. As they tried to flee in disarray, many were mown down; and those left lying wounded on the field of battle were later finished off.

Witnessing this unexpected turn in the battle, Osores mounted his horse and sped via Lajas in the direction of the hacienda Quilcate, where he was eventually arrested and imprisoned on the island San Lorenzo with the rest of his family.[73] Benel and his men engaged the government troops, but soon realised that all was lost and so retreated to El Triunfo. Likewise, the Vásquez bandits sustained a fierce gun battle with the soldiers before heading in the direction of Cutervo and establishing a base in the mountain retreat of Payac. Colonel Samuel del Alcázar and lieutenant Barreda were not so fortunate. While trying to retreat and link up with Benel in El Triunfo, they were detained at Montán by Anselmo Díaz and twenty of his brigands. After being relieved of their personal possessions and bound, Díaz ordered César Campos to take the two officers to Chota – because of his long-standing vendetta with Villacorta, the bandit leader was wary of entering the town due to the large number of *chetillanos* encamped there.

Raúl Zavala and Wenceslao Villacorta occupied Chota after their victory at Churucancha. Relieved by his good fortune, the commanding officer gave little thought to hunting down and eradicating those rebels who had man-

96

aged to escape. Instead he preferred to enjoy the spoils of victory and exact revenge on the townspeople. The store owned by Benel was looted, along with properties belonging to Osores and his allies. The victors also began to celebrate their success with alcohol. Thus when on 30 November 1924 del Alcázar and Barreda were dragged into the town roped behind a horse, Zavala was found drinking in the house of *leguiísta* lawyer Hermógenes Coronado with Villacorta and others. The inebriated commander ordered that the rebels be shot without a court martial, and after receiving some rough treatment the prisoners were stood against a wall.[74] Impatient to finish the business, Zavala interrupted del Alcázar's parting speech and ordered the firing squad to shoot. Barreda crumpled to the ground, lifeless; but del Alcázar, with blood seeping from his mouth and breathing heavily, needed to be finished off by a soldier who picked up a nearby stone and hit the bullet-ridden man on the back of the head.[75] Fittingly, a bungled execution brought the curtain down on what had been a quixotesque *montonera* 'revolution' in the best nineteenth century tradition.

### III

Beaten but not defeated, Eleodoro Benel resolved to continue armed opposition to the Leguía regime. Indeed, the caudillo was faced with little alternative for the government declared him *'fuera de ley'*, a wanted outlaw to be captured dead or alive. Fortunately for Benel, the fiasco at Churucancha had not decimated his clientele, and after an initial period of dispersion, his gunmen were able to regroup in Samana parish. Plans were then laid to repel government troops and seek revenge on local enemies. These developments naturally worried Fortunato Alvarado and his brothers. On 6 December the apprehensive *comisario rural* wrote a confidential letter to subprefect Macciotta urging that determined action be taken against the reforming rebel bands while they were still in a relatively disorganised state:

'the bandits who joined the rebellion have regrouped in Samana, Andabamba, Yauyucán and Ushushqui, where they are organised in groups of 60, 45, etc. They are led by Benel, his son and the Vargas brothers. The outlaws are strongly positioned in trenches and are preparing to fight the forces of law-and-order who are tracking them. Other small bands of brigands are stationed at La Lucma and Tongod. I take this opportunity to inform you that at La Lucma and Tongod I have a spy called Garino Celis. He advises me that in a house at La Lucma two extraneous men are billeted. They are well dressed and Celis does not know who they are. One of the strangers is ill. Because the column headed by captain Guerrero and my own men are not numerous enough to confront the bandits, it is vital that you intercede with the military commander so that he sends a minimum of one hundred soldiers to attack them. If this is not done,

97

with every day that passes the outlaws will increase in numbers and strength, making their persecution more difficult'.[76]

Alvarado's fears soon proved well founded. Shortly afterwards approximately a hundred troops under the command of Ezequiel Padrón marched from Chota to attack Benel in El Triunfo. Forewarned of their approach, the landlord assembled his men and rode off to intercept the soldiers, who had encamped for the night in the village of Andabamba. At nightfall the rebels surrounded the settlement and detained all those inhabitants whose loyalty was suspect. When the sun rose the *benelistas* opened fire, catching their opponents unawares. The ensuing gun battle lasted throughout the day with over twenty troops being killed.[77] Under the cover of darkness the remainder of Padrón's men slipped away, leaving behind all their mounts as well as a sizeable quantity of arms and ammunition. Two weeks later the army mounted another assault on Benel's citadel. This was led by a lieutenant Zárate, the officer commanding a cavalry unit based in the town of Santa Cruz. Again Benel was informed of their approach and organised a successful ambuscade involving approximately two hundred militiamen. On this occasion only a few minutes firing was sufficient to put the government troops to flight, with the rebels capturing additional mounts and firearms.[78]

Faced with these reversals, the government ordered another column of soldiers up into the highlands from Lambayeque. Under the command of Manuel Valdeiglesias, this contingent numbered four hundred troopers. They marched through the Chancay valley to Chongoyape, and then headed for the town of Santa Cruz. Upon arrival the soldiers were joined by *alvaradista* civilian pistoleers, and on 15 January 1925 they set out for El Triunfo. Yet again sympathisers in Santa Cruz gave fair warning to Benel concerning the movement of troops. Consequently, long before the government forces approached, the rebels were occupying a network of trenches and tunnels dug into the Changasirca hill nearby Yauyucán. The defenders held their fire until the scouting party sent by Valdeiglesias was almost upon them, and then destroyed most of the soldiers with a dense fusillade. In reply Valdeiglesias ordered an assault on the *benelista* positions. This was repulsed, and a battle commenced that lasted twenty-four hours. The outcome proved inconclusive. Suffering heavy losses, the soldiers finally managed to infiltrate the rebel fortifications and scatter the *benelistas*, most of whom managed to escape.[79]

Although undefeated, the rebels had exhausted most of their ammunition and found themselves in no position to repel a further attack. Benel therefore decided to abandon his burnt-out estate and retreat to the hacienda Silugán in Cuervo. Accompanied by his family, sixty *pistoleros* and over a hundred camp-followers, the landlord arrived in his northern properties following a strenuous four day march.[80] Meanwhile the brigands captained by Misael Vargas retreated to hide-outs on the *jalca* that ran down the centre of Hualgayoc province. Here they split up into groups between twenty to thirty strong in an effort to make their elimination more difficult. One band headed by Aurelio Vargas started to operate on the moors adjacent to Hualgayoc and Bambamarca, while Misael and Rosario Vargas captained other gangs in the zone around Llapa, San Miguel and the hacienda Quilcate.[81] Given their intimate knowledge of terrain, secure bases and an efficient network of informers, the Vargas brigands were able to frustrate all efforts to eradicate them. Nor could the military control their rustling activities. Vargas and his associates continued the business of lifting cattle in highland Hualgayoc for sale to meat traders based in San Miguel and Bambamarca. Alternatively, the fugitives took stolen livestock to haciendas in the Zaña valley, where they received backing from the administration in Cayaltí.[82]

If the hard core of Benel's gunmen dispersed and survived, many peasants on the periphery of the *clientela* established by the caudillo were less fortunate. Operating out of Santa Cruz, the army began a campaign to eliminate banditry in Hualgayoc. This resulted in numerous on the spot indiscriminate executions. The level of bloodshed increased due to the close co-operation existing between the military and private militias loyal to Marcial Alvarado and his faction. These latter groups moved swiftly to appropriate lands owned by Benel and eliminate sitting tenants. Traditional rivals were removed by denouncing enemies as 'bandits' to the army.[83]

While the *alvaradistas* and the military shed peasant blood in rural Santa Cruz and surrounding districts, Benel enjoyed two months of unaccustomed tranquillity secure in his remote estate. Holdings were allocated to those families who had migrated from El Triunfo with their patron, and his gunmen engaged in agricultural pursuits. Guards strategically posted overlooking the approaches to Silugán kept a look-out for hostile activity, but no army offensive materialised. The troops were still busy attempting to restore order in neighbouring Chota and Hualgayoc. Fresh dispatches soon started to arrive in Silugán from Oscar Benavides and other plotters in Ecuador, as did a certain amount of munition. Benavides informed Benel that three anti-Leguía army officers had slipped into Peru from Ecuador and a military uprising in the northern garrisons was immanent. Accordingly the exiled general strongly urged Benel to march on the key coastal town of Chiclayo. The occupation of Chiclayo, Benavides reasoned, would act as a catalyst sparking off army revolt.[84] Surprisingly persuaded by such facile arguments, Benel prepared for action.

Accompanied by twenty-five gunmen and the Vásquez gang from Lanche, on 11 April 1925 the caudillo left Silugán, skirted the town of Cuervo, and after a minor skirmish with some troops in Cochabamba, headed for El Triunfo. His plan was to link up with Misael Vargas and other anti-government forces before descending to the coast. Benel's sudden reappearance surprised the acolytes of Marcial and Fortunato Alvarado. Fidel Vásquez, a foreman employed by the Alvarados to oversee their interests in El Triunfo died riddled with bullets as the *benelistas* apportioned rough justice to their factional enemies.[85]

The news that Benel was back in El Triunfo and reestablishing contact with his followers caused panic among the Alvarado faction in Santa Cruz and was of grave concern to the government. Troops garrisoned in Santa Cruz were ordered to attack the rebel forces and subsequently a hundred infantrymen set out for Samana parish under the command of major Gerardo Flores. They were partnered by approximately an equal number of civilian gunmen from the band headed by Pedro Zuloeta, members of the Díaz gang, pistoleers hired by Marcial Alvarado and Noé Aguinaga, in addition to the bandit group from Polulo under the captaincy of Vidal Avellaneda and his son Moisés. *Benelistas* in Santa Cruz informed their patron of these moves and in order to avoid an inopportune conflict, the caudillo withdrew with his men to La Lucma. Anticipating such a move, major Flores ordered Vidal Avellaneda and fifty of his followers to cut off any breakout by Benel in a southerly direction. Encountering one another in the woods at La Lucma, a fierce gun battle developed between the pro-government irregulars and the *benelistas*. During the fracas Moisés Avellaneda had his leg shattered by a bullet and the rebels put their enemies to flight.[86] Major Flores and his soldiers, who had begun to follow Benel once they discovered he was no longer in Samana, were then ambushed by one of the bands organised by Misael Vargas. After suffering several losses, the troops gave up their pursuit and camped in the hacienda Quilcate. Now the road to the coast lay open.

Three days later, on 24 April 1925, Benel arrived in Niepos, well within striking distance of the town of Zaña and only two days march from Chiclayo. Quartered in the house of Father Portal, the local priest who supported the Aspíllaga faction within the Partido Civil, the caudillo made contact with clandestine anti-Leguía circles in Chiclayo and the hacienda Tumán. Their reports proved devastating. One of the three officers who entered Peru from Ecuador fell ill and they had all returned across the border. Consequently agitational activity in the barracks had not advanced and there would be no military *pronunciamiento*.[87] Feeling betrayed and disillusioned with the Lima politicians who had misled him, after four frustrating days in Niepos Benel commenced the long trek back up into the highlands.

The downcast rebel band journeyed to Silugán via Samana, Chota and Cutervo. They skirted the latter two towns judiciously avoiding military engagements with government troops and the groups of civilian gunmen organised by factional adversaries.[88] Rumours abounded that Benel was poised to overrun Chota and Santa Cruz, but the rebel caudillo rarely ventured outside the safety of his estate and its environs.[89] Instead his defensive frame of mind at this juncture was indicated by the adoption of certain precautionary measures. Dynamite induced landslides blocked the paths leading to Silugán. Bridges over rivers and streams were destroyed. Sentinels were posted on all approach roads to ensure against a surprise attack.

While Benel strengthened his defences, in June 1925 two new army units, one infantry and one cavalry, arrived in Cutervo. Commanded by major

Mauricio Cervantes, these soldiers had orders to eliminate the *benelistas*, the Vásquez gang and pacify the zone. To facilitate this objective the military pressed a prisoner in the Cutervo jail, Mercedes Salazar, to act as their guide. Salazar knew the countryside around Silugán and Cervantes hoped that he would lead the soldiers to Benel. However, the reluctant guide sympathised with the rebels and during a prison visit from his daughter instructed her to notify Benel about the impending attack and the route along which he would lead the army.[90] For two days the troops struggled in the direction of Silugán along narrow winding tracks through the forested mountains. On the third day, 6 July 1925, when they reached the mountain pass called Portachuelo del Cumbe, the column was ambushed by approximately two hundred *benelistas*. Hidden in trees and from vantage points overlooking the path, the rebels hurled sticks of dynamite and fired their rifles at the troops. Finding themselves attacked from all directions, panic spread through the ranks and the officers only succeeded in restoring discipline with the greatest difficulty. Once the soldiers reformed a battle commenced that raged all afternoon. Following an incident free night, at dawn the conflict erupted again. Pinned down on all sides, the troops efforts to scatter their attackers failed, and the tide finally turned against them with the arrival of civilian reinforcements organised by anti-Leguía partisans based in Cutervo.[91] At three o'clock in the afternoon one group of soldiers managed to break out of the rebel ring and retreat to Cutervo. The rest surrendered. Over a hundred troops lay dead, while their opponents suffered sixteen fatalities. Many wounded soldiers strewn over the battlefield were killed with machetes and knives. Those taken prisoner were marched to Silugán, where for a short period they endured forced agricultural labour before being turned loose. Due to this successful action, the insurgents acquired much needed ammunition, including machine guns, and during their sojourn in Silugán the captured soldiers taught the rebel militiamen how to operate these modern weapons.[92]

Now that the main army contingent in Cutervo was vanquished, the *benelistas* controlled a large portion of the province. Opportunity also arose to occupy the lightly garrisoned provincial capital, swell the rebel militia and threaten Chiclayo. But with the ill-fated Chota insurrection and the futile march to Niepos still fresh in his memory, Benel decided not to abandon the security of his mountain stronghold. Instead raids against local *leguiístas* were undertaken. Thus at six o'clock in the afternoon on 7 July when the mayor, governor and other minor officials of Callayuc awaited major Cervantes and his troops with food, they were surprised to see a column of thirty *montoneros* ride into the town. The rebels, who that afternoon had helped defeat the military, took the authorities prisoner. Ransoms of between twenty-five to fifty *libras peruanas* (Peruvian pounds) or two rifles per household head were levied on the populace. Alternatively they could join the rebel militia. Shortly afterwards the hacienda Caputango, which was owned by a *leguiísta*, was invaded by thirty-six *benelistas*, who robbed cattle and looted the property.[93]

Aware of the potential threat posed by anti-government rebels in northern Cajamarca, the Leguía regime adopted military and political measures to stabilise the situation. A new contingent of troops marched through Hualgayoc. Commanded by major Genaro Matos, this battalion numbered approximately six hundred. It arrived in Cutervo on 22 July 1925. Then peace feelers were extended to Benel. The government intimated to the caudillo that substantial concessions might be offered in return for an abandonment of his anti-Leguía activities and assistance in the extirpation of banditry. At the local level these negotiations were coordinated by the *leguiísta* deputy for Cutervo, Leoncio Villacorta, and field commander Genaro Matos.[94] Villacorta conceded that the Chota 'revolution' had political roots and that Benel could not be classified as a common outlaw. On the other hand, Benel's present resistance to the military was, somewhat illogically, regarded as non-political. Nevertheless, Villacorta suggested that the authorities would overlook this if Benel collaborated in pacifying the provinces of Hualgayoc, Chota and Cutervo. To facilitate disarmament and demonstrate good faith, all mounts and firearms captured from the army should be handed back. In return the government would guarantee the security of Benel and his family. They would be issued with safe-conduct passes allowing unrestricted travel throughout the republic.[95] Tentative agreement on these general principles was quickly reached, but Benel then sought to wring further concessions from the authorities. He demanded that the government investigate the assassination of Castinaldo Benel and punish those responsible. In addition the store in Chota should be returned, with compensation paid for goods looted. Likewise, the hacienda El Triunfo should be given back to its rightful owner. Finally, the government should agree to liquidate all opposing armed bands.[96] These extra requests were supported by Genaro Matos, who regarded the usurpation of Benel's property by the Alvarados and their allies as unjust.[97] Backing also came from the Villacorta clan, who supported their former ally out of sentiments of class sympathy. Villacorta offered to help implement the truce by acting as a guarantor of Benel's physical safety and overseeing the disarming of his enemies.[98]

The additional conditions presented by Benel were wired to Lima. On 26 July the government reply indicated acceptance in principle of the general terms agreed in Cutervo.[99] Negotiations to determine the detail of a pact then commenced in Chiclayo in early August. Through an intermediary, lawyer Miguel Puga, the rebel caudillo again hardened his terms. A pardon and safe-conduct guarantees, Benel argued, should be extended to the Vargas and Vásquez brothers. Although major Matos opposed any concession on this issue, it was acceded by the authorities.[100] Difficulties then arose over the level of compensation due to Benel for the ransacking of his properties by factional enemies in Santa Cruz and government troops. A total of S/.501,000 was requested, a sum regarded as exorbitant by the regime.[101] No mutually acceptable figure could be arrived at and the talks broke down.

Leguía then played the military card. Major Matos marched out of Cuervo in the direction of the Vásquez stronghold at Payac. His plan was to first destroy the Vásquez gang, and then attack Benel in Silugán. On 15 August the combined militias of Benel and Avelino Vásquez, who had concluded a mutual defence pact, sprang an ambush. In the ensuing confusion twenty-five infantrymen found themselves surrounded by the Vásquez gang. They surrendered, but with memories of the November 1924 Lanche massacre still fresh in their minds, the Vásquez showed no clemency. Despite kneeling and pleading for their lives, the conscripts were placed before a firing squad in groups of five.[102] With the *benelistas* assaulting the main column from well-selected positions, the government troops suffered numerous casualties. Even so, Matos was an experienced and determined officer. He rallied his men and after four hours of fierce combat managed to beat off the attack. The following morning Matos led his soldiers towards Callacate, a small town that lay on the route to Silugán. At Chilcacerca, where the mountain pass narrowed, the rebels launched a second ambuscade. Further losses were inflicted on the troops and Matos retreated to Cuervo with a much depleted force.[103] Over the ensuing days several minor engagements occurred, with the military coming off second best in each encounter.

Such reverses prompted Leguía to authorise a new round of negotiations in September 1925. Again Benel was represented by Miguel Puga, and progress took place at preliminary talks in Cuervo. Although no precise figure of indemnification was fixed, in early October major Mauricio Cervantes and the priest of Chongoyape, Britaldo Orrego, rode to Silugán to parley with Benel and finalise a pact. After some discussion a concord covering the principal points agreed upon the previous August was signed on 12 October.[104] Marcial Alvarado and his *clientela* vehemently opposed the concessions ceded to Benel. They feared that the return of their enemy would erase the economic advantages recently acquired and threaten their physical safety. Alvarado also argued that a pardon should not be offered to an individual responsible for the death of several hundred soldiers. Moreover, Benel intended to spark off another 'campaign of terror on behalf of the Partido Civil'.[105] For his part, Benel was sceptical of the government's motives and extremely wary of *alvaradista* jesuitry. During discussions with Cervantes and Orrego he took the precaution of reinforcing the sentinels scanning the approaches to Silugán. Benel also regarded the government promise to personally hand back the hacienda El Triunfo with suspicion. The rebel caudillo viewed this as a ploy aimed at enticing him out of Silugán in order to facilitate his arrest.[106] Even the withdrawal of a civilian militia strategically placed by Matos at the town of Pimpincos for deployment in a possible assault on Silugán failed to allay Benel's doubts.[107]

To help surmount understandable reticence and implement the terms of the peace agreement, on 25 October major Genaro Matos issued a decree ordering the disarmament of Cuervo, Chota and Hualgayoc provinces. A time limit of one month was fixed for this to be implemented. That same day

103

a force led by major Luis Brambilla unexpectedly occupied Samana and adjoining parishes. The soldiers first clashed with the brigands led by Gonzalo García, a gang twelve to fourteen strong and one of the several *benelista* splinter groups that appeared after their *patrón* left for Cutervo.[108] Brambilla's chief task, however, was to dissolve those armed bands hostile to Benel; unless this could be achieved the rebel caudillo would not lay down his arms. Those *alvaradistas* who had usurped Benel's property were driven from the hacienda El Triunfo, and over the following weeks the military successfully hunted down the gangs captained by Anselmo Díaz and Vidal Avellaneda. During November 1925 renowned outlaws such as Rosendo Mondragón, Vidal Avellaneda and Tarcilo Cabrejo were summarily executed by army firing squads, along with many of their accomplices. Hounded by the troops, many brigands attempted to survive by splitting up and fleeing Hualgayoc. Several sought refuge as labourers on the coastal sugar estates. Others retreated northwards to secluded zones in Jaén province. A number also hid on the moors and in the forests of Hualgayoc.[109]

Swimming with the tide in an effort to protect their interests and influence, the Alvarados reacted to this unexpected turn in events by denouncing to major Brambilla gunmen once in their employ.[110] Such tactics did nothing to ingratiate mayor Alvarado or his kin to Brambilla and Matos, with the result that local *leguiísta* faction leaders also began to suffer at the hands of the army. This prompted the governor of Santa Cruz, Arturo Orrego, to address a letter of complaint to subprefect Macciotta:

'I am informed that in mid-October major Mauricio Cervantes and don Britaldo Orrego, the priest of Chongoyape, journeyed to Silugán for discussions with don Eleodoro Benel. They tried to persuade him to hand over his arms as ordered by the government. We have knowledge that the aforementioned Benel has not turned over any weapons. He has only returned those horses captured from the column of troops, led by major Cervantes, attacked at Callayuc in early July. On 24 October major Luis Brambilla arrived in this district, accompanied by three officers and sixty troopers. His goal has been to collect arms from all those individuals reported to regional military commander major Genaro Matos. This was achieved without resistance on the part of those involved. However, this was not the case with respect to the followers of Benel, even though they are enemies of the government and have been denounced to major Brambilla by officials from Santa Cruz. On the contrary, the *benelistas* have been given all kinds of concessions. Moreover, they have fed false information regarding the authorities of this district to the military. The officers have listened to these lies and acted upon them. Such irregularities have resulted in a tenacious persecution by major Brambilla against mayor Marcial Alvarado. In order to avoid taunts and public humiliation, mayor Alvarado has chosen to leave town, thus abandoning his civic functions . . . .

104

Major Brambilla has launched a similar witch-hunt against citizens Noé and Juan Aguinaga, kicking the latter's mother, demanding the key to her shop and taking goods. On 9 November major Brambilla arrested the honest farmer señor Conrad Aguinaga in the hacienda Munana and brought him prisoner to Santa Cruz. The reason given was that he had provided hospitality in his house to Marcial Alvarado. On 31 October major Brambilla ordered *comisario rural* don Fortunato Alvarado to ride to Cutervo with lieutenant Arturo Ortega and six soldiers. They were delivering part of the arms collected in this district. According to *comisario* Alvarado, upon his arrival in Cutervo he was thrown in prison by major Matos. The *comisario* was released the following day, 1 November, and commanded by Matos to return to Santa Cruz. At 11 a.m. that very day the *comisario* was detained in the hacienda Llanduma and marched to Cochabamba to face commander don Raúl Zavala. Zavala had been informed about the law man's movements and instructed his soldiers to watch all the highways. Orders were issued to kill Alvarado if they came across him. The *comisario* was taken to Cutervo by commander Zavala and his men, thrown in the public jail and kept incommunicado with a sentry constantly watching over him. *Comisario* Alvarado was refused food or a bed for twenty-four hours. He suffered beatings and was repeatedly threatened. After six days in jail, and ignoring an order for his release that the commander had received, *comisario* Alvarado was transferred to Lambayeque. On the day of his arrival, the colonel in charge of the Military Region released the *comisario* Major Matos arrived in this town on 8 November with eight officers and 150 soldiers. He had orders from commander Zavala to apprehend mayor Marcial Alvarado and transfer him to Cutervo. This command also extends to eighty other individuals who attended a banquet offered in honour of commander Valdeiglesias and his officers to celebrate the victory obtained last January over the bandits captained by Eleodoro Benel Zuloeta. I should also inform you that commander Zavala has forbidden any telegrams to be sent from the provinces of Cutervo, Chota and Hualgayoc. In conclusion, the behaviour of the troops commanded by major Brambilla has been improper because of their partiality. Moreover, Brambilla has not paid for the rations consumed by the soldiers, such as meat and other commodities. Neither has the officer paid for the fodder eaten by their horses. I attach a separate sheet detailing these accounts. I should also mention the abuses, robberies and beatings given to peasants in the surrounding valleys by the soldiers, who due to a lack of morality and discipline, are violating the citizens' rights'.[111]

Anti-*alvaradista* activities by Brambilla and Matos created grave problems for the mayor and his allies, effectively undermining a consolidation of the faction's political and economic hegemony.

While his enemies were paradoxically under attack from government-backed troops, Eleodoro Benel remained unmolested in Silugán. Although captured army mounts were handed back, Benel's circumspect attitude vis-à-vis the regime's true intentions was evinced by his failure to return those firearms taken in battle. Only a relatively small number of well-worn rifles were given up. Ever distrustful, the caudillo declined to be drawn out of Silugán for any length of time, and sent a member of his *clientela*, Narciso Perales, to receive the hacienda El Triunfo from the military. This passed off smoothly. Unimpressed, Benel still refused to budge from Silugán.

Meanwhile, the military position of the rebels eased with the withdrawal of Genaro Matos and his troops to Santa Cruz in November 1925.[112] Cutervo was now policed by a much smaller garrison under the command of lieutenant-colonel Silva Santisteban. In September Matos had established the *Junta de Defensa Social*, a committee of prominent *leguiístas* who r ·ganised a *guardia urbana*. During his stay in Cutervo the major also formed three civilian militias, whose task was to assist the army in its campaign to 'extirpate banditry'.[113] However, the combined strength of these forces remained inferior to those led by Benel and Avelino Vásquez. This situation provoked one notable of Cutervo to address a delatory letter to major Matos:

'. . . because of you we find ourselves gravely menaced by brigands based in the parish of Lanche. They are threatening to invade this town. The outlaws are biding their time, waiting for the small detachment of troops to leave, so that they will be free to commit crimes and satiate their baser instincts. For the present, the bandits continue to rob livestock, expropriate land and take over all official positions. All this the outlaws have attained via the force of arms, in violation of the pact recently conceded to them'.[114]

The fears expressed in this letter materialised on 31 December 1925, when a column of *benelistas* attacked and overran the provincial capital, assassinating several pro-government partisans.[115] Despite such acts, rebel military superiority remained unchallenged throughout 1926. Undisturbed by the army, Avelino Vásquez and Benel continued to control a large portion of Cutervo province, filling the political vacuum left by the government and imposing their own style of gun-law on the populace. Further south the *benelistas* had also managed to survive. While those armed gangs linked to the Alvarado faction had suffered serious dislocation due to the efforts of the military, the bands led by Misael Vargas continued to function. Vargas personally captained a thirty-five strong gang that robbed in Hualgayoc and sold the proceeds in the coast. Although slightly reduced in numbers and constantly harassed by detachments of troops, the two groups headed by the other Vargas brothers also continued to operate in 1926.[116] Nevertheless, the political opponents of Leguía were in such a divided and disorganised state that they proved unable to exploit the situation.

# IV

Eventually, the Leguía regime tired of Benel's unwillingness to lay down his arms, take advantage of concessions already granted and make peace with the government. In late 1926 the military were instructed to prepare a new offensive whose goal was the elimination of Benel, Vásquez, and their *pistoleros*, and the complete pacification of northern Cajamarca. In January 1927 major Julián Gensollén and over two hundred troops marched from Lambayeque to the village of Querocotillo. From this base, a column of troops occupied and looted the hacienda Sillangate. The estate buildings and *trapiches*, or oxen-driven sugar-mills, were burnt, the tenants beaten and women violated.[117] An assault on the hacienda Minas, which was also owned by an anti-*leguiísta* landlord, immediately followed. The troops happened to arrive on the wedding day of *benelista* gunman Antonio Asenjo to one of the landowner's daughters. Several rebel pistoleers, including the bridegroom's brother César Asenjo, were attending the matrimony. When the army attacked the bandits were already merry on *cañazo*, or sugar cane alcohol, and taken by surprise. After a short gun-fight the Asenjo brothers and their fellow brigands perished.[118] Gensollén then attempted to march on the hacienda Silugán, but, shadowed by the *benelistas*, was unable to penetrate the high mountain passes leading to the estate. Afraid of suffering heavy losses, the battalion commander ordered his men back to the barracks at Lambayeque.

Shortly after these events, a detachment of the recently formed *guardia civil* made its way from the coast to Chota and on to Cutervo. Commanded by colonel Antenor Herrera, the column comprised eleven officers and 215 privates. Instructed by officers from the Spanish civil guard, this force was better trained and paid than the *gendarmes* they replaced.[119] Once installed in Cutervo, Herrera called up reinforcements and an infantry regiment commanded by Manuel Valdeiglesias was drafted into the province from Lambayeque. Confrontations between government troops and rebels consequently intensified after January 1927. The military had instructions to capture bandits dead or alive, with the result that anyone suspected of *benelista* sympathies ran the risk of on the spot execution. Many peasants died in their own fields. Other measures were also employed to terrorise the population. A number of detained outlaws were publically executed in the main square of Cutervo on successive Sundays when the local peasants came into town to shop.[120]

For three months no side gained military superiority. Lightning raids and ambushes by the rebels created difficulties for the army. Numerous losses were inflicted on the troops, while the pistoleers led by Benel and Vásquez proved hard to track down given their superior knowledge of the terrain. As the guerrilla war progressed, however, the government gradually attained the upper hand. The rebels lacked firearms and ammunition. Weapons and bullets captured from their opponents inadequately compensated for losses incurred in combat. Likewise, the execution of detained gunmen was not

107

offset by a flow of new recruits. The bulk of the *campesino* population, severely intimidated by military repression, failed to actively back the *benelistas*. With additional soldiers being sent into the battle zone, government troops heavily outnumbered their opponents.

In July 1927 colonel Herrera felt confident enough to launch a major assault on the hacienda Silugán. This was planned as a two-pronged attack, to be succeeded by a tri-directional assault on the Vásquez stronghold of Payac.[121] On 28 July the civil guard marched towards the hacienda Sedamayo. A series of ambuscades momentarily halted their approach, but the *benelistas* proved unable to wipe out the attackers. Then columns of soldiers advanced from the south. More of Benel's gunmen were killed or forced to flee further inland in order to escape assassination. Consequently, three days later when Herrera mounted his final assault on Silugán, the landlord could only count on the services of his family and fewer than thirty pistoleers. Although the rebels offered resolute resistance, they were overwhelmed numerically and compelled to abandon the estate. Most managed to escape the pursuing troops and hide in the surrounding forests.[122]

Herrera and Valdeiglesias then returned to Cutervo. After resting and rearming their troops, the officers set out for Payac. On 8 August the rump of the Vásquez and Benel gangs sprung an ambush nearby Callacate. The battle lasted from mid-morning until nightfall, and ended with the rebels slipping away under the cover of darkness. After burning the haciendas Payac and Mamabamba, the soldiers retraced their steps to Cutervo.

Thwarted in their efforts to eliminate Vásquez through military force, the authorities resorted to Machiavellian tactics. As Vásquez and his band had taken refuge in the mountains of Lalín, their capture would be difficult. Colonel Herrera thus suggested to subprefect Francisco Moreno that the bandits be lured into a trap by offering them an armistice. Two paid envoys, Vicente Muñoz and Rudorico Llatas were sent to Lalín to parley with Vásquez. A series of meetings were subsequently arranged between the bandit leader and Moreno.[123] The subprefect pointed out to Vásquez that a new army battalion and another unit of the civil guard had recently arrived in Cutervo. Inside a month all anti-government resistance would be crushed. Why continue with a futile struggle? In any case, the regime's main concern was to finish off Eleodoro Benel. Co-operation in eliminating Benel would be rewarded by giving the Vásquez clan political domination in Cutervo.[124] Eventually Avelino Vásquez and his brothers were persuaded by these arguments. They made a verbal pact with the subprefect and entered the town of Cutervo. To seal their arrangement with the authorities and demonstrate goodwill, Moreno suggested that a reception might be arranged by Vásquez. This took place in the house of Lorenzo Quispe sited on the outskirts of Cutervo. On 4 November 1927 Avelino Vásquez, his son Mercedes, pistoleer Manuel Maluquish, two cousins of Avelino and five other members of the gang, played host to subprefect Moreno, Antenor Herrera and twenty officers from the local garrison. The remainder of the Vásquez band feared a trap and refused to attend. Immediately after the start of the meeting the renowned brigand Pedro Flores smelt a rat and slipped away. His instincts proved sound. The first toast offered to the Vásquez by subprefect Moreno was the signal for the assembled officers to draw pistols concealed beneath capes and arrest their hosts.[125] Vásquez and his cronies had been foolish enough to attend unarmed as arranged.

Bound, the brigands were dragged to the *plaza* and stood on the steps leading into the church. A multitude of citizens quickly assembled, for news of the arrest swept through the town. Subprefect Moreno then asked the townspeople to decide the fate of the outlaws. Demands were made that they be shot. Tied together, the prisoners were then paraded in the streets and taken to the cemetery.[126] Without ceremony or the attention of a priest, Avelino Vásquez was placed against the rear wall. His ultimate wish was that the life of his young son be spared. Subprefect Moreno appeared to concede this request. One by one the brigands faced the firing squad. Terrified by the gruesome spectacle, Mercedes Vásquez attempted to flee, was recaptured, broke down and begged for mercy. Unmoved, the subprefect ordered the execution to proceed. The hysterical youth was then held with arms outstretched by two soldiers and shot in the head. Pistol in hand, subprefect Moreno then moved among the bodies delivering the *coup de grâce*.[127]

Since the army occupation of Silugán, Eleodoro Benel had been on the move. 20 August 1927 saw the caudillo and the remnants of his militia occupy the small town of Callayuc, which was burnt in reprisal for support given by the populace to the civil guard. After committing this act, Benel attempted to march eastwards and seek refuge in the jungle on the other side of the Marañón river. This manoeuvre was thwarted by a detachment of 120 soldiers armed with machine guns, who blocked the eastern passes.[128] Now without purpose or plan, the hapless band of dirty and hungry fugitives roamed the mountain forests between Payac and Silugán. Keeping clear of the roads and the civil guard by day, at night the rebels ventured down into valley fields to steal food. Demoralised gunmen started to leave their *patrón* and tried to flee to safe zones, so that by late September Benel's entourage was reduced to his family and seven pistoleers, five of whom were loyal peasants from the hacienda El Triunfo.[129] Trapped in a hopeless situation, partly of his own making, and realising that there was little chance of improvement, Benel then released five more of his retainers, giving them permission to make their own way back to Samana parish. After spending the night in the ruins of Mamabamba hacienda, in early November Benel also bade farewell to his wife and three daughters. The rains had recently commenced, the forced marches would become more arduous and uncomfortable, so the caudillo ordered them to seek refuge in Chiclayo. Thus the dejected band was finally reduced to Benel, his three sons, two pistoleers and the family hound. A few days later Antonio Estela and Arturo Coronel, the two remaining gunmen, were in turn told to make their own way to safety.[130]

Like some latter-day Aguirre, Benel continued to lead his sons aimlessly in circles around the mountains of Cutervo. One day they happened upon Antonio Cotrina. Cotrina was a former sympathizer of Benel and was asked by the landlord to buy clothes, food and ammunition in Cutervo town. The peasant was given S/.600 and told to rendezvous the following day at a place called Arenal de la Merendana, situated between Callayuc and Cutervo. The fugitives rested that night in the cottage of Jesús Cotrina, a *benelista* and brother of Antonio. Since the defeat of the rebels, Cotrina's loyalty had waned. He pocketed the S/.600 and informed the authorities of Benel's whereabouts. A column of troops rode out of Cutervo, along with an armed band of *leguiísta* hired gunmen headed by Alejandro Fonseca, Grimanez Berríos and Santiago Altamirano. The fifty-strong posse intercepted their quarry on 27 November 1927 at Arenal de la Merendana. A shoot-out developed and Benel received a flesh wound in the leg. Unable to escape, the rebel chief engaged the attackers, enabling his sons to make their getaway.[131] Rather than be taken alive, Benel blew his brains out with his last bullet. The cadaver was loaded onto a hastily constructed wooden cradle, tied behind a horse and dragged to Cutervo, where it was purposely paraded before the townsfolk. After a short wake in church, Benel's coffin was carried to the cemetery and interned with full military honours.[132]

Applauding the deaths of Vásquez and Benel, *leguiísta* newspapers loudly proclaimed the 'extirpation of banditry' in the department of Cajamarca.[133] Such affirmations proved premature. Although the killing of outlaw chiefs, successive military sweeps and widespread state repression, dealt a severe blow to brigand activity in Hualgayoc and neighbouring provinces, small groups of outlaws managed to survive. State power increased during Leguía's *oncenio*, but still exhibited important limitations. Opportunity for bandit pursuits grew after December 1927 upon the withdrawal of the army to the coast. Importantly, social relations and conditions underpinning brigandage remained unaltered. Numerous peasants and labourers probably saw their living standards decline even further with the onset of the world recession. Under these circumstances it is hardly surprising that banditry continued, albeit on a much reduced scale. Indicative of this situation is the subprefect's request in March 1930 for a greater and better equipped police presence in Hualgayoc. This was deemed necessary to contain growing brigand activity in the mountains linking Niepos, San Miguel and Hualgayoc.[134] Large bands of thirty or more outlaws were now a thing of the past, but livestock rustling and highway robbery still provided smaller gangs with a livelihood.[135] Vendetta feuds and violence also continued, even in zones where military repression had been greatest and a regular police presence was maintained. In Samana and surrounding parishes, for example, serious clashes occurred between gunmen loyal to the widow of Eleodoro Benel and factional enemies.[136] Traditional rivalries spilled over into armed conflicts in all districts of Hualgayoc. At first sight, the military campaigns waged between 1925 and 1927 appeared to have achieved nothing fundamental.

# CHAPTER 7

# Conclusion

Although patterns of continuity appeared dominant, significant changes were unfolding in Hualgayoc's politics by 1930. Leguía's *oncenio* witnessed a marked expansion in state power, even though the Peruvian state remained relatively weak compared to its Chilean neighbour. This development of the state was not confined to its repressive capabilities, although these undoubtedly increased with the founding of the *guardia civil* and the professionalisation of the armed forces. It was also demonstrated by a notable change in the balance of power from local to national, and from personal to institutional, political forces. According to Wolf and Hansen, *caudillismo* was rooted in the high degree of landlord autonomy within estate boundaries, which gave rise to a proliferation of political power centres.[1] In the department of Cajamarca these gradually became subordinate to the dictates of Lima after 1919 owing to the appearance of a larger and more assertive state machine, so that by 1930 the level of landlord autarchy at the political level had already entered into a slow process of decline. Prior to the 1920s many boundary disputes and factional rivalries in highland Cajamarca were effectively settled through armed confrontation. As a result of state development during the *oncenio*, these conflicts were increasingly resolved through the courts and intervention by the civil guard. Another hallmark of caudillo politics is the primacy of violence and assassination, to an extent that 'leadership can be achieved only through violence'.[2] Following Leguía's presidency this form of authority, which was based on bands of armed retainers, diminished in highland Cajamarca, while connections with more powerful government institutions and the judiciary grew in importance as a source of political muscle.[3] Leguía's *oncenio* proved a watershed in another crucial respect. From Independence through to the end of the *república aristocrática* in 1919, weak central government meant that local influence was all-important, to an extent that the executive in Lima depended on support from provincial *gamonales*, who in turn enjoyed a wide measure of autonomy in managing local affairs. After 1919 this balance altered, and although provincial power brokers retained leverage, now *gamonal* control was derived from more effective state backing, rather than the existence of a political vacuum as in the past. Hand in hand with added constraints on the activities of highland *gamonales* went a greater ability of the state to act independently of local political bosses. Thus, during and after Leguía's presidency the functions of social control formerly exercised by caudillos were gradually assumed by the state via the judiciary, the army and the civil guard. Simultaneously, state regularisation of political violence increased, as did the institutionalisation of political competition.

One other significant development in the 1920s was the growth of ideological politics in highland Cajamarca, a change that came into the open after August 1930, when Augusto Leguía was ousted as a result of a successful military revolt. Led by colonel Luis Sánchez Cerro, this coup was backed by leading figures among the traditional élite who had been excluded from power during the *oncenio*. Support for the dictator's overthrow was also forthcoming from the left. Prominent among the latter was APRA (Alianza Popular Revolucionaria Americana). Founded in Mexico in 1924, APRA espoused a populist-nationalist rhetoric that called for social and political reform.[4] This position was in marked contrast to that held by representatives of the oligarchy, who desired a return to the *república aristocrática*. To further complicate matters, Sánchez Cerro and the military officers around him encouraged popular mobilisation aimed at consolidating their popularity in southern Peru and Lima. With the idea of winning a future election in mind, they formed a political party called the Unión Revolucionaria. Such a disparate coalition could only fracture upon Leguía's downfall, and after a short period of uncertainty the traditional élite gained increasing influence within the Sánchez Cerro regime.[5] By November 1930 the *aprista* and communist left found themselves subject to state repression.

In Hualgayoc these shifts propelled the *leguiístas* out of office and brought a restoration of *civilista* influence in local politics. This transition was to be expected. Unforseen, however, was the rapid adoption of *aprismo* by prominent pro-Leguía partisans in the province.[6] After experiencing harassment at the hands of government troops in 1925 and 1926, during the military's attempt to implement the pact with Benel, a number of Hualgayoc's *leguiístas* became increasingly disillusioned with Leguía's administration. Another possible factor encouraging the Leguía faction to consider their political options, was a realisation that the government could not last for ever and was becoming increasingly unpopular. Into this situation of flux appeared *aprismo*. APRA's nationalist ideology and anti-oligarchic brand of populism appealed to important figures among the provincial petty bourgeoisie who had hitherto backed Leguía. They were also drawn by APRA's stress on organisation, hierarchy and discipline. Furthermore, the party's emphasis on political ideology, even though it was eclectic and not well understood, seemed to present an attractive alternative to the prevailing vacuous mode of personalist politics that eschewed doctrinal or programmatical issues. An environment conducive to the spread of APRA support was also being created in the 1920s by the influence of *indigenista* intellectual currents and the presence in Hualgayoc of a small number of political agitators of an *indigenista* persuasion.[7]

Influenced by these developments, the *leguiísta* subprefect of Hualgayoc, Angel Macciotta Rivasplata was clandestinely recruited by APRA some time in 1929, even though he continued in his official post.[8] Macciotta was later joined by long-standing opponents of the Partido Civil throughout the province. Among these figured Marcial Alvarado, Adolfo Ugaz, Leonardo

112

Orrego and Juan Aguinaga in Santa Cruz. Now calling themselves *apristas* the local Alvarado faction continued to harass traditional rivals and disturb the political peace. This led to complaints about their behaviour:

'During the Leguía administration the Alvarados and Aguinagas were the authorities in this district. Due to its criminal history, they are famous throughout the country, along with the equally notorious Benel. Today, under the banner of *aprismo*, they are trying to relive that epoch when the law of the assassin ruled and the principle of respect for authority was a myth'.[9]

Despite state repression, first by Sánchez Cerro, then, after his assassination on 30 April 1933, by incumbent president general Oscar Benavides, APRA continued to grow in Hualgayoc. By 1940 it was the dominant political force in the province. One of the factors assisting this expansion was APRA's ability to utilise established factional structures. The party gained vital support from local political power brokers like the Alvarados in Santa Cruz.[10] Thus, traditional forms of political organisation and behaviour helped give birth to new, more 'modern' ideological politics. To a certain extent, therefore, developments in Hualgayoc between 1925 and 1935 give credence to Hobsbawm's suggestion that endemic banditry and violence can lead to a questioning of the social order and serve as a precursor to political change.[11]

Less sustainable is Kapsoli's assertion that Eleodoro Benel and other participants in the events described in this book acquired the mantle of 'social bandits'.[12] According to Hobsbawm social bandits are:

'peasant outlaws whom the lord and the state regard as criminals, but who remain within peasant society, and are considered by their people as heroes, as champions, avengers, fighters for justice, perhaps even leaders of liberation, and in any case as men to be admired, helped and supported'.[13]

Moreover, it would 'be unthinkable for a social bandit to snatch the peasants' (though not the lord's) harvest in his own territory, or perhaps even elsewhere'.[14] Brigands in Hualgayoc inevitably became political, because their survival depended on the establishment of links with local patronage structures organised in factions. This connection meant that they regularly robbed and murdered fellow peasants if they happened to support a rival band. Bandits in Hualgayoc enjoyed little class independence. Rather they became tools of landlords and merchants, and were vulnerable once they became expendable, as the career of Raimundo Ramos demonstrates. Instead of being 'admired, helped and supported', Hualgayoc's outlaws were feared and tolerated, notwithstanding the later development of folk-hero mythology. Kapsoli's idea of Eleodoro Benel as some kind of Andean Robin Hood clearly does not fit the facts. Of all the bandits to emerge in northern Cajamarca over these decades, perhaps Avelino Vásquez best fits the image

113

of a social bandit. But from an early stage in his career Vásquez was linked to landlords supporting the most reactionary wing of the Peruvian élite. Coming from humble peasant origins, the booty from his robberies enabled Vásquez to amass land and wealth, which suggests that primitive accumulation rather than distribution to the poor formed his prime concern. Although at times he did operate with a degree of autonomy, Vásquez ended up fighting a primitive guerrilla war on behalf of the coastal sugar barons. As such, Vásquez is a figure of the utmost tragedy. His history highlights the weaknesses of peasants as political actors and the limitations of banditry as a mechanism for social change.

If the notion that noble robbers appeared in Hualgayoc between 1900 and 1930 is difficult to uphold, so too is the idea of Burga and Flores Galindo that Benel was a feudal landlord intent on resisting the development of the state.[15] Benel benefited from public works contracts and provided the timber to construct a telegraph wire from Cajamarca to Hualgayoc. As one of northern Cajamarca's leading businessmen, Benel stood to gain rather than lose by the rise of a stronger interventionist state. A more assertive state need not automatically have been detrimental to Benel's political and economic interests. What Benel wanted was a state machine that he could dominate at a local level. Strong or weak, that state he would support. If it fell into the hands of political and commercial rivals, then Benel would oppose the state. This situation arose due to the impossibility of distinguishing the provincial state apparatus from those individuals who happened to occupy official positions.

Finally, the validity of the claim that Eleodoro Benel and his followers were 'revolutionaries' hinges on which concept of revolution is adopted.[16] According to a traditional interpretation developed by Polybius, Machiavelli and others, a revolution signified a revolt that changed one clique of politicians or system of government for another. Social progress and economic transformation were regarded as incidental. Under this definition, Benel and his associates could be classified as 'revolutionaries'. But if a more modern concept of revolution is employed, one that entails the transformation of 'state organisations, class structures, and dominant ideologies', then obviously the movement led by Osores and Benel was far from 'revolutionary'.[17] Above all else, the revolt described in this book represented the last important *montonero* uprising in Peru at a time when emerging social forces were ushering in a new political era.

# Abbreviations

| | |
|---|---|
| ADC/FDP/CS | Archivo Departamental de Cajamarca/Fondo Documental de la Prefectura/Corte Superior de Cajamarca. |
| ADC/FDP/GH | Archivo Departamental de Cajamarca/Fondo Documental de la Prefectura/Gobernación de Hualgayoc |
| ADC/FDP/SpC | Archivo Departamental de Cajamarca/Fondo Documental de la Prefectura/Subprefectura de Cajamarca |
| ADC/FDP/SpH | Archivo Departamental de Cajamarca/Fondo Documental de la Prefectura/Subprefectura de Hualgayoc |
| ADC/FDP/P | Archivo Departamental de Cajamarca/Fondo Documental de la Prefectura/Particulares |
| ADC/FDP/Pr | Archivo Departamental de Cajamarca/Fondo Documental de la Prefectura/Prefectura |
| ADC/CSJC/CO | Archivo Departamental de Cajamarca/Corte Superior de Justicia de Cajamarca/Causas Ordinarias |
| ADC/FDCS/C | Archivo Departamental de Cajamarca/Fondo Documental de la Corte Superior/Criminales |
| ADC/JPI/CO | Archivo Departamental de Cajamarca/Justicia de Primera Instancia/Causas Ordinarias |
| BN/SI | Biblioteca Nacional/Sala de Investigaciones |

# Notes

## Chapter 1

1. S. Vílchez, *Fusiles y machetes* (Lima, 1960).
2. C. Vigil, *La rebelión del caudillo Andino* (Trujillo, 1978).
3. Ibid., pp. 3, 13.
4. Several authors have written on aspects of the events analysed in this volume. John Gitlitz has published a short article on Benel's rebellion against president Leguía. While this piece makes a number of interesting points, it says little that is new because it appeared before archival sources became available. More substantial is the undergraduate thesis written by Jesús Carranza Rimarachín and his associates. This dissertation contains a lot of important data, but is badly organised, fails to address the subject matter in a systematic fashion and does not draw on the prefectural documents which provide the best source material. Finally, Genaro Matos' study of the military campaigns against Benel and his allies is accurate and insightful, but does not thoroughly explore the social origins of brigandage and insurrection. See J. S. Gitlitz, '*Conflictos políticos en la sierra norte del Perú: la montonera Benel contra Leguía*', *Estudios Andinos*, no. 16 (1980), pp. 127–38; J. Carranza Rimarachín, E. Saenz, M. Varias and M. Orellana, *Economía, clases, lucha de clases y estado en Cutervo, Chota y Santa Cruz, 1919–1930* (BA thesis, Universidad Nacional 'Pedro Ruiz Gallo', Lambayeque, 1979); G. Matos, *Operaciones irregulares al norte de Cajamarca 1924–5 a 1927* (Lima, 1968).
5. According to Kapsoli, 'Some acted solely for loot and vengeance. Other bandits sought to expropriate the rich, the *gamonales*, to help and protect the peasantry. Among the latter the figure of Eleodoro Benel is the most outstanding example'. W. Kapsoli, *Los movimientos campesinos en el Perú, 1879–1965* (Lima, 1977), p. 78.
6. M. Burga and A. Flores Galindo, *Apogeo y crisis de la república aristocrática* (Lima, 1979), p. 8.
7. E. Hobsbawm, *Bandits* (Harmondsworth, 1972), p. 94. The question of 'social rebellion' would, however, need qualifying.
8. For a critique of this perspective see L. Taylor, '*Cambios capitalistas en las haciendas cajamarquinas, 1900–35*', *Estudios Rurales Latinoamericanos*, vol. 7, no. 1 (1984), pp. 93–129.
9. J. Bravo, '*El poder en el Perú*', in J. Matos (ed.), *La oligarquía en el Perú* (Lima, 1969), p. 189.
10. E. López Albújar, *Los caballeros del delito* (Lima, 1936); J. Varallanos, *Bandoleros en el Perú* (Lima, 1937); V. Zapata Cesti, *La delincuencia en el Perú* (Lima, n.d. 1940?); A. Carrillo Ramírez, *Luis Pardo, 'El gran bandido', vida y hechos del famoso bandolero chiquiano que acaparó la atención pública durante varios años* (Lima, 1970). López Albújar, for example, states that 'banditry, no matter from what angle it is analysed, is a protest, a rebellion, non-conformism or simply a means of earning a living. It is a protest against injustices perpetrated by the powerful and extortion by the strong . . . (banditry) is a manifestation of the latent communism that lies buried in the soul of all the disinherited'. López Albújar, *Los caballeros*, p. 53. The aforementioned book by Carrillo clearly treats Luis Pardo as a 'noble' robber. Surprisingly for an officer in the *guardia civil*, Víctor Zapata claims that 'Banditry in Lambayeque has always been distinguished by its gallantry, valour, finesse and the disinterestness of the brigands. Neither bloodthirsty nor cruel, these used, in most cases, to distribute their booty among the poor and hungry, thus showing that they were not lost to feelings of charity and had not hardened their hearts'. Zapata, *La delincuencia*, p. 175. Cited from Hobsbawm, *Bandits*, pp. 44–5. Outlaws from Hualgayoc

116

who operated in the neighbouring department of Lambayeque hardly fitted this idealised description, which will no doubt have to be substantially altered once documents in the proposed Archivo Departamental de Lambayeque become available. Two recent studies that try to place bandits within their social situation and adopt a more critical perspective are B. S. Orlove, 'The position of rustlers in regional society: social banditry in the Andes', in B. S. Orlove and G. Custred, *Land and power in Latin America* (New York, 1980), pp. 179–94; and A. Flores Galindo, *Aristocracia y plebe: Lima, 1760–1830* (Lima, 1984), pp. 139–62.

11. López Albújar, *Los caballeros*, pp. 40, 75–6, 92–3, 120–4, 24–5, 268–75.

12. The term *gamonal* originates from the word *gamonito*, a short thick parasitic sucker that grows near the roots of vines and other trees, absorbing sap meant to feed the fruit. The lack of research into the activities of local bosses means that literary descriptions, such as that of don Alvaro Amenabar in Ciro Alegría's *Broad and alien is the world* (London, 1983), still dominate our conception of *gamonal* activity.

13. Víctor Andrés Belaúnde, *Meditaciones peruanas* (2nd edition, Lima, 1963); and *La realidad nacional* (3rd edition, Lima, 1964).

14. 'The judge, the subprefect, the commissary, the teacher, the tax collector, all are in bondage to the landed estate. The law cannot prevail against the *gamonales*. Any official who insisted on applying it would be abandoned and sacrificed by the central government; here the influences of *gamonalismo* are all-powerful, acting directly or through parliament with equal effectiveness'. José Carlos Mariátegui, *Seven interpretive essays on Peruvian reality* (Austin, 1971), pp. 22–3. Also see ibid., pp. 30, 73, 159, 166.

15. José Tamayo Herrera, *Historia social e indigenismo en el altiplano* (Lima, 1982), chapter 2. Tamayo sees the *gamonal* in Puno as being of white or mestizo extraction. He exercises economic and political power at the local level, exploits the peasant population for personal benefit, terrorises them, and when necessary, commits cruel acts against them. The *gamonal* comes from a variety of occupational backgrounds, tends to have a higher cultural level than the peasantry, violates peasant notions of reciprocity, and maintains vital contacts with the provincial and departmental state apparatus. Ibid., pp. 152–3.

16. E. Hobsbawm, *Primitive rebels* (Manchester, 1978); E. Hobsbawm, *Bandits*. For a critique of Hobsbawm's concept of social banditry, see A. Blok, 'The peasant and the brigand: social banditry reconsidered', *Comparative Studies in Society and History*, vol. xiv, no. 4 (September, 1972), pp. 494–503.

17. L. Lewin, *Politics and parentela in Paraíba: a case study of oligarchy in Brazil's Old Republic* (PhD thesis, Colombia University, 1975), especially chapters 5 and 6; L. Lewin, 'Some historical implications of kinship organisation for family-based politics in the Brazilian Northeast', *Comparative Studies in Society and History*, vol. xxi (1979), pp. 262–92.

18. Ibid.; L. Lewin, 'The oligarchical limitations of social banditry in Brazil: the case of the 'good' thief Antonio Silvino', *Past and Present*, no. 82 (1979), pp. 116–46.

19. Ibid., p. 128. On this theme also see P. Singelmann, 'Political structure and social banditry in Northeast Brazil', *Journal of Latin American Studies*, vol. 7, part 1 (1975), pp. 66–76; J. Burger, *From banditry to agrarian reform: a study of banditry and rural unions in Pernambuco, Brazil* (PhD thesis, University of Essex, 1982).

20. Lewin, 'The oligarchical limitations', pp. 120–1; Lewin, *Politics and parentela*, pp. 13, 78, 94, 97.

21. From the 1870s to 1930 Paraíba experienced no major anti-landlord peasant movement. Lewin, 'The oligarchical limitations', pp. 141–3. Between 1900 and 1930 the only peasant mobilisation in Hualgayoc arose on the hacienda Llaucán. Significantly this was the one estate in the province that did not have a resident landowner. See chapter 4. Individual, as opposed to collective, peasant protest was quite common. Many individuals voted with their feet and changed their work situation. Alternatively, disgruntled labourers and tenants joined bandit groups allied to a rival landowner.

22. B. J. Chandler, *The bandit king: Lampião of Brazil* (College Station, 1978). On the recruitment of Lampião and other bandits to fight the Prestes column, see ibid., pp. 61–6, 72.

23. Works in English include J. Henderson, *When Colombia bled: a history of the violence in Tolima* (Alabama, 1985); P. Oquist, *Violence, conflict and politics in Colombia* (New York, 1980); J. M. Daniel, *Rural violence in Colombia since 1946* (Washington, 1965); R. Maullin, *The fall of Dumar Aljure, a Colombian guerrilla and bandit* (Santa Monica, 1968). In Spanish see G. Guzmán, O. Fals Borda and E. Umaña, *La violencia en Colombia: estudio de un proceso social*, vol. 1 (Bogotá, 1962), and the good recent study by G. Sánchez and D. Meertens, *Bandoleros, gamonales y campesinos* (Bogotá, 1983).

24. Sánchez and Meertens, *Bandoleros*, pp. 62, 68–9, 141–2, 238–9.

25. Ibid., pp. 236–7.

26. In Colombia this evolved into a struggle where modern ideologies came to play a significant role. This is partly explained by the thirty-year time lag between the movement led by Benel and *la Violencia* during the 1950s. On Colombian developments see ibid., pp. 118–56; E. Hobsbawm, 'The revolutionary situation in Colombia', *The World Today*, no. 6 (London, 1963), pp. 248–58.

27. Sánchez and Meertens, *Bandoleros*, p. 188.

28. P. J. Vanderwood, *Disorder and progress: bandits, police and Mexican development* (Lincoln, 1981).

29. See the essays in D. A. Brading, *Caudillo and peasant in the Mexican Revolution* (Cambridge, 1980). In Spanish a recent study of note is R. Falcón, *Revolución y caciquismo. San Luis Potosí 1910–38* (Mexico, 1984).

30. Ibid., for the case of Saturnino Cerrillo.

31. J. Tussell, *Oligarquía y caciquismo en Andalucia (1890–1923)* (Barcelona, 1976). An informative study exploring the interaction between local élites and power structures in Madrid is provided by J. Varela Ortega, *Los amigos políticos: partidos, elecciones y caciquismo en la Restauración (1875–1900)* (Madrid, 1977).

32. Ibid. The Italian experience is also very similar. See D. Mack Smith, *Italy: a modern history* (Ann Arbor, 1969), pp. 199–201, 220–1.

33. On 'El Tempranillo', the 'nobel outlaw' of Andalucía, see Hobsbawm, *Bandits*, pp. 43, 53. One interesting exploration into the growth of banditry to endemic proportions in Baja Andalucía after 1868 and its relation with local *cacique* controlled power structures is the book by J. Zugasti, *El bandolerismo* (Madrid, 1982). The author was appointed governor of Córdoba in 1870 and was consequently at the centre of the local political stage. One of his tasks was the suppression of banditry. Another useful book that details the role of brigands in Galicia, a region with a very different social structure, but one that nevertheless supported similar connections between bandits and *caciques*, is B. López Moran, *El bandolerismo gallego (1820–24)* (Vigo, 1984).

34. M. Pantaleone, *The mafia and politics* (London, 1966); D. Mack Smith, *A history of Sicily: modern Sicily after 1713* (London, 1969), chapters 50–5.

35. Ibid. Also see P. Arlacchi, *Mafia, peasants and great estates* (Cambridge, 1983) for a description of these phenomena in Calabria. On Sicily, see A. Blok, *The mafia of a Sicilian village, 1860–1960* (Oxford, 1974); H. Hess, *Mafia and mafiosi: the structure of power* (Westmead, 1977).

36. The career of Salvatore Giuliano provides a classic example of the importance to bandits of patronage by influential protectors. Once Giuliano became a liability to the *mafia*, they arranged his assassination. On the colourful exploits of this outlaw see G. Maxwell, *God protect me from my friends* (London, 1957). The Francesco Rosi film *Salvatore Giuliano* (1961) provides an excellent reconstruction of the bandit's life.

37. Giuliano's flirtation with Sicilian separatism and its part in his downfall is detailed in Maxwell, *God protect me*, pp. 57–79.

38. *Bandits*, p. 18.

118

39. Ibid., pp. 22, 67.
40. Ibid., pp. 24, 65.
41. Ibid., pp. 62–3, 65. According to Hobsbawm, 'even the best of bandits must demonstrate that he can be 'terrible''. Ibid., p. 63.
42. Ibid., p. 13.; *Primitive rebels*, p. 13. I return to the question of social banditry in the concluding chapter.
43. Ibid., p. 23.
44. *Bandits*, pp. 31–5.
45. *Primitive rebels*, pp. 17–18.
46. *Bandits*, p. 30.
47. ADC/FDP/SpH, 18 March 1892.
48. Ibid.

# Chapter 2

1. Due to restrictions on space, this account of Hualgayoc's economy and social structure is very brief. A more detailed analysis is forthcoming in L. Taylor, 'Earning a living in Hualgayoc, 1870–1900', in R. Miller and W. S. Bell (eds), *Region and class in modern Peruvian history* (provisional title, Liverpool, Institute of Latin American Studies, forthcoming 1986).
2. Ibid.
3. Ibid.
4. In the 1876 Census the population of Hualgayoc was calculated at 47,982, of which 37,603 lived in the countryside. Peasant freeholders comprised 69 per cent of the rural population, but many individuals classified as urban dwellers attained most of their income from peasant farming. For a more detailed discussion on this see Taylor, 'Earning a living'.
5. Ibid. The largest employers in coastal agriculture were the sugar plantations of Tumán, Cayaltí, Pucalá, Pátapo and Pomalca, located in the Zaña and Chancay valleys. On the development of the Peruvian sugar industry see W. Albert, *An essay on the Peruvian sugar industry, 1880–1920* (Norwich, 1976), pp. 1a–112a.
6. Taylor, 'Earning a living'.
7. A close examination of notarial and prefectural records reveals two notable exceptions to this general rule. These were the peasant movements that developed in the haciendas Chancay and Llaucán. See chapters 3 and 4 for further details. The most important land dispute along the pattern of clan rivalry arose in and around Samana parish, part of Santa Cruz district. Here a clash over hereditary rights combined with a dispute between tenant farmer and landlord to produce violent clashes, sparking off a spate of vendetta feuding that began before 1850 and lasted into this century, making an important contribution to the events described in this book. See 'Mateo Otiniano a nombre de Manuel Zulueta litigando con don Agapito Basquez sobre derecho a las haciendas de Polulo, Samana, Uticyaco pertenecientes a Chota', ADC/JPI/CO, 1850; 'Dn Manuel Agapito Basquez litigando con Dn José Antonio Chavarri representante de Manuel del Carmen Zulueta, sobre mejor derecho a las haciendas de Ninabamba, Uticyaco y Polulo', ibid., 1851; 'Manuel Zulueta litigando con Agapito Basquez sobre los terrenos de Polulo, Samana, Uticyaco y Polulo', ibid., 1857; 'Expediente seguido por D Manuel Agapito Vásquez sobre las haciendas Ninabamba, Uticyacu y otros', ADS/CSJC/CO, *legajo* 7, 1862. The former documents are classified according to date and the *legajos* are not yet numbered.
8. For the period under discussion, factional leaders were exclusively male in Hualgayoc.
9. One example was the governor of San Gregorio, who was eventually ordered to stop by the

119

prefect after many complaints by citizens. ADC/FDP/SpH, 9 October 1883; 15 October 1883. A colourful description of these types of abuses is provided by Abelardo Gamarra in the tale 'La visita de un subprefecto', in his *Partículos de costumbres de El Tuñante* (Lima, 1910), pp. 18–45.

10. J. Basadre, *Introducción a las bases documentales para la historia del Perú* (Lima, 1971), pp. 304–5.

11. ADC/FDP/SpH, 7 April 1855.

12. Ibid., 17 December 1856.

13. The history of the War of the Pacific in Cajamarca has still to be written. To date the best study is J. Dammert, *Cajamarca durante la guerra del Pacífico* (Cajamarca, 1983).

14. ADC/FDP/SpH, 2 May 1881. Throughout 1880 and 1881 Bambamarca experienced an intense period of inter-faction strife for control of the town, with frequent gun fights in the streets, resulting in various deaths. Houses and stores were also looted and fired. See ibid., 23 January 1880; 19 November 1880; 24 November 1880; 14 May 1881.

15. Ibid., 2 May 1881.

16. Ibid., 26 January 1881.

17. Ibid.

18. J. Basadre, *Historia de la república del Perú*, 5th edition (Lima, 1962), p. 2631. The War of the Pacific was also a catalyst in the development of social mobilisation and violence in the central Andes. On the *montonera* columns led by Cáceres, see Nelson Manrique, *Las guerrillas indígenas en la guerra con Chile* (Lima, 1981); and Florencia Mallon, *The defense of community in Peru's central highlands: peasant struggle and capitalist transition, 1860–1940* (Princeton, 1983), especially Ch. 3.

19. Dammert, *Cajamarca*, pp. 109–114; J. C. Guerrero, *1879–1883: la guerra de las ocasiones pérdidas* (Lima, 1975), pp. 28–31.

20. ADC/FDP/SpH, 14 May 1884.

21. Ibid., 1 April 1884.

22. For further details see 'Memoria elevada a la Dirección de Gobierno por el Prefecto de Cajamarca, Don Agustín Moreno', BN/SI, D5960. The alleged size of Puga's *montonera* seems exaggerated.

23. Ibid.

24. ADC/FDP/SpH, 4 June 1887. The *iglesistas* were known as 'blues', the Puga-Cáceres faction as 'reds'.

25. Ibid. Also see ibid., 2 June 1887; 29 June 1887.

26. According to Vílchez, 'In the late nineteenth century the followers of Cáceres and Piérola left the political environment in Cajamarca saturated with blood and arms. After the demise of colonel Becerra, whose guerrillas dominated the zone, in each area of the north powerful landowners remained in control. Their haciendas were fortresses defended by their *guapos* (gunmen)'. *Fusiles*, p. 15. Becerra was a captain in the *montonera* led by José Mercedes Puga.

27. In his *Memoria* for 1897–8, the subprefect of Cajamarca calculated that the livestock population was only one-tenth of the pre-1879 level. War and civil war explained this drop. ADC/FDP/SpC, 5 June 1898.

28. In Niepos, for example, valuables from the town church were sold and eighty men armed with the proceeds. The local *iglesista* caudillo in Llapa and San Miguel, Tiburcio Barrantes, also armed a column of his *clientela*. ADC/FDP/SpH, 20 May 1891; 4 February 1887; 16 December 1887.

29. Ibid., 9 October 1887; 20 January 1888. Vásquez participated in the *montonera* campaign of José Mercedes Puga. The bandit and his associates committed serious crimes against the local peasantry, as a despatch from the *iglesista* governor of Niepos to the subprefect in Hualgayoc illustrates: 'The Vásquez *montoneros* from Niepos and the Torres gang from the

village of Argolla, continue to daily commit all kinds of criminal acts against the populace. Ten days ago, one league distant from this town, Vásquez lassoed a woman, dragged her to a gorge and raped her. He also robbed twenty *soles* and a cow from her husband Esteban Torres. Assisted by a neighbour, the husband (who is blind in both eyes), followed his wife to beg for mercy. Torres approached Vásquez while he was violating the woman. The blind man pleaded that the outlaws should not do such a degrading thing to his wife. Upon hearing this the criminals kicked and punched Torres before shooting him in cold blood. The Torres gang from Argolla are acting in a similar manner. They seized a woman, tied her to some stakes, stripped and raped her. They then cut her arms and back with knives, eventually leaving her half dead . . . Bandit chief Agustín Vásquez has been given control of this district by Dr Puga, and is imposing substantial ransoms on whoever takes his fancy, bringing ruin to many citizens'. ADC/FDP/GH, 24 October 1884. During the civil war both Puga and Iglesias placed their own supporters in official positions, which explains why Niepos had two governors at this juncture.

30. ADC/FDP/SpH, 17 December 1887.

31. Ibid., 20 January 1888; 21 January 1888. The Vásquez gang obtained refuge in the haciendas Culpón, Chumbenique and Oyotún.

32. This fate befell San Gregorio and Niepos in 1896. Ibid., 28 June 1896. Bambamarca was invaded by the fifty-strong Tello gang in 1890. ADC/FDP/GH, 19 July 1890.

33. ADC/FDP/SpH, 16 March 1888.

34. Ibid., 5 May 1888.

35. Ibid., 29 May 1890; 1 December 1896; 22 December 1896; 5 November 1898; 17 December 1899.

36. On the concepts of authority and legitimacy see C. F. Andrain, *Political life and social change* (Belmont, 1970), pp. 130–40.

37. V. A. Belaúnde, *Meditaciones peruanas*, p. 66.

38. Ibid., pp. 237–8. This essay was written in 1914.

39. See Basadre, *Historia*, vol. vii, pp. 3096–7 for further details.

40. On the phenomenon of *caciquismo parlamentario* see Belaúnde, *Meditaciones peruanas*, pp. 244–49. Also see R. Miller, 'The coastal elite and Peruvian politics, 1895–1919', *Journal of Latin American Studies*, vol. 14, part 1 (May, 1982), pp. 97–120.

41. Writing in 1914 Víctor Andrés Belaúnde noted that central power was dependent on local interest, an arrangement which found 'the government scheming with provincial *gamonalismo*'. *Meditaciones peruanas*, p. 70. Mariátegui also makes this point. *Seven interpretive essays*, pp. 159, 170.

42. J. Basadre, *Elecciones y centralismo en el Perú* (Lima, 1980), pp. 23–4.

43. In 1874 the district of Hualgayoc sent sixteen *electores propietarios* to the provincial electoral college. Bambamarca sent ten, as did Santa Cruz. Niepos sent five, while San Miguel had fifteen *electores*. San Gregorio and Llapa had no representation. Each college vote represented approximately ten electors. Calculating from population figures provided by the subprefect, less than one per cent of the adult population was enfranchised. '*Datos tomados para la estadística de la provincia de Hualgayoc*', *El Peruano*, 16 October 1874; 17 November 1874.

44. To my knowledge the names of cows were not included on the electoral registers in Hualgayoc, as happened in Predappio near Forli. Mack Smith, *Italy*, p. 221.

45. The local *tinterillo* and caudillo from San Miguel and Llapa, Tiburcio Barrantes, was particularly adept at staging these events. For a description of his take-over of Hualgayoc town on the eve of the 1888 poll see ADC/FDP/SpH, 17 November 1888. A highly critical commentary on electoral practice in Peru is provided by Manuel V. Villaran, *Costumbres electorales, Mercurio Peruano*, 1 July 1918. Víctor Andrés Belaúnde lamented the crisis of parliamentary government in Peru. This existed because 'there is no clean election; because free voting does not exist in Peru; because elections are a farce decided by the government

or the majority group in Congress'. *Meditaciones peruanas*, pp. 70–1. Election to Congress was important because it gave the deputy for the province influence in the nomination of local political and judicial officials, access to public funds for local public works (which often benefited the deputy or his friends), and allowed him to raise issues of local concern in parliament.

46. Two members were appointed from each chamber of Congress, the Supreme Court nominated four members, with the executive providing the ninth incumbent. After 1899 the *Junta* was increasingly managed by the Partido Civil via its domination of parliament and the judiciary. Through a law passed on 25 November 1908 the judiciary's allocation of four members was suspended. Eight seats on the *Junta* were now nominated by parliament. Leguía, having lost control of Congress, abolished the National Election Council in 1911, and elections came under the control of local *Asambleas de Mayores Contribuyentes*. See Basadre, *Elecciones*, pp. 54–8.

47. The five occupational categories were landowners; professionals; farmers and labourers; manufacturers and artisans; and merchants. In theory the representatives of these social groups were to be nominated via random selection. Ibid., pp. 53–4.

# Chapter 3

1. Albert, *An essay*, pp. 36a–37a. The Chancay valley in Lambayeque should not be confused with that in the north of the department of Lima.

2. For more details on these developments see M. J. González, *Plantation agriculture and social control in Northern Peru, 1875–1933* (Austin, 1985).

3. Information used in this paragraph comes from Vigil, *La rebelión*, pp. 17–22; Gitlitz, *'Conflictos políticos'*, pp. 129–30; and J. Berrios Alarcón, *Monografía histórica de Chota* (Lima, 1967), pp. 85–93, 176–7.

4. Vigil, *La rebelión*, p. 17.

5. In 1907 Benel sold the authorities 700 beams for the construction of a school in Hualgayoc town. See ADC/FDP/SpH, 1 May 1907. He also retailed timber for use in public buildings being erected in Cajamarca. See Vigil, *La rebelión*, pp. 21–22. April 1911 saw Benel sign a contract to supply the state with 520 posts to be used in the laying of a telegraph line between the town of Hualgayoc and Cajamarca. The timber was cut using labour recruited through the *enganche* system. See ADC/FDP/SpH, 6 April 1911.

6. Gitlitz, *'Conflictos políticos'*, p. 130. The standard wage rate for agricultural labourers was S/.0.10 between 1900 and 1914. During the First World War and up to the early 1920s the average wage rate for this category of worker stood at S/.0.20. Carranza Rimarachín et. al., *Economía, classes*, p. 233.

7. Vigil, *La rebelión*, p. 18.

8. Ibid., pp. 20, 24.

9. Ibid., pp. 24–5. Also see *El Ferrocarril*, 20 April 1918.

10. Vigil, *La rebelión*, p. 24.

11. P. Macera, *Cayaltí 1875–1920: organización del trabajo en una plantación azucarera del Perú* (Lima, 1973), p. 221. At 1911 wage rates for cane cutters, S/.50 represented approximately one hundred days labour on the hacienda Cayaltí.

12. ADC/FDP/SpC, 12 May 1906. Smuggling was probably a further source of wealth for Eleodoro Benel, but no documentary evidence has so far been uncovered to substantiate this.

13. *Registro de Propiedad Inmueble de Cajamarca*, vol. 16, fol. 193.

14. Ibid., vol. 57, fols. 145–7.

15. More details on this are given in C. Burga Larrea, *Monografía de Santa Cruz* (Lima, 1940), pp. 23–5, 29–30 and 85–8.

16. Gitlitz, 'Conflictos políticos', p. 134.
17. ADC/FDP/SpH, 23 January 1900.
18. Ibid., 29 May 1900; 9 January 1901.
19. Ibid., 18 October 1900. The Villacorta *montonera* of 1900 sprang up in response to tensions unfolding in Lima within the governing *civilista-demócrata* coalition. For background information of this dispute at a national level see Basadre, *Elecciones*, pp. 61–6; and J. Basadre, '*Para la historia de los partidos: el desplazamiento de los demócratas por el civilismo*', *Documenta*, no. 4 (1965), pp. 297–300.
20. ADC/FDP/SpH, 12 March 1901; 1 April 1901. The situation prompted the subprefect to record in his *Memoria* for the administrative year 1900–1901 that Hualgayoc province 'Has for a long time been the theatre of grave disorders and anarchy'. Ibid., 27 May 1901.
21. Background information is forthcoming in Basadre, *Historia*, vol. vi, ch. cxxii.
22. For further details on these events from a *pierolista* perspective see Alberto Ulloa, *Don Nicolás de Piérola: una época de la historia del Perú* (Lima, 1950), pp. 339–45.
23. According to Basadre the 1903 elections did not lead to grave public disorder and the populace 'gave their assent, actively or passively, to the contest of 1903'. *Historia*, vol. vii, p. 3331. While this may have been a correct assessment of the campaign in Lima, attitudes in Cajamarca were more abrasive.
24. ADC/FDP/SpH, 12 January 1903.
25. Ibid.
26. Details concerning this alliance at a national level are forthcoming in Basadre, *Historia*, vol. vii, pp. 3329–30. After meeting official hostility on several campaign trips, Seminario withdrew his candidacy.
27. ADC/FDP/P, 14 May 1903.
28. ADC/FDP/SpH, 22 July 1903; 26 July 1903.
29. Ibid., 1 April 1903.
30. Ibid., 5 May 1903. The possibility exists that the subprefect was attempting to get the secretary removed in order to provide one of his friends with a job.
31. Ibid., 5 January 1904.
32. Ibid.
33. Ibid., 22 July 1903; 10 January 1905.
34. On these events see Basadre, *Historia*, vol. vii, ch. cxxxviii, and Ulloa, *Don Nicolás*, pp. 351–5.
35. ADC/FDP/SpH, 26 December 1906.
36. Ibid., 28 December 1904.
37. Juan de la Cruz Cadena to the prefect, ADC/FDP/P, 15 February 1906.
38. ADC/FDP/SpH, 26 December 1906.
39. Vigil, *La rebelión*, p. 20; Gitlitz, '*Conflictos políticos*', p. 131.
40. ADC/FDP/SpH, 10 September 1901.
41. Eleodoro Benel to the governor of Santa Cruz, ADC/FDP/CS, 12 May 1906; ADC/FDP/SpH, 6 June 1906; and Domingo Cubas to the prefect, ADC/FDP/P, 20 August 1907.
42. Ibid., 18 May 1906.
43. Domingo Cubas to the prefect, ibid., 20 August 1907.
44. ADC/FDP/SpH, 17 July 1907.
45. Details of these developments can be obtained in Basadre, *Historia*, vol. vii, pp. 3371–2 and Ulloa, *Don Nicolás*, pp. 365–8.
46. *Historia*, vol. vii, p. 3372.
47. ADC/FDP/SpH, 4 May 1908.

48. Ibid., 13 June 1909.
49. Ibid., 23 September 1908.
50. Ibid.
51. Background information on these developments is forthcoming in D. Gilbert, *La oligarquía*, pp. 40–3; and R. Miller, 'The coastal elite', pp. 103–6.
52. ADC/FDP/SpH, 4 December 1909.
53. Gerónimo Alvarado and others to the prefect, ADC/FDP/P, 16 April 1912.
54. Miller, 'The coastal elite', p. 103; Gilbert, *La oligarquía*, pp. 42–44.
55. These latter settlements had a history of rivalry with Samana parish and could therefore be mobilised by the Alvarado clan against Benel and his supporters. See footnote 7, chapter 2.
56. Data on the 1912 municipal elections in Santa Cruz contained in this and the following two paragraphs is taken from ADC/FDP/SpH, 17 April 1912 and 4 May 1912.
57. Ibid., 17 April 1912.
58. Ibid.
59. Ibid.
60. Ibid., 20 April 1912.
61. Ibid.
62. Ibid., 4 May 1912.
63. Ibid., 20 April 1912.
64. Ibid.
65. Ibid., 4 May 1912.
66. Ibid.
67. Ibid., 13 June 1912.
68. Ibid., 29 June 1912. Also see ibid., 20 July 1912.
69. Manuel Antonio Burga to the prefect, ADC/FDP/P, 25 July 1912.
70. ADC/FDP/SpH, 31 July 1912.
71. Ibid., 14 August 1912.
72. Ibid., 7 October 1912.
73. Ibid., 14 August 1912; 7 October 1912; 21 October 1912.
74. Data on the early activities of the Ramos gang appears in ibid., 27 November 1911.
75. Gitlitz, '*Conflictos políticos*', pp. 135–6.
76. ADC/FDP/SpH, 1 June 1912.
77. Dolores Benel to the prefect, ADC/FDP/P, 21 May 1912.
78. Ibid.
79. ADC/FDP/SpH, 26 October 1912.
80. Natividad Cabrejos to the prefect, ADC/FDP/P, 4 November 1912. Montoya y Batanero also had the temerity to imprison Adolfo Ugaz on 5 October for his participation in the 24 September *benelista* occupation of Santa Cruz. Along with José María Asenfo, Ugaz was charged with possessing rifles belonging to the state and, in the company of ex-subprefect Wenceslao Mori, of terrorising their factional opponents in the parish of Polulo. Ugaz was not without influence: on 12 October ex-subprefect Mori ordered and attained his and Asenfo's release, even though he no longer held an official position. Thus, within a matter of days the new *gobernador militar* became deeply embroiled in local politics and was clearly identified as a member of the Alvarado faction. In his letters to the prefect he began to vigorously denounce Ugaz and Benel as 'protectors of the criminals Galarreta and Vargas'. He also recommended that they be jailed 'for peace in this district will never occur unless these elements do not disappear'. ADC/FDP/SpH, 27 October 1912. This advice fell

on deaf ears: the prefect ordered copies to be forwarded to the authorities in Lambayeque and filed away the original. Aware of the threat that Montoya y Batanero posed to their local dominance, the *benelistas* mobilised against him, and succeeded in getting the *gobernador militar* ousted in late November 1912, when the subprefect took up residence in Santa Cruz.

81. Natividad Cabrejos to the prefect, ADC/FDP/P, 4 November 1912. Also see Natividad Cabrejos to the subprefect of Hualgayoc, ibid., 27 November 1912. Montoya y Batanero offered a different version of events, stating that the Galarreta and Vargas brothers were attacking the house of Dolores Benel when the troops arrived on the scene. During the ensuing affray Catalino Galarreta was shot dead. ADC/FDP/SpH, 26 October 1912.

82. Ibid., 16 January 1913.

83. Ibid., 4 December 1912.

84. Ibid.

85. Ibid.

86. Ibid., 28 January 1913.

87. Ibid.

88. Ibid., 6 February 1913.

89. Ibid., 11 February 1913.

90. Ibid., 2 February 1913.

91. Ibid., 16 May 1913.

92. Ibid., 2 January 1914.

# Chapter 4

1. Rent strikes occurred in 1871, 1873, 1874, 1878, 1890, 1896, 1897, 1902, 1904, 1905 and 1906. Further details on these and related events are provided in L. Taylor, 'Social organisation and peasant protest in the hacienda Llaucán, 1860–1960', mimeo, Cambridge, 1985.

2. In the words of Lorenzo Guadaña, a tenant farming in the hacienda Llaucán, brigandage and the unauthorised impositions made on the tenants by the lessee 'have converted the estate into a battlefield'. See Lorenzo Guadaña to the prefect, ADC/FDP/SpH, 5 November 1914. Guadaña's letter was written on 15 October 1914.

3. 'Escritura de poder especial que confiere Eleodoro Benel Zuloeta a Bernardino Guerrero Gayoso', *Archivo de la notaría de Gilberto Carranza Villavicencio*, Chota, *legajo* 1913–14, fol. 32, 27 September 1914. Juan Vigil, in an attempt to absolve Benel from responsibility vis-à-vis the December massacre, states that Benel became the lessee of Llaucán in 1912 and persuaded by the board of governors of the Colegio San Juan, refrained from taking possession of the estate for two years out of fear of provoking a bloodbath. See Vigil, *La rebelión*, pp. 26, 28. This version of events is incorrect.

4. Basadre, *Historia*, vol. viii, pp. 3769–70.

5. Vigil, *La rebelión*, pp. 26–7.

6. Ibid., p. 28.

7. Ibid. Also see Taylor, 'Social organisation', pp. 3, 15.

8. Vigil, *La rebelión*, p. 28.

9. Ibid., pp. 26–9. Eleodoro Benel also had a group of supporters settled on the estate, but these formed a small minority.

10. Andrés Díaz Bustamante to the prefect, ADC/FDP/P, 15 June 1914. Díaz was one of the wealthier tenants and was soon to become a prominent anti-*benelista* and pro-Alvarado peasant leader in the hacienda Llaucán.

125

11. Aurelio Zaldívar to the prefect, ibid., 1 July 1914. Zaldívar was also the lawyer of Eleodoro Benel.

12. After a fire destroyed the mining town on 17 June 1856, the hacienda Llaucán was bequeathed to Hualgayoc in January 1857. A new town called Nueva Hualgayoc was to be built on Llaucán and 100,000 *pesos* made available for this project. Politicking by influential men from Chota managed to persuade the government of Ramón Castilla to grant the estate to the Colegio San Juan in 1861. This caused great bitterness among the population of Hualgayoc, and became an issue promoting intense inter-provincial rivalry. For more details see Taylor, 'Social organisation', pp. 2–5. Evidence that this dispute was still alive in the early part of this century is provided by a reading of the pamphlet '*La hacienda Llaucán: su legítimo propietario*', Imprenta El Heraldo, Cajamarca, n.d. (1921?).

13. Lorenzo Guadaña to the prefect, ADC/FDP/SpH, 5 November 1914.

14. Ibid.

15. Ibid.

16. 'Escritura de finanza dada a Eleodoro Benel Zuloeta', *Archivo notarial Gilberto Carranza*, *legajo* 1913–14, fols. 39–43, 17 November 1914.

17. Copies of the telegrammes relating to the Llaucán events were later published in a special report that appeared in the Lima daily *La Prensa*, 30 December 1914, under the headline '*Los sucesos de Llaucán*'.

18. Ibid.

19. Ibid.

20. Ibid. By suggesting that César Miranda had been attacked the school authorities probably hoped that the landlord's brother, deputy Demetrio Miranda, would be stimulated into putting pressure on the authorities in Lima.

21. Ibid.

22. Ibid.

23. ADC/FDP/Pr, 23 November 1914.

24. Ibid.

25. *La Prensa*, 30 December 1914; ADC/FDP/Pr, 29 November 1914.

26. Ibid. He had been ordered by the *Director de Gobierno* on 23 November 1914 to 'adopt all the measures you deem necessary to restore peace and order to all citizens, respecting the rights of both sides'. '*Los sucesos*', *La Prensa*, 30 December 1914.

27. Given that most official documents relating to the massacre were removed or destroyed by those officials implicated in the incident, this account of how the massacre took place follows that presented by Vigil, *La rebelión*, pp. 29–31. This is the most detailed report available and the *benelista* sympathies of the author do not appear to have influenced his description of how events unfolded on the day of the conflict.

28. Ibid., p. 30.

29. No figure of the exact number killed during the Llaucán massacre exists, for the officials implicated had no interest in keeping records, while the peasants, for obvious reasons, buried their dead without notifying the authorities. According to Jorge Basadre, 'more than 150 Indians were murdered', but he gives no reference for this statistic. See Basadre, *Historia*, 6th edition (Lima, 1970), vol. xii, p. 327. Carlos Vigil holds that 300 people were shot dead on the field next to the *casa hacienda*, with a further 200 murdered during the second stage of the massacre, when the soldiers rampaged through the estate, making an overall death toll of 500 peasants. As this father was a trusted servant of Eleodoro Benel, he obtained information from individuals deeply involved in the conflict. Moreover, Vigil had no reason to exaggerate the loss of life brought about by the efforts of his hero to raise rents. The mother of Carlos Vigil, who as a result of the activities of her spouse was very well acquainted with factional disputes in Hualgayoc, puts the body count at 400. Given that these latter two sources were much better informed about the details of the massacre,

it is likely that the number assassinated on 3 December 1914 was well in excess of the 150 mentioned by Basadre. See Vigil, *La rebelión*, p. 31, and Carlos Burga, *Diccionario geográfico e histórico de Cajamarca* (Lima, 1983), p. 904. Conversations with peasants in the district of Bambamarca support this conclusion. The majority of those asked put the number killed at between 200 and 400.

30. Vigil, *La rebelión*, p. 31.
31. *El Ferrocarril*, 1 January 1915.
32. ADC/FDP/SpH, 16 December 1914.
33. '*Grave conflicto en Cajamarca*', *La Prensa*, 8 December 1914.
34. '*Los sucesos de Llaucán*', *La Prensa*, 2 February 1915, p. 2.
35. *El Ferrocarril*, 1 January 1915.
36. Ibid., 12 December 1914. Also see the edition of 23 September 1916.
37. '*En el senado*', *La Prensa*, 31 December 1914, p. 2.
38. Ibid.
39. Ibid. Afternoon edition.
40. Ibid., 13 January 1915, p. 15.
41. ADC/FDP/SpC, 8 November 1915.
42. Eleodoro Benel to the prefect, ADC/FDP/P, 19 December 1914.
43. '*Labor de la Pro-indígena*', *La Prensa*, 30 January 1915, p. 2; '*Asociación Pro-indígena*', *La Prensa*, 6 February 1915, p. 2; '*La acción de la Pro-indígena*', *El Comercio*, 14 December 1914, p. 1; '*Por los indígenas de Llaucán*', *La Prensa*, 14 February 1915, p. 6 and '*La Pro-indígena*', *La Prensa*, 26 May 1915.
44. See, for example, the speech by deputy Oswaldo Hoyos Osores in parliament on 4 December 1914, *Diario de los debates de la cámara de diputados*, 1914, pp. 433–4.
45. Jorge Basadre claims that 'The Indians got on very well with the new administrator and paid their rents without any problems'. *Historia*, 6th edn., vol. xii, p. 328. This is incorrect. See, for example, the 'Memoria presentado por los arrendatarios de la hacienda Llaucán al Sr Prefecto', ADC/FDP/Pr, 22 October 1916. In spite of the massacre and the hounding of the peasant leaders, resistance to rent payments continued in early 1915. The governors of the Colegio San Juan responded by organising a vigilante column in Chota to go and forcibly collect the rents. A local newspaper described this incident as follows: 'three hundred *chotanos* armed with rifles belonging to the State invaded the hacienda Llaucán on the afternoon of Monday 12 April. The attackers committed a series of abuses against the unfortunate Indians, forcing them to pay their rents at rifle point'. *El Ferrocarril*, 21 April 1915. Once again the citizens of Hualgayoc were backing the peasants as a means of furthering their traditional rivalry with Chota. Official reluctance to send government troops in the wake of the 3 December massacre, meant that the governors could only collect rents by forming a citizens militia around the theme of upholding '*intereses chotanos*' against the threat from Hualgayoc town. One other motive for this show of force was to intimidate the *llaucaneros* into dropping their demands for the parcellation of the estate.
46. *El Ferrocarril*, 20 April 1918.
47. Ibid.
48. Rivalry between the Benel and Osores clans went back to the War of the Pacific, when Benel's father supported the *iglesista* cause and the Osores family backed the Cáceres-Puga faction.

# Chapter 5

1. ADC/FDP/SpH, 16 February 1915.
2. Ibid., 12 January 1915.

127

3. Ibid.
4. Ibid., 16 February 1915.
5. Ibid.
6. Ibid.
7. Ibid.
8. Ibid., 4 February 1915.
9. Ibid., 20 February 1915.
10. Ibid.
11. For background data on the accession of Pardo to the presidency, see Basadre, *Historia*, vol. viii, pp. 3896–8.
12. Aurelio Zaldívar to the prefect, ADC/FDP/P, 7 December 1915, letter of the subprefect of Chota dated 17 December 1915. Also see Aurelio Zaldívar to the prefect, ibid., 4 December 1915.
13. Ibid., letter of the prefect dated 7 December 1915.
14. Ibid., letter of subprefect Touset, 17 December 1915.
15. Ibid.
16. Ibid.
17. José Demetrio Tello to the prefect, ibid., 24 April, 1915.
18. Ibid.
19. Ibid. For more incidents of factional violence in Bambamarca over these months, see Oswaldo Salazar to the prefect, ibid., 23 April 1915.
20. ADC/FDP/SpH, 27 July 1915.
21. Ibid., 21 September 1915. A local observer notes that by this time people attending a wake did not ask the cause of death. Instead they enquired 'who killed him and where did he get shot?'. Manuel Cabrejo, *Añoranzas Cruzeñas* (Lima, 1951), p. 54.
22. ADC/FDP/SpH, 21 September 1915.
23. Ibid.
24. Ibid., 18 October 1915. The Ramos brothers had been captured during a gun battle nearby Hualgayoc in late July 1915. It is probable that the guards were bribed by Raimundo Ramos.
25. See, for example, the letters of protest addressed to the prefect by the *campesinos* Francisco and José María Fernández, ibid., 20 March 1916. Also see Eulogio García Ramos to the prefect, ADC/FDP/P, 15 June 1916.
26. Ibid., 24 April 1916.
27. Ibid., 15 May 1916.
28. ADC/FDP/SpH, 8 May 1916.
29. Ibid., 4 September 1916 and 8 September 1916.
30. Ibid., 4 September 1916.
31. Ibid.
32. 'Juicio seguido contra Fernando y Gervasio Díaz por los delitos de homicidio y heridas perpetrados en la persona de Daniel Guardia y María Luisa Díaz', ADC/FDCS/C, 1916, *legajo* 63.
33. ADC/FDP/SpH, 16 October 1916. Bonifacio Medina was a *pistolero* working for Benel.
34. Cases of homicide before the court in Cajamarca reveal a total of 108 for the provinces of Hualgayoc and Chota in 1916. See ADC/FDCS/C, *legajos* 61–72.
35. ADC/FDP/SpH, 23 April 1917. Eulogio García had denounced Benel as a bandit and murderer to the authorities, which provoked Benel to take revenge.
36. Francisca Sánchez to the prefect, ADC/FDP/P, 15 January 1918. Aggression against the

García family commenced in May 1916, if not before. See Eulogio García to the prefect, ibid., 15 June 1916. Eulogio García was eventually killed by the *benelista* militia on 2 June 1917.

37. ADC/FDP/SpH, 23 April 1917.
38. Ibid.
39. Ibid.
40. Ibid., 14 May 1917.
41. Ibid.
42. Ibid.
43. Ibid.
44. Ibid.
45. Ibid. The difficulties facing Durand were illustrated during the previous week. He sent two suspected bandits associated with Benel to the Hualgayoc jail. These were then released by the local judge, who was a political ally of the landlord of El Triunfo. Ibid., 7 May 1917.
46. ADC/FDP/SpH, 2 April 1917.
47. Santiago Celis to the prefect, ADC/FDP/P, 29 May 1917.
48. Ibid.
49. 'Juicio contra Neptalí Becerra por los delitos de homicidio frustrado y lesiones en la persona de Asunción Terrones', ADC/FDCS/C, 1917, *legajo* 73. Letter dated 30 April 1917.
50. Ibid.
51. Ibid. For the parliamentary debates on these incidents see *Diario de los debates en la cámara de diputados, Primera legislatura extraordinaria de 1917*, pp. 297–8 and 460–1. The following month witnessed a number of serious ructions in Bambamarca. In one incident Juan Hernández and a gang of his associates attacked the home of their rival Campos Cabrera. After a fierce gun battle they gained entrance, sacked Cabrera's house and set it on fire. Details of this action appeared in the Cajamarca newspaper *El Norte*, 26 May 1917.
52. ADC/FDP/SpH, 20 September 1917 and 8 October 1917.
53. 'Juicio contra Domingo Ramos, Ramón Ramos, Vicente Azamera, Eleodoro Benel Zuloeta y otros por triple homicidio y otros delitos', ADC/FDCS/C, 1917, *legajo* 82, vol. i. The two volumes in this *legajo* contain over 400 pages of legal proceedings relating to the attack of 29 November 1917.
54. ADC/FDP/SpH, 14 December 1917.
55. Ibid.
56. 'Juicio contra Domingo Ramos, Ramón Ramos, Vicente Azamera, Eleodoro Benel Zuloeta y otros por triple homicidio y otros delitos', ADC/FDCS/C, 1917, *legajo* 82, vol. ii. Also see Vigil, *La rebelión*, p. 42 and ADC/FDP/SpH, 14 December 1917, which contains the report of Julio Vargas García, the *comisario* of Santa Cruz who had replaced Augusto Durand.
57. Vigil, *La rebelión*, p. 40.
58. 'Juicio contra Domingo Ramos, Ramón Ramos, Vicente Azamera, Eleodoro Benel Zuloeta y otros por triple homicidio y otros delitos', ADC/FDCS/C, 1917, *legajo* 82, vol. i.
59. Vigil, *La rebelión*, p. 41. A long report of the attack on El Triunfo and the subsequent legal proceedings also appeared in the local newspaper *El Heraldo*, 15 April 1918, 24 April 1918 and 27 April 1918.
60. Vigil, *La rebelión*, p. 42. Also see 'Juicio contra Domingo Ramos, Ramón Ramos, Vicente Azamera, Eleodoro Benel Zuloeta y otros por triple homicidio y otros delitos', ADC/FDCS/C, 1917, *legajo* 82, vol. i.
61. Ibid., vol. ii; Vigil, *La rebelión*, p. 42; ADC/FDP/SpH, 14 December 1917.

62. Vigil, *La rebelión*, p. 42.
63. Ibid.; ADC/FDP/SpH, 14 December 1917.
64. Ibid.
65. 'Juicio contra Domingo Ramos, Ramón Ramos, Vicente Azamera, Eleodoro Benel Zuloeta y otros por triple homicidio y otros delitos', ADC/FDCS/C, 1917, *legajo* 82, vol. ii; Vigil, *La rebelión*, p. 44.
66. ADC/FDP/SpH, 14 December 1917.
67. Ibid.; 'Juicio contra Domingo Ramos, Ramón Ramos, Vicente Azamera, Eleodoro Benel Zuloeta y otros por triple homicidio y otros delitos', ADC/FDCS/C, 1917, *legajo* 82, vols. i and ii; *El Heraldo*, 15 April 1918.
68. ADC/FDP/SpH, 14 December 1917.
69. 'Juicio contra Domingo Ramos, Ramón Ramos, Vicente Azamera, Eleodoro Benel Zuloeta y otros por triple homicidio y otros delitos', ADC/FDCS/C, 1917, *legajo* 82, vol. i, testimony of Eleodoro Benel dated 4 January 1918. Months later Santos Chuquimango made an affidavit claiming that the raiders carried off S/.6,000 in cash, jewelry and other valuables. See the testimony of Santos Chuquimango dated 5 October 1918.
70. ADC/FDP/SpH, 14 December 1917.
71. Ibid., 8 January 1918.
72. Vigil, *La rebelión*, p. 45.
73. ADC/FDP/SpH, 8 January 1918. Commenting on these events, Basadre states that 'a judge who was an ally of Benel persuaded the landlord to visit Hualgayoc in order to sign some documents that would resolve a legal matter. In the town the *gendarmes* seized Benel unawares and conducted him to goal in Cajamarca. A large crowd assembled to greet his arrival in the city and cheered Benel as he entered jail on 15 December 1917'. *Historia*, vol. xiii, p. 139. This version is incorrect both with respect to the way Benel was captured and the date he was imprisoned. Basadre takes this version directly from Vílchez, *Fusiles*, pp. 17–18.
74. 'Juicio contra Domingo Ramos, Ramón Ramos, Vicente Azamera, Eleodoro Benel Zuloeta y otros por triple homicidio y otros delitos', ADC/FDCS/C, 1917, *legajo* 82, vol. i. Decree of judge Gallardo, 14 January 1918.
75. Ibid.
76. Ibid.
77. Further details on the impact of the 1914–18 war on Peru are given in P. Henderson, *Latin America and the Great War: a study of the effects of World War I on economic and social conditions in Peru and Chile*, unpublished PhD dissertation, University of East Anglia, Norwich 1985.
78. Gilbert, *La oligarquía*, pp. 46–8; Miller, 'The coastal elite', p. 106.
79. M. Capuñay, *Leguía: vida y obra del constructor del gran Perú* (Lima, 1952), pp. 148, 183.
80. Only one member of the list standing on the Aspíllaga slate in Cajamarca was not a landowner. See *El Ferrocarril*, 13 February 1919.
81. Gilbert, *La oligarquía*, p. 48.
82. The *leguiísta* list of candidates for the senate in Cajamarca included two landowners, one merchant and four lawyers. See *El Ferrocarril*, 13 February 1919.
83. ADC/FDP/SpH, 2 February 1918.
84. Ibid., letter of the lieutenant governor dated 29 January 1918.
85. Eleodoro Benel to the prefect, ADC/FDP/P, 30 January 1918. In reply, Vargas stated that these claims were unfounded, and were made to get him removed from his post. The *comisario* alleged that as an outsider he was neutral with respect to local factional feuds. Ibid., letter of Julio Vargas dated 15 February 1918.
86. ADC/FDP/SpH, 2 March 1918.

87. Eleodoro Benel to the prefect, ADC/FDP/P, 12 July 1918. The brother of Eladio Estela was convinced that he had been murdered by the Ramos outlaws. See Eloy Estela to the prefect, ibid., 19 February 1918.

88. Eleodoro Benel to the prefect, ADC/FDP/P, 12 July 1918.

89. Ibid.

90. Ibid.

91. Ibid., 18 July 1918.

92. Ibid. Clearly Benel's problems with the Chota élite, that had accentuated as a result of the Llaucán affair, continued to provoke serious clashes.

93. On one occasion Raimundo Ramos claimed that his gang had murdered 110 people. See Gitlitz, 'Conflictos políticos', p. 136.

94. 'Juicio contra Domingo y Raimundo Ramos por los homicidios consumados en las personas de Manuel y Wenceslao Uriarte', ADC/FDCS/C, 1914, legajo, 55.

95. 'Juicio criminal contra José Angel, Ignacio i Rumaldo Ramos, Segundo i Andrés Luna, José Sinforoso Blanco i María Carmen Espinosa, por el homicidio de Domingo Llamoctanta i otros delitos', ADC/FDCS/C, 1917, legajo 73.

96. ADC/FDP/SpH, 19 December 1917.

97. Ibid., 20 December 1917. Report of lieutenant Conrado Contreras.

98. Ibid.

99. Ibid., 29 December 1917. Report of the governor of Bambamarca, Manuel Villulada, 21 December 1917.

100. Ibid. Also see ibid., 24 December 1917. The governor's unease was undoubtedly increased due to a spate of assassinations among government authorities. In November 1917 full-scale gun battles on the streets of Cutervo claimed the lives of a number of pro-government officials, while in the district of Lajas in Chota, the local governor was murdered by factional opponents.

101. 'Juicio contra Raimundo Misael Ramos, Arturo, Catalino, Moises Guevara y otros por delitos de homicidios perpetrados en las personas de Silvestro Apaéstegui, José Inocente Rodríguez, Estevan Rodríguez, Vicente Guevara, Adolfo Apaéstegui y María Margarita Rodríguez, y homicidio frustrado y heridas en las de Anastasio Guevara y Pedro Figueroa', ADC/FDCS/C, 1917, legajo 82.

102. Ibid. Affidavit of Dolores Rocha, 11 March 1918.

103. Ibid.

104. Ibid. Although robbery was the main motive behind this incident, it did contain a vendetta undercurrent. The Guevara clan maintained a blood feud with the Rodríguez family.

105. ADC/FDP/SpH, 6 May 1918.

106. Ibid., 20 May 1918.

107. Ibid., 22 October 1918.

108. Victoriano Hoyos Osores to the prefect, ADC/FDP/P, 16 November 1918.

109. Vigil, La rebelión, p. 45.

110. Ibid., p. 48. An account of Benel's escape also appeared in El Ferrocarril, 1 February 1919, 4 February 1919 and 6 February 1919. These reports suggested that Benel paid various individuals a total of S/.10,000 to buy his freedom, among them an ex-mayor of Cajamarca. It was also alleged that he had accomplices among the gendarmerie. Neither of these claims were proved. This escape greatly contributed to the creation of a Benel 'legend' in Cajamarca.

111. Vigil, La rebelión, pp. 48–9.

112. 'Las elecciones generales de la república', La Prensa, 19 May 1919, p. 1.

113. Ibid.

114. *Los Andes*, Cajamarca, 9 March 1919, p. 2. The Supreme Court in Lima had previously circulated a letter to all provincial judges reminding them that they could immediately suspend all officials who interfered in the electoral process. See Basadre, *Elecciones*, p. 91.

115. *El Heraldo*, 7 March 1919.

116. Ibid. For further details on the events leading up to this incident and descriptions of the battle itself, see the Cajamarca newspaper *El Heraldo*, 8 March 1919; 10 March 1919; 20 March 1919 and 16 July 1919. Also see Cabrejo, *Añoranzas Cruzeñas*, p. 54.

117. Basadre, *Elecciones*, pp. 92–5; Gilbert, *La oligarquía*, p. 48.

118. ADC/FDP/SpH, 28 October 1919.

119. *El Heraldo*, 8 August 1919.

120. For more details on these events see Basadre, *Elecciones*, pp. 99–109.

# Chapter 6

1. ADC/FDP/SpH, 16 April 1920. In this communication the *comisario* gets his names confused. The surname of Misael Vargas and family was Vargas Romero, not Ramos Vargas.

2. Ibid., 10 February 1920.

3. Ibid., 20 April 1920; 22 April 1920. It is possible that Ramos felt confident he would not be arrested due to the appointment of several of his protectors to official positions. Moreover, in mid-1919 the Alvarado faction established a militia of approximately forty men. They were consequently less dependent on the Ramos brothers to provide them with armed backing. This band centred its operations in the triangle formed by the town of Santa Cruz, the hacienda Chancay and the hamlet of Uticyacu. Ibid., 28 October 1919.

4. Ibid.

5. Ibid., 4 May 1920.

6. Ibid., 23 December 1919.

7. Ibid. This task was probably aided as a result of the growing economic difficulties besetting rural labourers, artisans and less prosperous peasant households. Whereas the prices of basic foodstuffs more than doubled between 1914 and 1920 due to the impact of war in Europe, the minimum wage paid to a majority of rural workers in this part of highland Cajamarca remained unchanged at twenty *centavos* from 1914 until 1924. See 'Oficio que dirige el alcalde del consejo distrital de Santa Cruz al alcalde del consejo provincial de Hualgayoc, sobre informe del jornal en Santa Cruz', *Libro copiador de oficios de la munici-palidad de Santa Cruz*, no. 38, 1920–4, fol. 358. On this issue also see Carranza Rimarachín et. al., *Economía, classes*, pp. 233–7.

8. ADC/FDP/SpH, 4 February 1920.

9. Ibid., 29 February 1920.

10. Ibid., 28 October 1919; 27 December 1919.

11. One indication of this state of affairs was the plea for official protection lodged by a nervous Zenón Burga, whose coastward bound muletrains were being seized and his men shot by *pistoleros* in the pay of Eleodoro Benel. Ibid., 15 June 1920.

12. Ibid., 31 October 1921. With small detachments of *gendarmes* billeted in the towns and afraid to venture far outside the urban centres, the rural areas were practically abandoned to the brigands and the caudillos who controlled them. Nor did the presence of troops in the district capitals provide much security, and they were frequently raided by outlaws. For example, at dawn on 16 January 1922 a *benelista* band under the direction of Zenobio and Mardoqueo Calderón assaulted the homes of Marcial Alvarado, Gerónimo Alvarado and Daniel Orrego. The local detachment of *gendarmes* only numbered five, and proved no deterrent. See the letter from Marcial Alvarado to deputy Javier Luna Iglesias, *Libro*

*copiador de oficios de la municipalidad de Santa Cruz*, no. 93, fols. 167–71. Letter dated 16 February 1922.

13. Ibid. Letter of the district council of Santa Cruz dated 29 October 1921. As yet the Zuloeta gang were operating independently of either of the two competing factions in Santa Cruz. Later they would ally themselves with the Alvarados against the *benelistas*.

14. ADC/FDP/SpH, 26 September 1922.

15. Ibid., 21 February 1922.

16. Ibid. Marcial Alvarado summed up one such failure in the following manner: 'On 29 March the *gendarmes* sent from Chiclayo by the Interior Ministry to apprehend the bandits who have long brought ruin and desolation to this district, returned without achieving anything . . . rather than improving matters they have worsened this population's predicament. Due to the inefficient performance of the troops, the bandits remain intact, have been incensed, and threaten to overrun the town. This could bring unfortunate consequences'. Alvarado also mentioned that several of the *gendarmes* were too afraid to face the bandits and should be removed. Ibid., 4 April 1922. Also see ibid., 1 April 1922.

17. For instance in 1919 a member of the *leguíista* controlled *Congreso Regional del Norte*, demanded that troops be drafted into Hualgayoc to restore order. Armed bands, 'who have embraced crime and form the shock troops of a local political tendency that was defeated on 4 July', were terrorising the populace. The brigands were controlling liquor smuggling and preventing the collection of taxes. In addition, 'salt, rice and sugar cannot be transported from Lambayeque, because the aforementioned bandits have their sentries stationed on the roads'. *Diario de los debates del Congreso Regional del Norte, Legislatura de 1919*, pp. 224–7. Session of 14 October 1919. Three years later señor Enrique de la Piedra voiced a complaint that, 'in the district of Santa Cruz, in the department of Cajamarca, brigandage has increased alarmingly. It is causing heavy losses to traders in Lambayeque, which is closely integrated economically with Santa Cruz'. *Diario de los debates en la cámara de senadores, Legislatura de 1921*, p. 130. Session of 27 January 1922.

18. ADC/FDP/SpH, 30 January 1923.

19. Ibid., 25 January 1923.

20. Ibid.

21. Letter of Feliciano Chules dated 22 August 1923, in *Libro de tomas de razón del consejo distrital de Santa Cruz*, vol. 3, 1923, p. 24. One of the sections invaded by Benel was reputed to extend for more than one hundred *cuadras*, or blocks. This was on the strategically placed mountain of Cuchupaccha that overlooked the trails leading from the hacienda El Triunfo to Santa Cruz. See 'Oficio que dirige Marcial Alvarado al diputado nacional por Hualgayoc, Javier Luna Iglesias', *Libro copiador de oficios de la municipalidad de Santa Cruz*, no. 93, 1923, fols. 498–9. Letter dated 28 March 1923.

22. ADC/FDP/SpH, 18 December 1923.

23. Gilbert, *La oligarquía*, pp. 58–9, 123–5.

24. B. Caravedo, *Clases, lucha política y gobierno en el Perú, 1919–33* (Lima, 1977), pp. 82–3.

25. For a presentation of the official viewpoint, see '*La reelección de Leguía: por que la dicta la conciencia nacional; por que es ella una exigencia del porvenir del Perú*', *Ministerio de Gobierno*, Lima, 1 January 1924.

26. Backing from these other political groupings was stressed by Leguía in his acceptance speech, no doubt with the intention of trying to legitimise a controversial political manoeuvre. See A. B. Leguía, *Discursos y mensajes del presidente Leguía* (Lima, 1926), pp. 265–6, 279–80.

27. For opposition reaction to the reelection of Leguía, see A. J. Andia, *El tirano en la jaula — de la constitución al vandalismo* (Buenos Aires, 1926). According to Pardo, Leguía was 'a heinous child spawned by the Partido Civil. First he was formed by love for *civilismo*, later by hatred of *civilismo*. Consequently, within Leguía passions clash with an unnatural violence'. Ibid., p. 152.

28. The notables of Polulo to the prefect, ADC/FDP/P, 25 January 1923.
29. Vigil, *La rebelión*, pp. 51–2.
30. Ibid.
31. Ibid., p. 53.
32. Ibid., p. 54.
33. ADC/FDP/SpH, 6 November 1923.
34. Ibid.
35. Ibid., 15 November 1923.
36. Ibid. Fernando was Castinaldo Benel's other christian name.
37. Vigil, *La rebelión*, pp. 53–4.
38. ADC/FDP/SpH, 29 April 1924. Letter of Eleodoro Benel to Gregorio Vargas dated 11 April 1924.
39. Vigil, *La rebelión*, pp. 56–8. Another important link in the anti-*leguiísta* underground was Juan Vílchez, who edited the newspaper *El País* in Chiclayo. Economic backing for the rebellion came from the Pardo and Aspíllaga families.
40. Ibid., p. 57.
41. ADC/FDP/SpH, 18 December 1923.
42. Ibid.
43. Ibid.
44. Margarita Vargas to the prefect, ADC/FDP/P, 21 January 1924.
45. Ibid.
46. Arturo Alarcón to the prefect, ibid., 14 May 1930.
47. ADC/FDP/SpH, 19 April 1924. Report of the governor of Santa Cruz dated 16 April 1924.
48. Ibid.
49. Ibid.
50. Ibid., 22 April 1924.
51. Marcial Alvarado to the prefect, *Libro copiador de oficios de la municipalidad de Santa Cruz*, no. 93, fols. 446–7. Letter dated 26 May 1924.
52. Other members of the so-called 'revolutionary committee' in Chota were Alberto Cadenillas, a lawyer, and Antero Acevedo, a public employee.
53. Jorge Berrios Alcarcón, *Monografía*, p. 87.
54. For further details see Basadre, *Historia*, vol. xiii, p. 20. Locally the position of the rebels was weakened by the incorporation of Leoncio and Wenceslao Villacorta into Leguía's *clientela*. In 1919 Benel and the Villacorta clan fought together. By 1924 they had become political rivals.
55. ADC/FDP/SpH, 29 April 1924. Straightforward acts of brigandage were also common-place. In May 1924 a married couple travelling to Santa Cruz were ambushed by a thirty strong band captained by Misael Vargas. After stripping the victims of their possessions, the man was shot. The bandits then raped the woman before shooting her. Ibid., 13 May 1924. Also see ibid., 14 October 1924 for details of similar incidents.
56. Ibid., 20 May 1924.
57. Letter dated 11 November 1924. See '*Documentos incautados a los revolucionarios de Chota que lee el Ministro de Gobierno Jesús M. Salazar antes la Cámara de Diputados*', *La Prensa*, 4 December 1924, p. 10. For additional details on these negotiations see Miguel Cabrejo, *Añoranzas Cruzeñas*, p. 52–6.
58. Ibid. The terms of the pact read as follows: 'Eleodoro Benel Zuloeta, Anselmo Díaz and brothers, Misael Vargas and brothers, as well as their followers, most solemnly agree, under religious oath and giving our word of honour, to not attack or trouble one another in any

way during the campaign of national regeneration. We celebrate and are bound to abide by this agreement because at this perilous time for the nation, our patriotic duty is to overthrow the tyranny that is causing the nation so much damage and leading Peru to ruin. The supreme command of the revolution decrees that any act in breach of this pact is treason and will be treated as such. We sign this treaty in the presence of national delegate Arturo Osores and consent to it being kept in his possession'. This letter dated 13 November was signed in the hacienda El Triunfo by Benel, Díaz and Vargas. Ibid. Benel thought that Osores had made a grave error in communicating with Anselmo Díaz, rightly suspecting that the bandit would betray them to the authorities. See Rimarachín et. al., *Economía, clases*, p. 368.

59. ADC/FDP/SpH, 18 November 1924. Alvarado's letter to the subprefect was written in Santa Cruz on 12 November 1924.

60. Ibid.

61. Vigil, *La rebelión*, p. 73.

62. Matos, *Operaciones*, p. 62.

63. Ibid. A single *benelista* was killed in the affray. When the rebels were trying to smash open a door to the shop owned by Catalino Coronado with their rifle butts, a weapon accidentally fired. The bullet hit one of the Cotrina brothers who happened to be standing close behind. Vigil, *La rebelión*, p. 78.

64. Chávez, *Monografía*, vol. iii, pp. 249–50.

65. Alvarez and Benel had clashed earlier in the year when the *gendarme* commanded a column of troops who, aided by the outlaw bands led by Anselmo Díaz and Pedro Zuloeta, attacked the farm of Misael Vargas in Ushushque. Once assistance arrived from El Triunfo, the troops were overwhelmed and fifteen *gendarmes* captured. The prisoners were roped together and frog-marched back to Chota by Vargas and his men, where they were left on the outskirts of the town. A note from Benel addressed to the subprefect was pinned on the uniform of the officer in command. It read 'In future, please do not disturb'. Vigil, *La rebelión*, p. 79; Vílchez, *Fusiles*, p. 18; Basadre, *Historia*, vol. xiii, p. 139.

66. Ibid., p. 137; Vigil, *La rebelión*, p. 80.

67. The Vásquez brothers came from humble peasant stock, who through force of character and physical prowess became the undisputed leaders of the *caserío*, or parish, of Lanche. Although they have on occasions been classified as 'social bandits', already by 1908 they were gunmen hired by the district committee of the Partido Civil in Cutervo, which was dominated by the wealthy landowners Manuel and Pedro Montenegro. See *La Voz*, Chota, 29 March 1908. Paradoxically, the presidential candidate of the Partido Civil in that election was Augusto Leguía. Avelino Vásquez first entered into serious conflict with the authorities in 1910 for resisting attempts to conscript him into the army. On this occasion Avelino's brother Tadeo used his rifle to good effect and scattered the recruiting party. By 1912 Avelino was already regarded as a dangerous outlaw wanted for crimes of armed robbery and homicide, but the Vásquez brothers fighting qualities and their influential protectors enabled them to avoid capture. The highly conflictive electoral contest of 1917 in Cutervo witnessed the now better organised Vásquez gang successfully battle to control the *asamblea de mayores contribuyentes*, so enabling their *patrón* Manuel Montenegro to secure election as a deputy. By 1920 the Vásquez band were recognised as the most feared brigand group in Cutervo, a reputation reinforced when they ambushed subprefect Alejandro Bustamante on a mountain road near the village of Callacate on 24 May 1923. Bustamante 'was undertaking a piratical tour through outlying villages under the pretext of conducting an administrative survey. His victims appealed to don Avelino Vásquez for assistance. In a surprise attack the subprefect and many *gendarmes* were killed. The survivors fled, abandoning their arms, ammunition and the booty they had extorted'. Vílchez, *Fusiles*, pp. 20–1. Twenty days later Vásquez and his men invaded Cutervo, gunning down the governor and overcoming the *leguiísta* faction after a fierce shoot-out. They then 'stayed in control for a long time, organising in Cutervo an autonomous

government, independent of the national government headed by the dictator don Augusto B. Leguía'. Ibid. According to Vílchez, 'Don Avelino Vásquez administered justice in his own style. Long-standing land disputes were solved. Boundaries were fixed and agreements signed. People were told to respect the decisions reached or they would be shot'. Ibid., p. 22. It was to do away with Vásquez's little autocracy and restore government authority that major Rosas entered Cutervo province in November 1924. Having reached the parish of Lanche, a detachment of troops commanded by captain Ezequiel Padrón found that the Vásquez gang had already left to join the rebels in Chota. The military then committed an indiscriminate massacre. Machine guns were set up in a corner of the village square. Padrón ordered the soldiers to open fire into the surrounding houses and the local school. Well in excess of thirty *lanchinos* were murdered, among them children in the school and their teacher Olinda Rivera y Piedra. Ibid., pp. 23–4; Vigil, *La rebelión*, p. 85.

68. Ibid., pp. 90–2.

69. For further details on the battle at Churucancha, see ibid., pp. 95–9 and Matos, *Operaciones*, pp. 62–7.

70. According to Vigil, Benel argued that 'we must finish them off before they finish us off', and requested del Alcázar 'to give me command of the troops for two hours, just two hours . . . and you'll see how I'll scatter them like birds . . . To win a battle, colonel, you don't just need maps and certificates, you also need *pantalones* (trousers, i.e., guts)'. Vigil, *La rebelión*, p. 98.

71. See footnote 67 above.

72. Anselmo Díaz maintained a vendetta feud with Villacorta. Fearful that he might be attacked by Villacorta's stronger force, Díaz retired to Lajas and did not participate in the battle of Churucancha.

73. Osores stayed on the island until 1929, when some North American ex-clients of his persuaded Leguía to allow the aging lawyer to be deported to the USA. Basadre, *Historia*, vol. xiii, p. 138.

74. Ibid., pp. 137–8. Barreda and del Alcázar were not the only people to be executed. A reign of terror enveloped the town as many citizens were placed before firing squads either in the local jail or against the cemetery wall. Others were dragged from their homes and dispatched in the street before the eyes of their wives and children. It is alleged that this repression claimed more lives than the Chilean occupation of Chota in August 1882. After these events the soldiers were nicknamed *matachotanos*, or *chotano* killers, by the local population. Vigil, *La rebelión*, pp. 106–110; Vílchez, *Fusiles*, p. 23.

75. Vigil, *La rebelión*, pp. 99–100.

76. ADC/FDP/SpH, 9 December 1924. The two men referred to in this communication were probably Arturo Osores and his son.

77. Vigil, *La rebelión*, pp. 111–13.

78. Ibid., p. 114. Subprefect Macciotta supplied his superiors with a list naming 94 men integrated into Benel's gang and 91 who rode with Misael Vargas. He also mentioned that the *benelistas* were robbing cattle in the highlands and selling them in the valleys of Jequetepeque and Zaña. Funds thus acquired were spent on arms and ammunition. ADC/FDP/SpH, 23 December 1924.

79. Consequently, both sides claimed victory. See Marcial Alvarado to the officer commanding the Lambayeque barracks, *Libro copiador de oficios de la municipalidad de Santa Cruz*, no. 39, fol. 78. Letter dated 20 January 1925. For a *benelista* version of events, see Vigil, *La rebelión*, p. 115. According to this source two of Benel's daughters fought alongside their father. Vigil claims that well over a hundred soldiers died, while eighteen *benelistas* lost their lives. Ibid., pp. 116–9.

80. Ibid., p. 120.

81. ADC/FDP/SpH, 3 February 1925. The brigands received protection from the *hacienda* administrator, who kept denying their existence to the subprefect. Also see Marcial

Alvarado to the landlord of Quilcate, *Libro copiador de oficios de la municipalidad de Santa Cruz*, no. 39, fol. 76.

82. ADC/FDP/SpH, 4 August 1925.

83. Vigil, *La rebelión*, p. 123. See *Caretas*, nos. 654 and 655, 30 June and 6 July 1981, for photographs showing the burning of the hacienda El Triunfo; groups of individuals accused of banditry and bound with wire just prior to their execution; as well as pictures of peasants being shot by firing squads.

84. Vigil, *La rebelión*, p. 124.

85. Ibid., p. 123. On the clash at Cochabamba, see the governor of Querocoto to the subprefect of Cutervo, *Libro copiador de oficios de la municipalidad de Cutervo*, no. 9, fol. 57. Letter dated 17 April 1925.

86. Ibid., p. 121; ADC/FDP/SpH, 25 May 1925. Gangrene infected Avellaneda's wound and he was carried to Cajamarca to have his leg amputated.

87. Vigil, *La rebelión*, p. 126.

88. This failure to strike a decisive blow against Benel's band while their morale was low infuriated Marcial Alvarado. The mayor complained that 'when Benel and his gang returned from Niepos, they passed only half a league from Chota riding tired mounts, without being in the slightest bit harassed by the troops stationed there. Although the authorities in Chota know that the rebel is at present encamped between Silugán and Salabamba, which is located in Chota province, they do not bother to chase Benel'. ADC/FDP/SpH, 2 June 1925. This information was passed on to Alvarado by one of his spies. Two weeks earlier Alvarado advised subprefect Macciotta that 'Benel and the armed group that ride with him, managed to outwit the pursuing troops. They passed very close to Chota en route to Salabamba, sited two leagues from Cutervo. The civilians from that district (i.e. gunmen employed by Villacorta — LT), who are searching everywhere for the insurgents, could not make contact'. Ibid., 19 May 1925.

89. Ibid., 26 May 1925. Subprefect Macciotta told the prefect that in Hualgayoc 'the bandit groups have created a total state of panic among the population', consequently even tougher measures against brigandage needed to be pursued. In the same letter he also passed on a complaint from the Alvarados about one of the military commanders in Santa Cruz. It stated that 'I have no confidence in this lieutenant because he is constantly in the company of Julio Aguinaga and Enrique Caballero, relatives of Benel, who, I suppose, pass on to him all sorts of information. Thus, our efforts to hunt the outlaws cannot be kept secret'. Ibid., 23 June 1925. Macciotta requested that the officer be removed. The subprefect ended by informing his superior that he had received news from Cutervo suggesting that 'the famous bandit (Benel — LT) continues with his plans of recruiting gunmen with the objective of attacking Chota, Cutervo or Santa Cruz on 24 June'. Ibid.

90. Vigil, *La rebelión*, p. 127.

91. Further details of this encounter are provided in ibid., pp. 127–31; Matos, *Operaciones*, pp. 74–79.

92. Ibid.; Vílchez, *Fusiles*, p. 24.

93. Rimarachín, et. al., *Economía, clases*, pp. 387–8.

94. Matos, *Operaciones*, p. 128.

95. Vigil, *La rebelión*, p. 133; Matos, *Operaciones*, p. 128.

96. Ibid., pp. 128–30. As if to emphasise that he was a patriot, Benel also agreed to give military support in 'the southern conflict'. This referred to the tense Tacna-Arica frontier dispute with Chile. Ibid., pp. 133–4.

97. Ibid., pp. 131–2. Throughout Matos appears to have regarded Benel with higher esteem than the Alvarado clan, possibly due to his higher social status.

98. Ibid., pp. 133–4.

99. Ibid.

100. Ibid. Miguel Puga was a cousin of Eleodoro Benel.

101. Ibid.

102. Ibid., pp. 120–6; Vigil, *La rebelión*, pp. 135–6.

103. Ibid., pp. 136–7; Vílchez states that in these two clashes the army lost two hundred men. See *Fusiles*, p. 151.

104. Vigil, *La rebelión*, pp. 140–2; Matos, *Operaciones*, pp. 161–2.

105. Marcial Alvarado to Celso Chirinos, *Libro copiador de oficios de la municipalidad de Santa Cruz*, no. 68, fols. 241–3.

106. Vigil, *La rebelión*, p. 141.

107. Matos, *Operaciones*, p. 202.

108. ADC/FDP/SpH, 4 August 1925; Vigil, *La rebelión*, p. 143. The García gang specialised in rustling cattle for sale to meat traders employed by the coastal sugar estates. They drove the stolen livestock to Bambamarca each week for sale in the Sunday market.

109. Ibid., pp. 144–5.

110. As happened to Pedro Zuloeta. In November 1925 Fortunato Alvarado notified the authorities that Zuloeta 'assisted by a group of fifteen men, is sowing panic and terror among the populace, rustling, raping women and sacking properties. Booty from their robberies is sold in San Miguel and Llapa'. ADC/FDP/SpH, 15 November 1925.

111. Ibid., 30 November 1925. The governor's letter was dated 27 November 1925. A total of S/.1,052.86 was claimed for rations and forage.

112. Matos, *Operaciones*, p. 336.

113. Ibid., pp. 289–99.

114. Ibid., pp. 335–6.

115. Vigil, *La rebelión*, p. 145; Vílchez, *Fusiles*, p. 25.

116. ADC/FDP/SpH, 4 May 1926; 16 August 1926.

117. Vigil, *La rebelión*, pp. 148–9.

118. Ibid., pp. 149–51.

119. Vílchez, *Fusiles*, p. 26.

120. Ibid.

121. *La Prensa*, 28 September 1927; 3 October 1927.

122. Vigil, *La rebelión*, pp. 161–4. Silugán was sacked and fired. All adults who fell into the hands of the military were assassinated. The troops then spread out into the surrounding hamlets killing and looting. According to Vigil, dozens of other peasants suspected of *benelista* sympathies were taken prisoner and marched to Cutervo. Some were murdered on the army's return journey and had their testicles cut off for show to the population. The head of Francisco Pérez, with its eyes open and sporting a terror-stricken mien, was paraded on a pike around the *plaza* of Cutervo. Ibid., p. 164.

123. Vílchez, *Fusiles*, pp. 150–2.

124. Ibid., p. 153.

125. Ibid., pp. 153–4; Vigil, *La rebelión*, pp. 169–70.

126. Vílchez, *Fusiles*, p. 154–5.

127. Ibid., p. 156. Their bodies were left lying on the ground. Members of the Vásquez clan paid a wage of fifteen *centavos* to four men to intern the corpses. When Moreno discovered this he had the four unfortunates stood up against the cemetery wall and shot, arguing that they were rebel sympathizers. Ibid., p. 27; Vigil, *La rebelión*, p. 171; Basadre, *Historia*, vol. xiii, p. 140.

128. *La Prensa*, 3 October 1927.

129. Vigil, *La rebelión*, p. 164.

130. Ibid., p. 171.
131. Ibid., p. 12. Segundo Benel and his two brothers travelled south to the hacienda Jancos in the province of Cajamarca. Although the landlord, Edilberto Castro Pol, was a *leguiísta*, he was also a close friend of Eleodoro Benel and so gave refuge to the fugitives.
132. Ibid., pp. 13–15; Matos, *Operaciones*, pp. 383–5.
133. See, for example, *La Prensa*, 3 October 1927; 12 October 1927.
134. ADC/FDP/SpH, 18 March 1930. On San Gregorio district see ibid., 14 November 1932.
135. To survive bandits sought protection from local landlords, power-brokers in official positions and through pay-offs to the civil guard. Rustling sustained by these connections continued to plague peasants in Hualgayoc until the 1980s, when in several districts the rural inhabitants finally took matters into their own hands and formed vigilante groups. On these see J. S. Gitlitz and T. Rojas, 'Peasant vigilante committees in Northern Peru', *Journal of Latin American Studies*, vol. 15, part 1 (1983), pp. 163–97.
136. ADC/FDP/SpH, 29 November 1929; 3 December 1929; 31 December 1929; 5 February 1930 and 31 May 1931. It was alleged that Domitila Bernal controlled a sixteen-strong gang led by her three sons and Eduardo Mego, one of Benel's most trusted gunmen.

# Chapter 7

1. E. R. Wolf and E. C. Hansen, 'Caudillo politics: a structural analysis', *Comparative Studies in Society and History*, vol. ix, no. 1 (January, 1967), p. 170.
2. Ibid., pp. 170, 175–7.
3. The political history of the Puga family illustrates this change: in the 1870s and 1880s José Mercedes Puga imposed his political will by riding at the head of a *montonera* column comprised of his dependents,while in the 1940s and 1950s his grandson Rafael Puga sustained his political influence via connections in Congress, as well as central and local government. Rather than using a personal army to squash dissenters, Rafael Puga relied on the *guardia civil*.
4. Background information is forthcoming in S. Stein, *Populism in Peru* (Madison, 1980), chapters 4–6.
5. Ibid., pp. 93–4.
6. The connection between *leguiísmo* and *aprismo* has also been noted by B. W. Loveday, *Sánches Cerro and Peruvian politics 1930–1933* (University of Glasgow, Institute of Latin American Studies, Occasional Paper no. 6, 1973).
7. On the *indigenista* movement see J. Deustua and M. Renique, *Intelectuales, indigenistas y descentralismo en el Perú, 1897–1931* (Cusco, 1985). In 1922 Carlos Malpica Rivola began to agitate among the peasants on the hacienda Llaucán. He was influenced by the propaganda of the Asociación Pro-Indígena, and quickly gained support among Llaucán's more politicised peasants, such as Lorenzo Guadaña and Juan Rojas. Malpica was appointed governor of Hualgayoc district by the *leguiístas* in 1926 and shortly afterwards became one of the first *apristas* in the province. He stayed loyal to the party all his life. An octogenarian, he died in summer 1985 while occupying the post of mayor of Cajamarca town on the APRA ticket. ADC/FDP/SpH, 19 January 1926.
8. ADC/FDP/SpH, 11 May 1933. This was prior to the formal foundation of the party in Peru in 1930. Macciotta was probably recruited by Malpica. The ex-subprefect participated in the abortive APRA uprisings of 1932 and 1933. Being an 'important member' of the party apparatus in the department, Macciotta was jailed following the 11 March 1933 revolt in Cajamarca town. See the confidential list detailing the occupational background and political activities of the subversives, ADC/FDP/SpC, 19 March 1933. Malpica was also involved, but managed to avoid detention.

9. ADC/FDP/SpH, 13 March 1934.
10. Also of importance was the constant flow of migrant labourers from highland Hualgayoc to work as seasonal labourers on coastal sugar and rice estates. Here they came into contact with APRA dominated unions and social clubs.
11. *Bandits*, pp. 28–9.
12. Kapsoli, *Los movimientos*, p. 78.
13. *Bandits*, p. 17.
14. Ibid., p. 18.
15. Burga and Flores Galindo, *Apogeo y crisis*, p. 8.
16. Vigil, *La rebelión*, pp. 3, 13.
17. T. Skocpol, *States and social revolutions* (Cambridge, 1979), p. 3.